Looking West

Looking West

The Journey of a
Lebanese-American Immigrant

Albert Nasib Badre

E. L. Marker
Salt Lake City

Published by E. L. Marker, an imprint of WiDo Publishing

WiDō Publishing
Salt Lake City, Utah
widopublishing.com

Cover design by Steven Novak
Book design by Marny K. Parkin

ISBN: 978-1-947966-13-0

Printed in the United States of America

Contents

Photos

Part III
On Exploring Religion and Spirituality

Part IV
On Reaching for the Realm of the Mind

For My Family

Prologue:
Fourteen Years Later

*A*S MY FLIGHT APPROACHED BEIRUT IN THE EARLY EVENING, I looked down from the plane's window, dazed by jetlag and the cloud of cigarette smoke that surrounded me and saw the glittering skyline of a sprawling metropolis—the Beirut I had left as a boy of fourteen. As my eyes started tearing uncontrollably, I wondered, Will this be the same Beirut that I left all those years ago? After all, I had changed, why not the city?

The plane descended, and I could see the city's hilly landscape meandering down to the blue Mediterranean. It was the landscape of my childhood. Nearly a lifetime had passed since I left Beirut for the United States. So many changes had taken place in my life. When I had left, I could barely converse in English and had given little thought to what my life would be like as an immigrant in America. Now I was returning, an American citizen, with an American wife, and a respected professor at an American university. I was now a product of two cultures—American and Lebanese—both of which I loved.

Would Beirut be the same today, in 1974, as it was when I left in 1960? Had I accomplished what I youthfully boasted I would all those years ago? As I watched Beirut approach, my mind traveled back to 1960, to the day my life changed forever.

Part I
On Looking toward the West

1. A Momentous Decision

JANUARY 14, 1960, WAS A COLD AND RAINY THURSDAY IN BEIrut. The weather had been oscillating between a light drizzle and a drenching rain for six days straight. Winter is the rainy season in Lebanon, so this came as no surprise, but I was looking forward to the rain abating. I enjoyed being able to play outside in the sun and the fresh, crisp air that came after such a rainy spell.

I was home from school for the regular two-hour lunch recess and was wet and hungry; I certainly had no idea this would be a pivotal day in my life. All I cared about at that moment was lunch, the main meal of the day.

My mother sat down with my two older brothers and me at the table, and as we were waiting for our cook to bring out the food, she informed us, "Papa is at an all-day meeting downtown. He'll be back for supper, and then we will tell you about a decision we have made that is of momentous importance for our family."

I was too hungry to be curious. I could smell the appetizing aromas coming from across the narrow hallway that connected the dining room to the large kitchen. Our cook, Shafia, had prepared two dishes for lunch, along with a salad, as was customary.

Just then, the door from the hallway flew open, and round and stocky Shafia came in carrying a sizable hot platter, followed by Josephine, our maid, her petite frame straining under another platter and a tray. They placed it all on the table in front of mama, who always sat at the head of the table.

Mama filled each plate, beginning with my oldest brother, Sami, and then moving on to Ramsey. At fourteen, I was the youngest, so my turn always came last. After she had served my brothers, she looked at me with her sparkling blue eyes, a trait said to have been handed down from some twelfth-century Crusader and asked me to hand her my plate.

We were having *kusa mihshi* (stuffed zucchini in tomato sauce) and *yakh'nit bameh* (okra stew), one of my least favorite dishes, for lunch that day. I begged her to just let me have the *kusa*, arguing I would throw up all over the dining room table if forced to eat the greenish cooked vegetable with its slimy texture. The wet skin of cooked *bameh* reminded me of the excretion left behind by a crawling snail.

Mama tried to convince me that *bameh* was good for me, but I was adamant; I would not eat it. Likely remembering the last time I was forced to eat *bameh*, she relented and gave me some extra *kusa* instead. My brothers were used to my complaining and ignored the exchange, already digging into their own lunches.

The dining room was a very important room in our house. It was where the family gathered twice a day for the main meal at lunch and for a lighter fare at supper. We would enter the dining room from the living room, where the floor was covered with Persian rugs. I often spent hours on those rugs, practicing playing marbles, as playing marbles for keeps was a popular game in our neighborhood.

The dining room had three huge French windows, and a large china cabinet stood against one wall. On the other wall was a sideboard with drawers full of silverware, white linen napkins, and napkin rings. We each had our own napkin ring, and we boys knew where to sit by looking for where Shafia had placed our rings. My two baby sisters, Leila and Maria, were too young to sit with us at the table and did not have their own rings yet.

After lunch, I went to my room to continue reading the Arabic translation of a Sherlock Holmes mystery I was currently immersed in before I had to head back to school for another two hours. Mama went to take her customary after-lunch nap, which papa would have done as well if he had been there. I gave no further thought to mama's "decision of momentous importance" and quickly forgot all about it.

As I walked home from school that day, I kicked a small stone all the way from the school's gate to the entrance of our building, lost in thought. I was thinking about an essay I had to write for one of my classes and decided to write about Mount Sanin and how it rose from the sea. The previous summer, we had climbed Mount Sanin and, much to our surprise, discovered fossils of fish and other sea life lying on the ground among the rocks at the peak.

When I got home, I went straight to my room with the intention of doing homework, but got distracted by the new issues of *Tom and Jerry* and *Little Lulu*. I loved comic books, even though I did not read English very well; I could simply follow the story by looking at the pictures. Comics were popular among many of the children of Ras Beirut. But for the most part, these were Arabic comic books published in Egypt. Some American comic books were translated into Arabic, but I never saw any of these, and never had interest in them anyway. American comics such as Li'l Abner, Superman, Donald Duck, Little Lulu, and Tom and Jerry were popular mostly among the older children, those well versed in English, in my family circle of friends. Sami, who read English well, wanted the original English version because he said they're more authentic. I loved going through Sami's English-language comic books, following the pictures and making up my own stories. Little Lulu was my favorite comic character. I imagined Lulu, the heroine, to be an independent tough girl who stood up to the boys. She was a girl with her own independent mind. I loved that image of Lulu.

I was in my room, sitting at my desk with the new *Little Lulu* issue when Sami came in. "Supper's ready; let's go find out what this 'decision of momentous importance' is," he said. I was jolted by the sudden memory of Mama's earlier statement, which I had completely forgotten about.

Lunch and supper were the times when our family had serious discussions and when my parents announced important family events, such as when mama found out she was pregnant again after nine years, or when my parents bought an apple orchard in the mountains.

For me, "serious family discussions" were sometimes unpleasant as they often involved my academic performance. It was not unusual for papa to reprimand me for not getting an A on a test and insist that I explain—in detail—how I had studied for it, which usually resulted in me admitting that I had hardly studied at all. The "serious discussion" then ended with the reminder: "Nasib, your only goal in life right now should be to get As in all your classes; nothing else matters. When you get back to your room, write down, in detail, how you plan to study from now on and show it to me before bedtime."

"But Papa, I already wrote a detailed plan last time," I would object.

"Well, it clearly didn't work," Papa said. "Write another one and remember the rule in this house: only 'A' students get allowances."

So, as I followed Sami into the dining room on this particular evening, I was extremely nervous. Had Papa found out about all my school shenanigans over the years? Had my escapades finally caught up with me? Perhaps my parents finally found out about the bell incident several months earlier.

One day, on my way home from school, one of my friends had dared me to ring the doorbell of a dark-looking house with a huge, cluttered garden filled with unkempt bushes and overgrown trees. Not willing to stand down from a challenge, I rang the bell, then ran around the corner and hid.

The next day, as I walked home from school alone, I decided to ring the bell again and see what would happen, mentally daring anyone to catch me. I had noticed two classmates walking right behind me but didn't give them any thought.

This time, no sooner had I rung the bell, than a fat, wrinkled older woman, most likely the household's maid, came running out, chasing after me with a rug beater. Of course, she could hardly walk, let alone run, and had no chance of catching up with me. As I raced around the corner, I saw her talking to one of my classmates who had been behind me. I didn't give it any thought, feeling certain that they wouldn't rat me out. I made it home in one piece, feeling triumphant after my adventure. As it happened, my feelings of triumph were premature.

The next morning, I was immediately called into the principal's office when I arrived at school. Evidently, my schoolmates had indeed told the lady who I was, and she had contacted the principal to complain about my behavior.

My answer to the principal's inquiry as to why I would do such a thing was, "I wanted to find out whether the bell worked. The first time

I rang it, no one answered, so I decided to try again." Of course, the principal did not believe a word, choosing instead to believe the adult who had reported my infraction; but, as usual, I got away with just a warning.

The principal greatly admired my father and was a little intimidated by him, as Papa was not only a respected professor of economics and a member of the Ras Beirut intellectual circle of movers and shakers—members of the academic community that worked and lived around Ras Beirut, the American University of Beirut neighborhood—but also the chief economics advisor to the president of the Lebanese Republic. The principal's respect for my father and my family was likely the reason why I was never seriously punished for all of my shenanigans in elementary school.

Now, as I walked slowly toward the dining room, my apprehension building, I wondered: had I *really* gotten away with just a warning? Were my parents going to announce I had been expelled from school? Had they enrolled me in a boarding school up in the mountains, away from all my neighborhood friends? And what about my school friends? I'd had the same friends for eight years; would I have to find new ones?

Then I checked myself and thought, *it wasn't that bad. All I did was ring a bell.*

As we sat down at the dining room table for the lightest meal of the day, I glanced at Papa, who wore a serious expression. He was a large man with a firm and stern, yet kind, round face, a balding head, and a large nose. He was dressed in his usual three-piece gray suit and seemed to have a lot on his mind.

As Papa tore off a piece of pita and scooped up a bit of hummus, he looked around the table. I was worried, and my fear began to manifest physically as stomach discomfort. I was almost on the verge of crying.

Between bites of hummus, cheese, and olives, he simply announced, "Your mother and I have decided to move the family to America this coming summer. The opportunities will be better for you boys, but if you prefer not to move, we'll forget about it."

"Excited" didn't even begin to describe my feelings as Papa uttered the words *move the family to America.* Not only was I relieved I was not in trouble, I was elated at the prospect that what had once seemed like an impossible dream might actually now come true.

Still, I needed to see my older brothers' reactions to be sure this was a good idea. In the siblings' hierarchy, I was number three, and my role was usually to follow and imitate.

Looking across the table, I saw that Ramsey was grinning; he was just as excited at the news as I was. Ramsey was three years older than me. For the most part, we seemed to exist on different planets, each with our own groups of friends and activities, but when it came to family matters, we had evolved a special, nonverbal form of communication. A wink, a frown, a raised eyebrow between us could say more than words ever would. I admired Ramsey's competitiveness and his uncanny drive to succeed. He had the biggest heart, and along with his generosity came a genuine sense of fairness in treating others.

My oldest brother, Sami, was clearly also pleased, but I could never read him as well as I could Ramsey. Ramsey and I were closer in age, and we shared more interests. In many ways, Sami always seemed more like another responsible adult in the house, and I never thought of him as a playmate. He has always been the reliable one among us, looking out to see how he can help, always kind and responsible.

Still, after a brief exchange of glances, the three of us shouted, almost in unison, "Not go to America? Are you kidding?"

After our initial outburst of enthusiasm, we all fell silent, waiting for Papa to tell us more. He drew out our anticipation as he silently reached for the pitcher of ice water and slowly poured the water into his glass. He always made sure only two ice cubes fell into the glass. He then informed us he would not be joining us for our first three years in the United States; he had commitments with the university and the government he needed to wrap up during the first year; the next two years, he accepted a position with the United Nations as the economics advisor to the UN Secretary General in the Congo. Then, as if to punctuate all was said and done, he put the glass to his mouth, drinking its contents in one long swallow.

Mama followed up: "We'll be going to live in Albany, New York, where my friend Arpené and her family live."

We children called all of my parents' longtime friends "Auntie" and "Ammo" (Uncle), so to us, she was Auntie Arpené. A member of the large Armenian community in Lebanon, Auntie Arpené and my mother had been friends since they were in elementary school together. The Armenian community in Lebanon was made up of the descendants of refugees who had fled the Ottoman genocide in Turkey at the beginning of the twentieth century, a horrific episode in history that we had learned about in sixth-grade history class.

Auntie Arpené was a short, thin woman with a pretty, round face, a permanent smile, and long, light-brown hair. She was famous in my family's circle of friends for frequently using the wrong gender-specific pronouns whenever she tried to converse in Lebanese Arabic, her second language. For example, whenever she addressed Mama and wanted to say "you," she would use *inta*, the masculine "you," instead of *intee*, the feminine "you." Everyone would laugh, Arpené more than anyone else.

Mama snapped me out of my reverie and continued her description of our future in America: "We'll start organizing and preparing for the trip immediately. I'll contact the U.S. embassy tomorrow and start telling people the news."

It was real! It was true! We were moving to America! I couldn't wait to get to school the next day and tell all my friends, especially my best friend, Misbah.

After supper, I went to my room to study, but I had a hard time concentrating on the assignment in my civics textbook. I was very excited and could not stop thinking and dreaming about this new adventure. Mama had told us we would travel to America on a ship, which was doubly exciting, as I had never been on one before. I kept picturing ships sailing away and disappearing beyond the horizon. I wondered what was beyond it. After an hour of trying to focus on my homework and being continuously interrupted by my thoughts and dreams about the voyage to America, I gave up and went to sleep.

I shared my bedroom with my oldest brother, Sami, who was five years my senior. As brothers, and when it came to family affairs, Sami, Ramsey, and I were very close. But when it came to friends and activities, if Ramsey and I were on different planets, Sami and I were not even in the same universe. He was hardly ever in our room when I was there. Even at bedtime, I saw very little of him. I went to bed in the evening before he did, and he got up and left before I was awake in the morning. He was in his third year at the American University of Beirut at the time, studying business, and he had his own friends and concerns.

That night, I went to sleep with the thought, *I'm going to America!* racing through my brain. Throughout my life, countless other people had visited America: papa; mama; mama's sister, Auntie Eva; her husband, Charles, or "Ammo Sharl" as we children called him; their son, my cousin Habib; my schoolmate, Raid; and my school principal, Mr. Ataya. I had only dreamt about *me* going to America. The idea was almost too far-fetched. We children had learned America was made for children, a land of fun, with Disney World and Coney Island. Our image of America was shaped to a great extent by the American movies we watched. We felt that in America they made movies for children. Films such as *Cinderella; Twenty Thousand Leagues under the Sea; The 7th Voyage of Sinbad; Davy Crockett, King of the Wild Frontier;* and the Superman and Tarzan movies influenced the games we made up and played. Western movies with heroes such as Roy Rogers, Hopalong Cassidy, and The Lone Ranger and Tonto gave us the impression the American West was populated by Cowboys and Indians. We often made up games where the hero would be one of the characters from these movies. From America came our most popular toys, such as the Hula-Hoop, Mr. Potato Head, Matchbox cars, and pogo sticks. We children were convinced America was one giant toyland.

Now, people—my friends, my cousins, others I didn't even know— would be talking about me. "Nasib Badre is going to America," they would say, wishing they could go, the way I used to wish whenever I heard someone was traveling to the United States.

2. Breaking the News

THE NEXT MORNING, I WOKE UP ANXIOUS TO SHARE MY EXCIT-
ing news with anybody and everybody. I rushed down the stairs
from our second-floor residence on Rue Artois—a grand name for a
street that was, in reality, very narrow, almost an alley that could only
accommodate one car at a time—to the street. The name dated to the
French mandate, a period of French colonial occupation that lasted
from 1923 to 1946.

In our neighborhood, Ras Beirut—"Ras" meaning "the head of" or
"the tip of," since this part of the city jutted out into the sea—families lived
in five- or six-story buildings. There were very few single-family homes
like the one I got in trouble for ringing the doorbell of. Usually, each
floor was a single residence, each with as many as five or six bedrooms.
We lived on the second floor of the Halim Hannah building, across the
street from the three-story building my grandparents lived in and owned.
They also lived on the second floor of their building, and they rented out
the first and third floors. We often waved and yelled at each other from
across the street while standing on our respective balconies.

We lived several streets away from my prep school, the International
College (IC), and near the American University of Beirut (AUB) cam-
pus, where papa worked. My walk to IC along narrow streets filled with
residential buildings and stores took about eight minutes. Each day, I
walked through the heart of our neighborhood, which extended from
Hamra Street in the east to the seacoast in the west, and from Abde'l
Aziz Street in the north, where the AUB hospital was located, to the
Manara, a nineteenth-century lighthouse, in the south.

Our residence was only two blocks west of Hamra Street itself. Hamra
was the hub of Beirut café culture, where people regularly gathered at

its many restaurants and coffeehouses. Hamra was also the place to go shopping for clothes, accessories, camera equipment, jewelry, shoes, furniture, books, groceries, and anything else one could imagine. This entire area of Ras Beirut was filled with shops, hotels, clubs and movie theaters. It was what gave Beirut the title The Paris of the Middle East in the 1950s. This neighborhood was also our playground growing up.

The tramway, a trolley that ran from the Manara to the Bourj, Beirut's city center, connected our Ras Beirut neighborhood to the rest of the city. It clamored along noisily, always ringing its bell. My friends and I often took the tram to the *souks* (markets) near the city center. We weren't actually interested in shopping in these overcrowded bazaars; we just loved watching the art of haggling.

As I stepped outside our building's gate this particular morning, I was pleased to discover it was finally sunny. It had been raining for six days straight. As I set out, I noticed the tiny grocery store kitty-corner to our building was open. I often stopped there after school to get a Pepsi and candy or a cookie. Now I thought, Oh, good! I'll go tell Im Jozef the news.

Im Jozef, which means, "mother of Joseph," owned the store along with her husband, and she was always there, sitting behind the counter. I never saw her stand up or leave her post behind the counter, so I never knew what she looked like below her chest. To me, Im Jozef was always a person with half a body, an ancient-looking woman with a wrinkly face and disheveled gray hair.

I never paid for the candy or anything else that Im Jozef was kind enough to give me. One day I told our maid, Shafia, about Im Jozef's generosity, only to discover from an amused Shafia that Im Josef kept a record of everything she "gave" me and sent a bill to my parents at the end of each month.

This morning, I burst in and excitedly told her about our impending voyage. The first words out of her mouth were to ask if I would be able to find my favorite candy in America, a chocolate-covered wafer, which I got almost every day on my way home from school.

Earlier that year, I dropped by to get my favorite treat after school, but to my great disappointment, there were none in their usual spot on the shelf. When I inquired, Im Jozef told me it had been discovered the candy was being sold in Israel in violation of the Arab boycott. As a result, Lebanese stores were no longer allowed to carry it.

After the 1947 war between Israel and the surrounding Arab countries, the Arab nations declared a boycott on any business or company that did business in and with Israel; any products sold in Israel could not also be sold in the Arab world. For example, for a long time, Pepsi was not sold in Israel, but Coke was. As a result, Pepsi became very popular in Lebanon.

Up until then, I had known next to nothing about the ongoing Arab–Israeli conflict. Now, it had a direct impact on me, even if it was only in the minor realm of candy availability. I'll never forget that day when the irresistible wafer candy bar personalized world politics for me.

After visiting Im Jozef, I continued on to school. Just before I turned the corner onto Jean D'arc Street, I heard the street vendor Abu Ali yell, "*Kastana mishwyeh!*" (roasted chestnuts), and smelled the unique aroma emanating from his cart. Abu Ali was a short older man who always wore a bulky gray wool knitted hat. He often smiled as he greeted his customers, displaying two missing front teeth.

That morning, the scent of the roasted chestnuts was deliciously appetizing and made me hungrier than I should have been that early in the day. Still, I approached the old man to tell him about my family's plans. He simply replied by assuring me I would never find *kastana mishwyeh* as fresh as his in America.

As I reached Bliss Street, which was named after the American Presbyterian missionary, Daniel Bliss, the founder of AUB, I saw my friend Raid. He was standing in front of the Uncle Sam's Restaurant, the only place in Beirut where we could get an American hot dog.

Uncle Sam's was located across the street from the AUB main gate and was a favorite destination for the residents of Ras Beirut. Whenever we were there, someone would almost always repeat the story of what had happened when Mr. Khoury, the owner, tried to introduce the hot dog to his Lebanese customers.

Shortly after he began serving hot dogs, the police informed him that they would be shutting down his restaurant. When he protested, they explained it was against the law to serve dog meat in Lebanon. Mr. Khoury finally managed to convince them hot dogs were not made with dog meat and were, in fact, a sausage made of pork and beef. After that, the hot dog at Uncle Sam's became very popular in Ras Beirut.

This morning, my classmate Raid was waiting for me. When I came up to him, he asked if I was coming to football practice that afternoon. I told him I was and then asked him if they played football in America.

Two years earlier, Raid had lived in the United States for a while when his father, a history professor at AUB, spent a six-month sabbatical at a university in Boston.

Raid casually replied that they did, but from what he saw, they ought to call it handball, since they used their hands to move the ball most of the time, not their feet.

At that, I told him the news we were moving to America. Laughing, I joked I had better learn their version of football. It wasn't until I arrived in the United States I learned that what I had always called "football," Americans referred to as "soccer."

As Raid and I approached the school, I saw my best friend, Misbah, coming from the opposite direction, hurrying to catch up with us.

"Misbah," I shouted as he crossed the street to meet us at the school gate. "You'll never guess the great news I have to tell you!"

"I know," Misbah said as he came up to join us, "the *manaeesh* you ate this morning made you forty percent smarter."

Every morning, all the kids stopped to get *manaeesh* on their way to school. We believed having the pita-like bread covered in thyme, sumac, and sesame seeds mixed with olive oil in the morning made us twenty percent smarter, and we usually made sure to have some on the mornings before tests. But today I had not stopped for any; I was too excited about my news.

"No, the great news has nothing to do with *manaeesh*; my family will be going to live in America," I exclaimed.

Misbah slapped me on the back excitedly as the three of us joined others entering the schoolyard and said, "I was looking at pictures of Coney Island in New York the other day. America is the greatest place to live."

"Is this the same Misbah," I asked, "who just the other day was singing the praises of the Soviet Union, boasting that Russia is the strongest
and greatest country in the world? And that if it comes to a showdown,
Russia will demolish America?"

"Get serious, Nasib. America is where we should all live. Have you
seen pictures of Disneyland, the home of Mickey Mouse?" We children knew America was where all our favorite cartoon characters lived.
Whenever we went to the movies, we looked forward to the cartoons
that preceded the feature film, even more than the film itself. We loved
Donald Duck and Mickey Mouse, and almost all of us wanted to be
close to where we imagined they lived—in America.

I could tell that Misbah was happy for me, and regardless of his
political leanings, he also yearned to go to America. In fact, within
a few days, I realized that almost all of my friends were wishing they
could travel to the United States with me. For my part, I had yet to realize how much I would miss them.

Misbah, Raid, and I walked down the narrow asphalt road that ran
through our school campus. This morning, like every morning, it was
buzzing with students. The three buildings that made up our school
sat quietly in a straight line, patiently waiting for the bell to ring before
devouring and silencing the noisy crowd approaching them. The first
two buildings contained classrooms for the seventh through twelfth
grades, with the second one also housing administrative offices. The
third building was primarily a dormitory for international students.

On one side of the three buildings was a football field, still echo-
ing with a high-pitched, "Pass the ball," and showing the remnants of
the many failed attempts at growing grass. Adjacent to the field was a
basketball court and a gym. Beyond the high school facilities, the road
wound downhill to the elementary school building, athletics field, and
playground. I had spent six of my eight years at the IC in that very
elementary building. It was also where I first met Misbah and Raid.

Just as we reached the first building, we ran into our fourth-grade
teacher. All these years later, her name escapes me, but I will always
remember her shapely figure. She was of Palestinian origin, with a naturally pretty face and long brown hair. She used to sit on top of her desk

at the front of the classroom and cross her ankles. I felt very lucky to have been assigned a seat in the very front row. I had a massive crush on her, as I'm sure every boy in the class did. We often compared her to the movie queen of the time, Tarzan's Jane.

As she started down the steep stairway to the elementary school grounds, we greeted her with the usual morning greetings, "*Sabah El Khair.*" She returned our greetings and told us how happy she was to see us, as we were three of her best students ever. Misbah and I looked at each other incredulously and started laughing. "Doesn't she remember?" we asked each other.

Misbah and I had bonded and become best friends in fourth grade when we got in trouble over what we had dubbed the Secrets Notebook. This was the first of many schemes, plans, projects, and ideas we cooked up throughout our years of friendship. The Secrets Notebook was where we wrote critical, humorous, and sometimes mean comments about teachers and other students.

Nobody had access to the notebook except for the two of us, as we guarded it carefully. Despite that, we made sure our fellow classmates knew about it and let them see us writing in it and whispering to each other over it. Sometimes we even simply pretended to say something, just to incite their notice. Classmates who did not want anything bad written about them went out of their way to be extra nice to us and win our favor.

One day in class, I wrote a comment about our attractive young instructor in the notebook: "She is a bore, but you have to admit, she's a knockout." When I passed the notebook to Misbah, our teacher saw the exchange. She came over, took the notebook from him, glanced at the open page, and stormed out the classroom door. Within minutes, Misbah and I were called to the principal's office.

The principal played his role as the tough disciplinarian with a "don't mess with me" attitude superbly. He was of average height, but muscular and with a stern face. He liked to flaunt his physical abilities whenever he had an opportunity. Before he became the principal, he had been in charge of school athletics and had been a weightlifter. Once during a school assembly, he had us watch slides of him lifting weights, showing us his physical strength and encouraging us to be like him. He was a rugged man from Schweir, a Christian mountain village, which also happened to be my family's ancestral village.

Students dreaded being called into the principal's office. He often used a stick cut from a *rimmani* (pomegranate) tree to punish unruly children with several lashes to the buttocks. We called it The Rimmani. The entire student body was terrified of it, and it was the subject of numerous whispered conversations in the hallways and during recess.

As we were busy filling the pages of The Secrets Notebook, the prospect of consequences never crossed our minds. But now, because of the teacher we most wanted to impress, we had to face the principal and the dreaded Rimmani.

The principal's office was on the other side of the building, down a very long hallway from our classroom. We walked that hallway as slowly as we could, hoping in our naïve way that if we went slowly enough, we would never reach our destination. Of course, we could not stop the inevitable.

As we entered the principal's reception area, Ms. Kalaf, the office administrator, who generally greeted us with a wide smile, now looked at us with a grimace, her wide eyes communicating her great displeasure. "Go right in," she said, "The principal is waiting for you."

There was an expression of fury and disgust on his face when we entered his office. He lectured us about our behavior, pointing out that IC students come from decent families and they *never* write inappropriate comments about teachers. Then he smacked the top of his desk with The Rimmani and told Misbah to turn around for his punishment. As he was administering the penalty to Misbah, the principal looked at me and said, "This is the kind of punishment you'll get the next time you do something like this." I got off with merely a tongue-lashing, while Misbah got The Rimmani version. As usual, I had been spared the worst. Years later, we both delighted in telling the story as a humorous episode in our youth.

Chuckling at these recollections, the three of us continued on toward our own school building. As we walked, Misbah glanced over at me and again assured me he was delighted by my family's decision to move to America. "Now," he declared, "I'll have someone to visit there!"

Still, I could tell he was conflicted. On one hand, he thought America was a great place to live. Yet at the same time, he wondered aloud why my family would want to leave Lebanon. He seemed uncomfortable with the idea my family and I would leave for good. He even waxed poetical on the subject at one point: "With its seacoast and fertile mountains, Lebanon is the most attractive country in the Arab world! Leaving it permanently is inconceivable, a heresy by every measure."

At his vehemence, I wondered, Could he be right? After all, we'll be leaving cosmopolitan Beirut, 'The Paris of the Middle East,' and going to Albany, New York, nowhere near the sea and likely far from beautiful mountain villages where we can spend our summers.

Seeing I was receptive to this line of thought, Misbah continued, "Here, you are somebody. You have lifelong friends, you're recognized as a top athlete in our school, your family belongs to the academic social elite, your father is a respected intellectual, and people know who you, Nasib Badre, are. When you get to America, no one will know you or anything about you; you'll have to start all over again. The boys in your class will already have their own friends, activities, and interests, and they will totally ignore you; you'll be alone and miserable."

I tried to dismiss what Misbah was saying and thought, He's just trying to spoil my great adventure because he's jealous. Our impending voyage, and telling my friends all about it, was of paramount importance to me, and I could not be swayed from thoughts of all the excitement and fun I would have in America. I wanted Misbah to understand that I, like the rest of my family, aspired to and believed in the values of Western culture, and that we were going to follow through on what we believed by adopting Western values and living in the West.

But his misgivings about the permanency of our move did give me pause. While I was excited by what I saw as a great adventure, I wanted to be able to explain what was so right about permanently moving to America and what was so wrong about staying in Lebanon. I couldn't think of one good reason for my argument, but this didn't dampen my excitement.

As I sat in school that day, I thought about my school friends and especially about Misbah, our long friendship, and our political arguments over the years.

Misbah and I had played together, confided in one another, and argued with each other for five years. In fact, we frequently argued fiercely, often about politics, America, and the Soviet Union. We knew we came from different cultural and religious communities, with our families on opposite sides of the Christian/Muslim divide that was Lebanon, but we never talked about it or let it interfere with our friendship. Instead, we argued about the politics of the day dividing our cultural communities, always reflecting our own community's cultural loyalties, whether Eastern or Western.

We were politically naïve, and our arguments were often childish and lacked factual accuracy, but we were interested in politics even when we were still in elementary school. We took opposing positions on almost every issue, but our arguments usually sounded more like a debate over who would win a football game.

Misbah: Abdel Nasser will make sure that Lebanon becomes part of the United Arab Republic.

Nasib: Not in your dreams or my nightmares; America will never let that happen.

Misbah: Russia will put a stop to anything America tries to do.

Nasib: America will wipe Russia off the face of the Earth with one blow.

Misbah: But how can they do that after Russia has already blown America into smithereens?

Nasib: America has ten thousand times more missiles than Russia.

Misbah: Nuh-uh! Russia has one hundred thousand more missiles than America. Besides, they're ahead of the Americans in science; they proved it with Sputnik.

Misbah and I frequently invented facts—like the number of missiles the United States and the Soviet Union had—just to win an argument. But at the same time, we were aware of what was going on in our world. Our arguments became much more intense in 1958, when we were twelve and civil strife between Christians and Muslims broke out in Lebanon. As a result, the school year ended early, and I did not see Misbah again until the next fall, after the conflict was over. My family spent that summer in Dhour Schweir, our ancestral village in the mountains. We felt safe in our Christian village, and we often spent our summers there anyway. The conflict lasted the entire summer.

After the short civil war ended and summer drew to a close, school opened again, and everything went back to normal. It was like nothing had happened at all. My first conversation with Misbah was as co-captains of the sixth-grade football team, deciding which positions we should each play that year.

Many years later, as a graduate student in Ann Arbor, Michigan, I finally realized my incessant arguments with Misbah were not simply those of children playing politics; they were—sadly and seriously—reflections of our communities' indoctrinations and the deep divisions that had plagued the Lebanese landscape for generations.

The Christian community from whence I sprung insisted that Lebanon was a Phoenician, not Arab, nation and looked to the West, and specifically to America, for inspiration and support. Misbah's community of Sunni Muslims was pro–Arab Nationalist and held the charismatic Egyptian President, Gamal Abdel Nasser, as their hero. They looked to the Soviet Union for protection from "Western imperialism."

What puzzled me the most at the time was that many in the Muslim community—especially my Muslim friends and their families—were themselves immersed in imported Western culture. They listened to American and European music, watched American movies, dressed like Westerners, read translated Western literature, and even chose Western schools such as IC for their children's education.

~

On my way home from school the day after my parents' "America announcement," as I thought of it, I was keenly aware of my surroundings, which on a normal day I would have taken for granted. Little things I encountered on my daily route home from school suddenly took on a greater importance, and I wondered how often I would see them again.

I considered the bearded beggar with his filthy face, unkempt hair, and ragged clothes that sat cross-legged and hunched over on the sidewalk just outside the school gate every afternoon as we headed home. To us, he was a strange kind of a beggar, as we never saw him actually beg for money. Instead, he sat there hammering perfectly good coins into the asphalt of the sidewalk. When we asked him why he did this, he never answered. We concluded he did not speak Arabic and became increasingly certain he was not even a real beggar.

We loved to come up with theories about his real identity. These ranged from the idea he was a spy quietly listening to the chatter around him, to the romantic notion he was a millionaire who simply enjoyed pretending to be a beggar. The story that eventually took hold of our imaginations and became the most popular theory was he was a Nazi criminal hiding out in Beirut. As a result, we named him Heinrich.

I felt conflicted. Of course I wanted to go to America, the land of rock 'n' roll, Mickey Mouse, and hot dogs, but here I had friends and a history that rooted me and my family closely to our kin and the city. How would it be to give up my conversations with Misbah, walks home from school, and even encounters with Heinrich?

3. Reasons for Immigrating: Politics and Religion in Lebanon

WHEN I GOT HOME FROM SCHOOL THAT DAY, I WENT directly to my parents' bedroom to talk to Mama about our coming trip.

On my way, I ran into Papa, who looked somewhat despondent. I guessed his expression was due to the fact he wouldn't be with us for the first three year there, as he had mentioned the previous night at dinner. Conversations with Papa usually revolved around my performance in school, so to cheer him up, I told him that my plan was to be a straight-A student in my first year in America.

"You'll be lucky if you can learn American English in your first year," he said. A touch of apprehension set in, dampening my excitement slightly.

What I did not realize at the time was this was the start of not only a geographical voyage, but also a personal and cultural transformation, a journey that, above all, would require I become fluent in a language with which I had zero practical experience. I did not appreciate the extent to which not knowing American English and not having experienced American youth slang would put me at a disadvantage.

I was not cognizant of it at that time, but I was the only one in my family with this serious difficulty. My parents both spoke fluent English. Papa had done his graduate studies in America and taught courses at the American University of Beirut in English. Mama had majored in English literature in college, and she had taught English at the university. My brothers, Sami, who had already finished his third year at the American University of Beirut, and Ramsey, who was about to enter college, both had a solid English vocabulary and spoke the language very well. Leila and Maria were still babies and would have no problems assimilating.

At the age of fourteen, I was the only one who would struggle with the language barrier.

I went on in to see Mama. I told her I was really excited about our move, but I wanted to hear more about why and how their decision came about.

Mama lay back on the bed, kicked off her shoes, and began by reiterating what Papa had said about there being more opportunities for us in America. Many Lebanese immigrated because professional job opportunities were almost nonexistent in Lebanon at the time, even with family connections. Most connections were religiously based, and Protestants like us were not well connected in the overall picture. Most Lebanese worked in services like tourism, farming, or the merchant trade, all of which were handed down within families. We had none of this, and intellectual and professional jobs were very limited.

Mama and Papa had started thinking about the possibility of moving when they were in New York during Papa's sabbatical at the United Nations during the 1957–58 year, when he headed up the U.N.'s Middle East unit. During her six months in America, she came to firmly believe the United States was an open society, a place where tolerance for different religions was the norm. She wanted to live in a society where she could openly practice her Roman Catholic faith without interference.

I had long been vaguely aware of Mama's Catholicism; I often saw her reciting the rosary or reading a Catholic pamphlet. Pictures of Mary and Jesus, as well as a wooden crucifix adorned the walls of my parents' bedroom. Catholic books and pamphlets sat on the table next to her bed.

Mama converted from Presbyterianism to Catholicism in January of 1952 while on a trip to Paris to see her sister Eva and her brother-in-law, Charles Malik. Ammo Sahrl, who at the time was the Lebanese Ambassador to the United States. He was in Paris attending a U.N. meeting, so it seemed like the perfect opportunity for the sisters to see each other. Ammo Sharl's brothers, one a Dominican and the other a Jesuit priest, were also there, and Mama spent many days and nights discussing religion with them. Their conversations were apparently enough to convert her to their faith.

From the day of her conversion on, Mama lived a truly devout Catholic life. Many times, I would enter her room to ask her something or simply give her a hug, and I would find her quietly praying or reading the Bible or *The Imitation of Christ* by Thomas à Kempis.

The Protestants of Ras Beirut did not approve of her becoming a Catholic, and I first realized that not all Christians were the same when I noticed her Catholic life and practices were not discussed or even mentioned openly in our Protestant community. She would not talk about her faith among our Protestant friends and relatives, except for when she had to occasionally correct a misconception.

I remember some conversations in social gatherings in which some-one would disparage Catholics as worshipers of statues and images. Mama would try to explain this was not true, but people didn't want to listen and stuck with their own ideas and misinformation. I knew what Protestants said about Catholics was incorrect, because I never saw my mother worshiping statues.

At the same time, I also noticed when it came to political arguments and conflicts with Muslims, all Christians—Catholics and Protestants—stood together as one. Despite any internal fractiousness, at the end of the day, the Christian/Muslim divide ruled supreme.

I experienced this divide in my political arguments with Misbah. To me, Misbah was simply a Muslim, and to him, I was simply a Christian. I don't know if he knew I was a Protestant; he never asked, and it never occurred to me to inform him. Similarly, I never thought to ask him whether he was a Sunni or Shia Muslim, and he never told me until many years later. All I knew at the time was he belonged to the Muslim com-munity, and so he automatically had opposing political views from mine.

For papa, the reality of Lebanon's religiously dominated political climate discouraged him. We lived in a society where religion reigned supreme, and the religion you belonged to defined who you were. Even though the Protestants of Beirut largely belonged to Lebanon's profes-sional class, their influence was limited because they were a minority religious group. The Maronite Christians—an Eastern Rite of the Cath-olic Church and the largest Christian denomination in Lebanon—and the Sunni Muslims were the majority religions in Lebanon, and thus, they constituted the majority political classes. As with everywhere else, those in the ruling classes made sure important decisions favored them.

Papa often spoke sarcastically of the Lebanese "confessional democracy," comparing it to the pigs of George Orwell's *Animal Farm.* "In Lebanon," he would say, "everyone is equal, but the Sunnis and Maronites are more equal than anybody else." This was likely at least partially what papa meant when he said, "The opportunities in America will be better for you children"—opportunities to live and work without the religious biases of others interfering.

It was only after we immigrated to the United States that Mama confided to me her life as a Catholic in our predominantly Protestant community of Ras Beirut had been very stressful. She had encountered difficulties, even hostilities, from Protestant friends. Some individual members of the Presbyterian Church even criticized Papa for allowing his wife to convert, challenging his status as a member of the Session.

In 1958, my mother was relieved of her position as an English teacher at the Beirut College for Women, a Presbyterian-founded college. The pastor put pressure on the college president to let her go, arguing if my mother continued to teach, she might influence the students to become Catholics.

Of course, while I was aware of Mama's hush-hush Catholic practices, I knew nothing of my parents' ongoing stress associated with her conversion. They did their best to shield us children from it, and they were largely successful. It wasn't until I was an adult, after many long conversations with my parents, I became fully aware of why my mother's catholic conversion caused stress and friction. It was due to the Badre family's historic and deep ties to the Protestant presence in Lebanon dating back to the nineteenth century.

My great-grandfather, Youssef Badr (1841–1912), had converted from Greek Catholicism—an Eastern Rite of the Catholic Church—to Presbyterianism and became the first Lebanese Protestant minister. Our family's ties to the Protestant presence in Lebanon led us to constantly look to the West for our intellectual and spiritual sustenance. Appreciating and yearning for Western culture was a part of who we were.

The Badre family's desire to associate itself with the West was evident in the repeated stories I heard about our origins. The narrative of our so-called "Europeans origin" was always told as part of the story of the

Badres, whether to hold it up as the truth or to expose it as myth. Our family story traveled to America with us and was told there many times, always with my parents enjoying the ritual of debating fact and fiction.

Over the years, I have also repeated the family story numerous times, always making sure to cast doubt on its veracity. Such accounts of European origins were not unusual among Lebanese Christians, who took pleasure in tying family lineage to historical events such as the Crusades. In cases where such occidental connections were hopelessly implausible, the fallback alternative was to link your heritage with the Phoenicians—but never to the Arabs.

According to the story, the Badres were descended from an Austrian nobleman named Alexif who came to Lebanon as a knight during the Crusades. This nobleman first came to Jbeil (Byblos), one of Lebanon's many towns where Crusaders eventually settled.

This aristocrat's descendants left Jbeil to settle in Khinshara, a village across the valley from the Badres' eventual ancestral village of Schweir. In Khinshara, the family name was Al-Kassouf, presumably an Arabized version of Alexif. Somewhere along the way, one of these descendants was named Badr Al-Kassouf, and one or more of his children adopted his first name as the family name. Thus, the Kassoufs of Khinshara became the Badrs of Schweir, descendants of Western nobility.

The Khinshara and Kassouf parts of the story have been verified as being historically accurate, but the part about the nobleman Alexif is always narrated with the caveat it is most likely untrue. Even as a child I wondered, If the Alexif story is in doubt, why keep repeating it, even if just to refute it? Was it to fulfill our family's aspirations for a connection with the West? To convince ourselves we had every right to a Western identity and culture?

After conversing with Mama, I left my parents' room with a much more complete understanding of what motivated my parents to decide we should move to America. It was not only we children would have better opportunities for careers in America, as Papa had told us when he made the America announcement. It was Mama's Catholicism and Papa's distaste for the confessional structure of Lebanese society that drove them to decide we should move.

4. The Realm of the Mind

IN MARCH OF 1960, A FEW MONTHS AFTER THE "MOVE TO America" announcement, we received a package in the mail from the U.S. embassy. It contained a cover letter from the consul requesting we make an appointment at the embassy for our entrance interview and to get our green cards. The large envelope also contained pictures of Albany, our destination in the United States, and literature about upstate New York and New York City. There was also a special pamphlet about "the mighty woman with a torch," the iconic Statue of Liberty.

The words of the poem by Emma Lazarus, inscribed at the base of the Statue of Liberty, had a lasting impact on me:

... From her beacon-hand
Glows world-wide welcome. . .
. . . cries she
With silent lips. "Give me your tired, your poor,
Your huddled masses yearning to breathe free,
The wretched refuse of your teeming shore.
Send these, the homeless, tempest-tossed to me . . ."

I had learned to read English in school, but translating this poem was difficult, even with an English-Arabic dictionary. Papa ultimately had to help me. When I was finally able to read and understand it, I felt these words were directed at me personally. The bold, proud lady with her torch was welcoming me to the land of better opportunities my parents promised.

Reading this poem, I realized for the first time I wanted to be recognized for achieving something special, and I felt sure I could only achieve this ambition in America. I believed my father's statement about opportunities, and I felt America was the land of boundless opportunities to achieve whatever one dreamed. I felt inspired, and that evening at the dining room table, I declared that when I grew up in America, I wanted to work in "the realm of the mind."

Papa asked, "What do you mean, 'the realm of the mind'?"

"I mean the realm of ideas," I replied, struggling to explain my thoughts and newfound ambitions. "I want to become a great thinker and write books. I could study history and relate my findings to current social and political issues. Then I could write books about my conclusions."

No one at the table took me seriously. After all, I was a youngster, and no one had heard me talk like this before. When kids my age in our social circle were asked what they wanted to be when they grew up, they usually gave answers like "a doctor" or "an engineer." Children generally didn't claim they wanted to work in "the realm of the mind."

However, by the age of nine, I was already interested in politics and history. I loved reading and had a ritual for reading the countless books I purchased in the bookstore across the street from my school. I would occasionally skip sitting down for supper with the rest of my family and instead ask Shafia to prepare a baguette sandwich—sometimes made with ham, butter, and several thinly sliced pickles, other times simply with butter and jam—for me and bring it to my room with a bottle of Pepsi. I would sit in bed with an Arabic translation of an English book—often one of the Sherlock Holmes books I was so fond of—and eat, drink, and read until I eventually turned off the light and went to sleep.

The next morning, as I walked to school, I would imagine myself as one of the characters I had read about the night before. After reading a Sherlock Holmes mystery, I would sleuth the street, noticing how people dressed, the brand of shoes they wore, their facial expressions, and whether they looked tired, anxious, or in a hurry. Then I would use my observations to make guesses about their lives, who they were, what they did for a living, and if they were rich or poor.

My reading list included Arabic translations of many of the British and American classics, but I did not ignore Arabic authors, either. *Isma Ya Rida*, or *Listen, Rida*, by Anis Frayha made me fall in love with the simple life of the Lebanese mountain village he described. The author narrated stories to his son, Rida, about village life in Lebanon. It made our summers in various Lebanese mountain villages much more appealing. I often went around the villages, looking for people and faces that would fit Frayha's characters and imagined stories about them similar to those in the book.

I also spent many baguette nights with *Gone with the Wind.* I fell in love with Scarlett O'Hara, who demonstrated what adversity women could overcome through shear strength of will. I was already familiar with strong and determined women among my relatives, especially my mother, who was both very strong-willed and a trailblazer in her own right, so Scarlett resonated with me deeply.

Mama often spoke to us around the dining room table about the challenges she faced in her daily life. We frequently asked her to repeat the story of how she led the effort to establish the first national kindergarten in Lebanon—my first school. We loved to hear of how she had successfully defended "those innocent children" from eviction by the building's owners, German missionaries who wanted to use it to start their own school. One day, she arrived at the school to find they had removed the kindergarten's sign and hung their own sign in its place. Mama in turn removed their sign, put her sign back up, and stood right in the gateway to the schoolyard, daring the missionaries to lay a hand on her. In the end, she prevailed.

My firsthand experience with Mama's trailblazing determination came when my parents bought their first car in 1952, a black English-made Humber Hawk. Mama insisted she wanted to drive, even though women did not drive in Lebanese society at this time. As usual, Papa supported and encouraged her, and she ultimately became our family's driver and the first woman driver in Lebanon. Whenever we got into the car to go to the mountains, the beach, to visit friends, or just about anywhere, Papa, who didn't like driving, sat in the front passenger seat, and we three boys sat in the back.

As Mama drove, the men in the street would point at her and shout in Arabic, "Look, a woman, a woman!" Sitting in the back seat, Ramsey and I felt important and would pretend we were big shots, waving at people when they stared in astonishment and pointed.

Mama didn't shy away from all that attention, either. In fact, she became quite well known in our Ras Beirut neighborhood for her signature car honk: "toot-toot-to-toot." People would always know the Humber Hawk and Mama were nearby when they heard the "toot-toot-to-toot."

Whether others recognized it or not, we knew our mother was wonderful and extraordinary, just like Scarlett O'Hara in that wonderful book.

Those countless evenings in bed with a sandwich and a book were the start of my life-long interest in ideas and intellectual discourse. Many of the beliefs I adopted as a result of my "book and baguette" phase have stayed with me my entire life and become the basis for later convictions and behaviors, including my love for baguette sandwiches.

Between 1956 and 1960, my intellectual curiosity grew. On the eve of our journey to the United States in the spring of 1960, I had made up my mind to pursue a career in what I termed "the realm of the mind." Little did I know my intellectual pursuits and interests would make me a very lonely and socially isolated teenager in America.

5. Together at San Michelle Beach

IN LATE MAY, MAMA AND I, ALONG WITH LEILA AND MARIA, and our two maids, Shafia and Josephine, went to San Michelle Beach early one morning to prepare our cabin for a large gathering later that day.

My little sisters were the jewels of our family. When Leila was born in 1954, I was nine years old and she took my place as the baby in the family. Leila's birth was an absolutely momentous event. She was the first girl to be born into the family of my mother and all my mother's siblings. Before that, it was a boys' world and boys in the family were my playmates. After Leila was old enough to run around, I loved playing silly games with her. The game we created and played incessantly was one where she would chase me around the house with a rug beater until I let her catch me, both of us falling down in laughter. She loved the "falling and laughing" part, and wanted to do it over and over again. When Maria was born two years later, she became the family's official baby. She was too young for me to play with her, but she loved it when I would carry her, dancing and singing, and making her laugh. Maria was so cute everybody wanted to hold her, carry her, and hug her. She was hugged at least a dozen times a day. Because of that experience, Maria still hugs everybody multiple times a day. To her, hugging is as essential to life as breathing. When you go to visit Maria, she hugs you three times, once when you arrive; then you'll be sitting, visiting, doing nothing, she'll come up and hug you; then when you leave she hugs you.

Our beach cabin was always the destination for large gatherings during the spring, and this would be our last beach party before our departure for America. All our relatives would be there, except for the Maliks, who were in the United States at the time.

The cabin at San Michelle sat on a white sandy beach close to the water. We entered the cabin through a small sitting room adjacent to a moderate-sized kitchenette on one side and a bathroom on the other. The sitting room was sparsely furnished with a couch, three chairs, and a table. From there, we went out to a balcony that contained a long table and several wooden beach chairs. The balcony faced the sea and had tieback draperies, which we used in the late afternoon when the setting sun in the west became too intense.

As soon as we arrived, I immediately slipped into my bathing suit and ran as quickly as I could down to the water for an early morning dip. Morning was my favorite time of day on the beach—it was the best time to look for seashells and other debris the night tides had washed ashore.

After a short swim, I floated on my back in the waves. Engulfed by the two blues, the sky and the water, I started thinking about where I was and where I would be going in a matter of weeks. *We're not just traveling; we're really leaving Lebanon for good. I will be leaving Beirut, where I was born and have lived all my life; my neighborhood of Ras Beirut; Dhour Schweir, my ancestral hometown; leaving my relatives and friends.*

Still, the prospect of going to America excited me more than the prospect of leaving everyone I knew pained me. I was going to the land of the Hula-Hoop and rock 'n' roll. I'd be living in the same country where Elvis Presley, Chuck Berry, and Mickey Mouse lived. I didn't just have to read about Disneyland—I could hop on a bus or a train and actually go there! Of course, I had not yet realized the vast size of America when compared with the small country of Lebanon.

As I daydreamed about my coming adventure, I saw the silhouette of the Lebanese mountains in the distance. I was sure my new American friends would be amazed that during early spring, we could sunbathe at noon and go skiing in the afternoon alongside the famous cedars of Lebanon, which are mentioned many times in the Bible. I knew it was fairly unlikely I could repeat the experience in my new home: Albany, New York, was close to the mountains, but far from the sea.

I also thought it unlikely I would be able to enjoy the kinds of summers we had in Lebanon. Shortly after school ended for the year and we had had our fill of the beach, we'd be on our way to the mountains, where we would spend the next three months. At the start of each summer, we children were exhausted from the rigors of school and ready to have fun and reunite with our summer friends. The friends we had at the summer resorts came from all over Lebanon and were, for the most part, not friends from school. By the end of summer though, drudgery would start to set in, and we couldn't wait to get back to Beirut, school, and our school friends.

Floating on my back, engulfed in the blue seawater, and lost in my deep thoughts, I was abruptly roused by someone calling my name. It was my cousin Amin, whom we called "Mooney." The Sabras had arrived.

We were close with my mother's sister Auntie Ellen, Ammo Fuad, and their two sons, Mooney and George. Not only did we share the beach cabin with them, but for three summers, we had also shared a house in Brummana.

Auntie Ellen was eight years younger than Mama. She was a reserved and quiet woman with a lovely face, light brown hair and hazel eyes. Most importantly though, she was kind to us children. Whenever I could, I used to go to the Sabra's house because I loved spending time with Auntie Ellen.

Ammo Fuad, a physician and our family doctor, was a sturdy-looking man. He was not very tall, but he seemed taller because of his manner. I was particularly fond of him because he always found a way to relate to us children, whether by talking to us about Western dance and music, playing the piano and leading us in song, wrestling with me and my brother, Ramsey, or just being a fun person. He often sided with the children against our parents when we wanted something, and he even occasionally intervened on our behalves when we were in trouble.

I was once spared a severe reprimand because of Ammo Fuad's intervention. It was our first summer in Brummana, and my brothers, cousins, summer friends and I spent a great deal of time playing badminton in the front yard. We were rather loud and earned a few serious complaints from the German couple that lived in an apartment on the lower level of our house.

One day, as some of us were playing a doubles match, the German couple walked by on their way to their apartment. One of our friends,

Ramzi, said in Arabic, "Here comes the male and female dogs." In Arabic, if you call someone a "dog" or "the son of a dog," it's a great insult. Ramzi said it in a very low voice, but then I repeated it in my usual very loud voice.

Of course, the couple heard me, and that day we discovered they knew Arabic. They immediately went to Mr. Baz, the athletics director and general manager responsible for summer rentals, who in turn got in touch with Papa. Through the grapevine of my friends, I was informed he was beside himself with anger at what I had said.

I managed to stay away from the house for the entire day. As dusk approached, I waited in the woods nearby, hoping I could eventually sneak in without Papa noticing. As I cowered behind a bush near the house, I heard a voice: "What are you doing out here?"

Ammo Fuad Sabra had just returned from Beirut, and as he got out of his car, he had spotted me.

"I'm waiting here until Papa goes to bed," I informed him, launching into the entire story of what had happened.

After he heard me out, Ammo Fuad said, "I'll talk to your father; wait here."

Fifteen minutes later, he came back out and said, "Your father will not punish you. Just go in now and be quiet."

I went in, still expecting a good scolding from Papa, but he merely looked at me with furious eyes and said, "Go to your room." I thought he would come up later and punish me, but he never did, and I think it was all thanks to Ammo Fuad.

After my cousin Mooney called out to me from the shore, I swam back to the shallow water, where Auntie Ellen was standing with Mooney and baby George, and decided to splash her and pull her into the water to play with us.

Her reaction to my antics was one of fearful anger. She scolded me and told me never to do that again. I had never seen Auntie Ellen angry before, and I did not know what I had done wrong. Later, when I told Mama what had happened, she explained that after a traumatic experience going down a waterslide and splashing into a pool of water when she was a baby, Auntie Ellen was uncomfortable around splashing water.

Now, as I swam closer to the shore, she told me Mama wanted me to come up and join the guests who had already arrived.

We walked back up to the cabin together and saw mama's younger brother, Khalo Fuad (In Arabic, an uncle is only called *Ammo* when he is the father's brother, an adult relative, or a friend of the family. The mother's brother we called *Khalo*); his wife, Auntie Wadad; and their sons, Hibbo and baby Kamal, had arrived. Khalo Fuad and the boys were already in their bathing suits and were heading down to the water to meet us.

"Nasib," Khalo Fuad greeted me, "are you ready to see if you can catch me in the water?" With that, he started running toward the sea.

A handsome man with a Roman nose and piercing dark eyes, Khalo Fuad's wit was unmatched in my family circles. He was very outgoing and would often crack jokes and set an upbeat mood for everyone at social gatherings. He frequently led our gatherings with music, playing the piano by ear, or, when there was no piano, his accordion. He had a natural gift for playing music by ear, as did my mother. They had inherited their musical talent from their father, my Grandfather Habib, who also often played the piano and sang at family gatherings.

After Mooney, Hibbo and I played in the waves with Khalo Fuad for a while, we came back to the cabin to find Auntie Wadad sitting in the sun on the porch in her bathing suit. She smiled and told Hibbo to put a towel on his shoulders because she felt a strong breeze. Auntie Wadad was always worried her children would catch a cold.

I loved visiting Auntie Wadad during lunch. Whenever I heard she was preparing *laban immou* (lamb cooked in yogurt and rice), I would go to their house for lunch instead of going home. It was both my favorite meal and her very best dish.

Just as we were about to sit down to join Auntie Wadad on the veranda, Papa arrived with my two brothers, Sami and Ramsey. Seeing her, he immediately asked Auntie Wadad to sing "Ya Laurie Houbiki," a song made famous by the Lebanese diva, Fayrouz. She protested there was no piano in the cabin to accompany her, but papa insisted her voice was a million times better alone than polluted by the sound of a piano.

The adults in our family often said her voice was similar, in fact, even purer than that of Fayrouz. If she had been willing to go professional, she would have become a very rich woman. But she wouldn't hear of such a thing, because in our family circles, to be a paid entertainer was beneath a person's dignity.

Convinced by my father, Auntie Wadad commenced singing. By the time she was done, Sami and Ramsey were already in their bathing suits. Ramsey ran out to the water and shouted, "Let's play tag! Nasib, you're it."

Both of my brothers were excellent swimmers, and they loved to show off their skills by swimming against the waves, teasing me by daring me to catch them. I remained "it" for the entire time we played that day; I was never able to catch either of them.

More family and friends continued to arrive. I lept out of my lounge chair when I saw the Nassifs—Ammo Anis and Auntie Nida with baby Lena in her arms—arrived. Their older children, Nadim and Samir, fell over each other laughing as they raced ahead toward the cabin. "Nadim, Samir, get changed! Let's go for a dive," I shouted as I ran toward them, practically falling over them in the sand.

The Nassifs were part of our extended family, the Badr–Sabra clan, which consisted of two core families. We became a noticeable presence in Ras Beirut with the 1949 double wedding of Mama's brother, Fuad Badr, to Wadad Sabra and Mama's sister, Ellen Badr, to Wadad's brother, Fuad Sabra. Auntie Nida was Auntie Wadad and Ammo Fuad's sister.

One of the last guests to arrive at our beach party was my father's cousin, Ammo Jamil, a short man with a round face, wide nose and slanted eyes. You could pick him out in a crowd immediately with his pencil-thin mustache and wavy, whitish hair. He was the only one on the beach wearing a suit jacket and tie.

A simple, quiet man, Ammo Jamil was a businessman of sorts, though not very ambitious or very successful. We saw very little of him in Beirut during the school year, but he was very much a part of my summer life in the mountains around Dhour Schweir, where he owned a clothing store for women and children right off the town square. I had even worked for him in his store for three weeks during the previous summer.

As he came over to where I was standing on the beach, he told me how delighted he was about our trip to America and informed me he was in partnership with his brother, Raif, who had immigrated to Florida and inherited a women's clothing factory and outlet store from their Ammo Ameen Badr.

He looked at me with raised eyebrows and said, "Why don't you go work for him? You did very well in my store last summer." He was referring to the day I had been left alone in the store and sold over 3,000 Lebanese pounds' worth of clothes, equivalent to about $1,000. Of course, I saw none of that money, as I was only being paid a very small hourly wage.

By mid-afternoon at San Michelle, as the sun was starting to tilt toward the west over the blue Mediterranean, all our guests had finally arrived, and the real party started. With Khalo Fuad on the accordion and Mama on the banjo, Auntie Wadad began to sing, starting with the song "Linban ya Akdar Hilou" ("Lebanon Green and Beautiful"). Then, Ammo Fuad Sabra led us in "Drunk Last Night," his signature song and one he never failed to sing whenever there was a Badr–Sabra gathering. He followed with the then-popular dance song "Mambo Italiano, Hey Mambo."

While dancing the Lebanese *debkee* or the Latin cha-cha was a common element of Badr–Sabra parties, this time the cabin was too crowded for dancing. Instead, we focused on singing, telling jokes, reciting poetry and eating.

Usually food on the beach consisted of ham, cheese and *labni* sandwiches and soft drinks. But this was a special occasion, so in addition to the sandwiches, Mama and the maids brought all kinds of cooked Lebanese cold dishes. It was truly a feast!

At one point, Ammo Anis asked papa to recite the poem he had composed for the Badr–Sabra double wedding. Papa had a gift for composing beautiful poetry in the Lebanese Arabic genre *al-irradi*. His two most memorable *irradi*s were the one he composed for the double wedding and the one in honor of his cousin Raif Badr's first return visit from America in many years. It had been the first time Raif saw his father, Faris Badr, whom we called Jiddo Faris, in fifty years. By then, Jiddo Farris was a very old man, blind with glaucoma, and all he could do was feel his son's face and hear his voice. On both occasions, people both laughed and cried when Papa recited his poem.

Forty-four years after Papa himself immigrated to America, he resurrected his talent for poetry in his nineties and composed a beautiful poem for the wedding of my son, David, and daughter-in-law, Sejal.

No sooner had Papa finished reciting the double-wedding *irradi*, than the two Fuads, the beneficiaries of that poem, led us all in the song "Ya Mustafa," which was very popular in Lebanon at the time. After that, we all sang the song, "Abdo Habib Gandoura" ("Abdo Loves Gandoura"), popular in Lebanon during the late fifties, with Mama on the *derbbakee*, a Lebanese drum, and the rest of us clapping to the beat.

At the end of the evening, we concluded the festivities with "This Land Is Your Land" by Woody Guthrie, in honor of my America-bound family.

As we drove home in our Humber Hawk, I thought back on the countless Badr–Sabra parties. Those parties had long-since become legendary in Ras Beirut, as partying and singing always climbed to a whole new level whenever the Badr–Sabra clan and their friends gathered. We sang and danced whenever we got together, be it Christmas Eve, New Year's, or just a Sunday afternoon.

I wondered what kind of parties awaited us in America.

6. Saying Goodbye

THE MORNING OF OUR DEPARTURE, FRIDAY, JULY 14, 1960, WAS a sunny and humid day in Beirut, and I woke up full of anticipation. I dressed quickly and went out to the large front balcony that faced my grandparents' house to take one last look at our neighborhood.

I saw Abu Younis, a rugged old man with a wrinkled face and a permanent hump, walking toward our building's entrance. He had arrived with his small truck, which in turn pulled an old, beat-up, wooden truck bed, as he always did whenever we had large, heavy items to move. I always wanted to ask him whether his hump was the result of years of carrying furniture and boxes on his back, but I never mustered the courage to do it. He had assisted with our big move from our American University of Beirut campus house to our new residence in the Halim Hanna building. Also, at the start and end of every summer, Abu Younis would show up to move belongings to and from our rented mountain houses.

"I'll start loading the crates," Abu Younis called to Papa.

"Yes, go ahead," Papa shouted back without raising his head. He had just finished inspecting the full inventory of twenty-four pieces: ten large wooden boxes, three china barrels, and eleven trunks and suitcases. With a notebook and pen, Papa had been engaged in his favorite leisure activity: working with numbers. He had assigned an alphanumeric code to each crate, box, and suitcase, recorded each piece's contents and weights, and then calculated the weight totals. It was a simple version of what he most enjoyed doing in his free time: solving problems in algebra, calculus, discrete mathematics, number theory, and probability and statistics workbooks. I once asked him why he spent so much time doing math, and he replied he enjoyed the challenge of solving problems. Plus, it was a good way to keep his mind sharp.

As I watched Abu Younis loading our luggage, it suddenly occurred to me I hadn't packed anything myself. In fact, I hadn't even thought about packing. *Had my parents packed my toys and books?* I asked Papa, who in turn told me to ask Mama. When I asked her, she explained, "We have a weight limit, and your clothes are more important than your toys, so we focused on packing them."

"But what about my scooter and my stamp collection?" I protested. "I can't leave my marbles; I played hard to win each one! And what about my train set and my bicycle?" I took my bicycle everywhere: to the beach and to the mountains during the summer. I often hopped on it to go visit friends and relatives around Ras Beirut. My bicycle, which I had named Nelly, was my friend. *I can't leave it behind.*

Mama assured me I could get a new bicycle in America and they would replace all my toys with bigger and better ones. I was upset about leaving my things behind and tried to protest a little more, but the excitement of the moment took over again when I heard Papa telling Abu Younis, "I'll meet you at the port in an hour, and we can process the cargo to be loaded onto the ship."

This was the day I had been anticipating for months; I would be traveling on a ship for the very first time!

The ship would be leaving port at two o'clock that afternoon. At exactly ten that morning, Ammo Fuad Sabra and Khalo Fuad Badr came by with their cars to drive us to the Beirut port. My brothers and I rode with Ammo Fuad Sabra, while my parents, Leila, and Maria went with Khalo Fuad Badr. Papa was coming with us for the first night as far as Alexandria, Egypt. Then, he would return to Beirut.

As we approached the Beirut port, I began to smell an odor that was like no other in the city. I had never been to the port before, and I had been expecting the familiar smell of the beach. Instead, it was a foul smell, a combination of fish, old urine, and rotting garbage. The smell of old urine was very familiar; I occasionally smelled the wretched odor on my way to school when I passed an alley or a corner where a beggar had urinated. But now, combined with the other smells, the odor was horrible and overpowering.

"What *is* this smell?" Ramsey asked Ammo Fuad, just as aghast as I was.

"This is the way harbors smell," he informed us. "You'll get used to it soon and will stop noticing it."

I thought to myself, I hope the odor doesn't go onto the ship with us.

Just a moment later, a huge, white, beautiful ship appeared right in front of us. I could see the name *Esperia* painted along the side. This was the Italian ship that would take us away from Lebanon. I had never seen a passenger ship up close before; I had only seen ships from the coast, and they had appeared to be tiny specks moving very slowly in the distance, eventually disappearing beyond the horizon.

Our two cars stopped in the vessel's shadow; a huge entourage was already waiting to bid us farewell. Most of the Badre-Sabra clan was there, as well as many close family friends. I noticed that my young cousins—Mooney, Hibbo, George, and Kamal—were not there. I asked my Aunties Ellen and Wadad if someone was bringing them later, only to be told they would not be coming. After all, it would have been difficult to drag them all the way from their summer vacation homes in the mountains.

Also absent from the gathering were the few relatives from Deir Mimas—the Crusader town in southern Lebanon and the ancestral home of Mama's mother's family, the Nemirs—who still remained in Lebanon. Most of the Nemirs had emigrated to the United States and Brazil at the turn of the twentieth century. Only my grandmother's family and her sister Saleemi's family were still in Lebanon.

As I stood on the dock looking at the faces of my relatives, it suddenly occurred to me the Badre extended family would no longer be a part of my daily life as it had been throughout my childhood. We had all lived in Ras Beirut within blocks of each other, and it was customary to drop in at each other's homes at any time of the day for tea, coffee, and sweets. I usually saw an aunt, an uncle, a cousin or my grandmother a couple of times a week. In the evenings, I sometimes dropped in at one of my relatives' houses to find the adults playing a card game called *Quatorze*. We spent our summers together in the same mountain resorts, and we often got together to dance, sing and eat on special occasions or just to have a party because we felt like it.

Gazing at our relatives, I noticed that all my female relatives—except Mama—were teary-eyed, which perplexed me. "Why are they crying?" I wondered. "This is a happy occasion; nobody has died."

When my Auntie Melia, my favorite great aunt, had died in the summer of 1956 in Dhour Schweir, all of our relatives had gathered for her funeral. I remember standing next to Ammo Fuad Sabra in the back of the assembly of mourners and asking, "Why are all the women crying?"

"Women are supposed to cry at funerals," he whispered in response.

At that thought, I looked into the tear-stained face of my grandmother, Teta Hana, and suddenly wondered whether I'd ever see her again. Only a week earlier, she had told me I should be very thankful to be going to America, because it was the best thing that could happen to a Lebanese Christian. Yet there she was, crying.

Teta was a very special person in my life. Even though she was very old, I loved spending time with her, and she always seemed to have all the time in the world to give me. She was a loving, albeit strict, woman, who did not put up with any nonsense from her grandchildren. If I were visiting her and I misbehaved—like the time I kept banging on the piano keys—she would send me home. But whenever she was pleased with something I had done, she would take me to the kitchen, open the cookie jar, and let me put my hand inside and take one or two cookies. She baked the most delicious cookies.

Now, standing face-to-face with her beside the big ship, I thought of all the times we had spent together. Would I ever play the card game *basra* with her again? Would I ever again go visit her just to talk when I was bored?

Sadly, this would in fact be the last time I saw my grandmother. She died three years after we left Lebanon.

I was caught up in this swirl of memories and farewells, and soon it was time to board the *Esperia*. We all went through the Lebanese ritual of hugging and kissing the air three times on both sides of the cheek, with the slightest rubbing of cheeks.

I still distinctly remember the roughness of Khalo Fuad's unshaven face scratching against mine as we went through the hug/kiss routine. He and Auntie Ellen, Mama's brother and sister, were two other close favorites whom I was saying goodbye to for the last time. Auntie Ellen passed away before my first return visit to Lebanon fourteen years later. Khalo Fuad was not in Lebanon during the first visit and died before I could visit Lebanon again in 1980.

As we stood on the upper deck of the ship, looking down and waving goodbye, it hit me, for the first time in my life, I was no longer on Lebanese soil. From the Beirut coast, I had always been able to see ships sailing west, and I often wondered where they were headed and how far they would have to travel before they reached land again. When I next reached land, it would be an entirely new one.

7. Lebanon from the Sea

THE SHIP'S HORN BLASTED FOUR TIMES, INDICATING OUR journey was underway. As the *Esperia* slowly pulled away from the harbor, the sea became larger and larger, while the Beirut I had lived in for my entire fourteen years receded and grew smaller. I saw Beirut as I had never seen it before. The city rose from the seacoast, climbing upward toward the east. Beirut had always felt flat to me, even though I used to climb, almost daily, the long, steep steps from my school near the seacoast to the higher-elevation main streets of Ras Beirut.

Ramsey was leaning against the ship's railing beside me, looking back at the slowly shrinking Beirut. "Look over there, to the right," Ramsey suddenly blurted out, pointing. "There's AUB." I looked and could see the American University of Beirut campus where Papa had taught.

"Do you remember playing *cockyelli*?" he asked. We had often used the entire campus to play *cockyelli*, which was like hide-and-seek, except the person who was "it" had to find and tag *all* the players before he was no longer "it." If you got tagged, you went to "jail." You could be freed from jail with a shoulder touch by anyone who was not yet tagged, so the jail was more like a revolving door than a holding cell. The game often went on all afternoon and into the evening with the same person being "it."

Looking back at the AUB campus, I also remembered the football games and track meets there. On Saturdays during the academic year, I often went with my friends to watch players from the Engineering, Liberal Arts, Medicine, and Business colleges compete.

In the spring, we would attend the annual music and folk dancing festival put on by the students and faculty. On winter nights, when it was cold and rainy, the place to be on a Saturday night was AUB's West Hall to watch American and British plays put on by students and faculty.

Theater and the arts flourished at AUB, as it had many poets, artists, dramatists, and musicians. In addition, students and professors in fields other than the arts participated. Papa, an economics professor, both wrote plays and acted in them. He told me once, after performing in a play he had written, a Hollywood producer who was in the audience that night came backstage and invited him to go to Hollywood. He told my father he had genuine acting talent, but Papa gracefully declined the offer.

As the coastline grew smaller, I pictured the streets of my own neighborhood, Ras Beirut. When I was six years old I had to learn which streets to take from our home at the Halim Hanna building to the IC elementary school. At first, I walked with my brother Sami, but learning to walk the route on my own did not take long; it was an easy five short streets. I soon became intimately familiar with the entire Ras Beirut neighborhood, and by riding the tram, I became acquainted with greater Beirut. Walking the streets to school every day, I would pass by the Nassifs' house, one block away from ours. I spent a great deal of time after school and on Saturdays after football practice in the Nassifs' front yard playing marbles with the neighborhood kids on a large patch of dry, packed dirt next to a muddy, wet area with an assortment of flowerbeds. We played marbles for keeps and tried to avoid the muddy ground with its thick flowerbeds and bushes. I lost many marbles in that patch.

Whenever I visited the Nassifs, nothing delighted me more than being greeted by their dog, Rex, a little brown Dachshund, of whom I was particularly fond. He always greeted me by jumping up to me, wagging his tail, and licking my hands.

Rex was the only dog I trusted at that point in my life. When I was five, I had been badly frightened by an experience I had with a dog. I had been out walking with our maid when we passed the office of Ras Beirut's *mukhtar* (mayor). The *mukhtar*'s German shepherd was sitting on the sidewalk. He looked friendly, so I approached him.

Up until then, my entire experience with dogs had been limited to playing with Ammo Cedric Haddad's dog, Spotty, a beautiful and friendly Dalmatian, during a couple of summers we spent at the village of Abey. I would get down on the floor and wrestle with Spotty and take him with me everywhere I went. Spotty and I walked to the village center every day, and on the way, I would throw my ball for him to retrieve.

In my young mind, all dogs were like Spotty, so when I saw the German shepherd, I put my hand out to pet him. He growled and bit my hand. I shrieked in pain and started crying. The *mukhtar* came out to see what happened. He attempted to ease my pain with offerings of candy and a red ointment he applied to my wound. Still, I felt completely betrayed by all dogs and never trusted one again until I met the Nassifs' Dachshund.

I looked away from the general area of our neighborhood and in the direction of the Beirut City center. Even as fairly young children, my friends and I would take the tram from the AUB main gate to the city center, called the Bourj. We would get off at the Bab Idriss transportation hub, with its adjoining *souks* (markets) and walk a few blocks to the Bourj. Papa once told me Bab Idriss had been one of the six gates in the wall that surrounded Beirut from medieval times up to the nineteenth century.

My friends and I often took the tram to see a movie at one of the Bourj's theaters. We never missed a dubbed cowboy, Tarzan or old Charlie Chaplin film, and we looked forward to the cartoons that preceded the films just as much as the films themselves.

After the movie, we would go down the narrow stone streets to the *souks* with their wall-to-wall shops. We would hang out just as I would later learn youngsters did in America. We loved to eat *caak b'simsim*, a round, hollow bread baked with sesame seeds on top; we would ask the vendor to tear the bread open and sprinkle a bit of thyme in the hollow part.

I could hear and feel the ship's great engines moving faster and faster. As l watched Beirut slowly disappear, I could see with my mind's eye the city's architecture, the buildings displaying their ancient facades of stone and their elegant wrought-iron work, adding beauty to their balconies and windows.

I looked up and away from the city and realized I could still see the top of Mount Sanin towering over the metropolis. Not only was I seeing Beirut from this new perspective, as a city rising on a hill away from the sea, but I also realized for the first time in my life, I was looking at Beirut from outside Beirut, facing east.

Despite my swirling thoughts, memories and emotions, the *Esperia* kept moving away from the Lebanese coast, caring little for my internal state. Now Lebanon merely looked like a small mountain sprouting from the sea, with the city a speck of light at its center.

I thought back to when I first realized I lived in a country called "Lebanon." Before that, it never actually occurred to me I lived in a nation at all. I knew I lived in my neighborhood of Ras Beirut; I even knew my home was in the larger city of Beirut. But in third-grade geography, I first discovered my nationality.

Our lesson in Lebanese geography took the form of a road trip through the four coastal cities: Tyre; Sidon; the capital, Beirut; and Tripoli. What really stuck in my mind from that lesson though was the map of Lebanon we drew that day had no neighboring countries; the only geographic body adjacent to Lebanon we labeled on our map was the Mediterranean Sea to our west. This signaled to my child's mind the region around us was insignificant and irrelevant to our existence.

In general, I felt I lived at the eastern fringe of the Western world and I should look toward the West, embracing its culture, music, literature, and art.

I didn't begin to appreciate Lebanon's unique cultural identity and nuances—and its connection to the Arab world—until the fourth grade, when we began studying Lebanon's history. At first, studying history was a tiresome activity, in which the only purpose seemed to be to memorize events, dates, and names so we could do well on class exams. However, that changed for me the day we started the section on Lebanese Independence.

When the teacher asked us to open our history textbooks to the chapter on Lebanon's independence, I saw, to my very great surprise, a photo of women marching, with my mother and her sister Eva featured prominently at the front of the group. As soon as I recognized Mama's face, I shouted, "That's my mother!"

When I got home that day, I showed Mama the picture in my history textbook and asked her to tell me about it. For the first time, I discovered my mother, Lily Badre, had been an activist for Lebanese independence. She had participated in the Lebanese Women's Union march to protest the French imprisonment of the newly elected president of the Lebanese Republic, Bishara al Khoury, and the prime minister, Riad as-Solh on November 11, 1943. Prior to that, Lebanon had been under the French Mandate, and the French government was not pleased that the Lebanese had unilaterally abolished their control by electing their own officials. After eleven days of protests and international pressure, the French finally released Khoury and Solh and recognized Lebanese independence.

After my outburst in class, I was a celebrity among my classmates for a few days. Unfortunately, all this attention went to my head, and I tried to get my classmates to pay me fifty *piasters* for my mother to autograph her picture in their textbooks. I collected zero piasters, was reprimanded by the principal and punished by my parents. I had to come straight home after school and stay in my room until suppertime for an entire week.

But despite the negative consequences of my moneymaking scheme, I was now interested in Lebanese history like never before. I continued reading our history textbook and learned Lebanon had not always been an independent country. In fact, to my astonishment, I discovered it had not been a country at all until the establishment of Greater Lebanon after the First World War when the League of Nations and the war's victors "mandated" the region to France.

The entire Middle East was taken from the former Ottoman Empire (now Turkey) and divided among the allies. England got Egypt, Palestine, and Jordan. France got Syria and Lebanon. At the time, "Lebanon" just included the Christian enclave of Mount Lebanon. As part of the mandate, the coastal cities of Beirut, Tripoli, Sidon, and Tyre—all of which were majority-Muslim communities—were added to it. Thus, France created modern Lebanon.

By the sixth grade, I understood Lebanon was a country where many different Muslim and Christian sects had to live, work and govern together in a power-sharing system based on religious communities. We learned about the unwritten covenant agreed upon in 1943—which is still in effect today—called the "National Pact," which decreed the president of the republic, the most powerful political position, would always be a Maronite Christian and the Sunni Muslims got the second-most important position of prime minister. This arrangement did not sit well with my Muslim friends.

My friend Malek, whose uncle held a seat in parliament, came out of class complaining his uncle, who was Muslim, could never become president and this limitation was outright unfair. I pointed out that my father couldn't become president either, because even though he was Christian, he was not a Maronite. In response, Malek insisted Christians were all the same and had an advantage in Lebanon over the Muslims. I didn't tell him, but I rather agreed with him.

As the Esperia continued moving and I could no longer see the Lebanese coast, I tried to imagine the city of Albany, New York, where Mama's childhood friend, Arpené Hovnanian, lived. Auntie Arpené had already found an apartment for us on the second floor of a house owned by Italian immigrants.

Papa had told us in America, everything seemed larger than it did in Lebanon. I envisioned tall buildings, wide city streets, and huge movie houses. Would I be able to walk the city streets with my new friends all day and night the way I did the small, friendly streets of Beirut? I wondered if Albany was close to Disneyland. How far was it from Coney Island and the giant amusement park there?

Despite any misgiving I may have had, I was really and truly headed to the United States.

Part II
On Being an Immigrant

8. Journey to a New Land

THE FUTURE AND THE PAST ABRUPTLY FADED, REPLACED BY the excitement of the present moment as Ramsey said, "Let's go explore the ship."

"Let's go see our cabins," Sami followed up. "The suitcases should be there by now."

From the deck, we entered a narrow hallway that led to a very large room. I had never been on a ship before and was astonished to see what looked like a huge living room with furniture just like that found in a home. This was the passengers' lounge, and there was enough furniture for many living rooms. It was hard to believe we were at sea; it felt more like a floating house.

Adjacent to the lounge was a huge dining room. It was like a restaurant, and next to the square wooden dance floor were a piano and several other instruments, including two guitars and a drum. Sami, who loved to dance, grinned at Ramsey and said, "Hey, that's where we'll be dancing!"

"I can't wait to do the cha-cha," Ramsey responded with a huge smile.

I was about to jump into my brothers' conversation, when our mother looked at Sami and informed him, "The dancing won't just be here. We have an invitation from the captain to a dinner dance in the first-class dining room on our second night."

All of a sudden, I desperately wanted to look around for girls my own age. I wondered how I would approach a girl to ask her to dance. I had hardly ever said hello to a girl, let alone ask her to dance.

My first and only experience with girls and dancing had been during the previous summer in Lebanon with my cousins, Joyce and Grace Said. They lived in Cairo, Egypt, during the school year but summered in Dhour Schweir, along with all of our relatives. One day, Joyce and Grace decided to have a dance party and invited us.

My brothers and I spent several days before the party practicing various dances. Sami was my teacher, and I learned to dance to songs like "Witch Doctor," "See You Later, Alligator," and "Sixteen Tons." I also learned to dance the cha-cha.

As a result of those lessons, I felt quite comfortable about the prospect of dancing on the ship, but I was still very nervous about meeting and asking a girl to dance with me.

From the lounge and dining room, we went down a few steps to a hallway leading to the tourist-class accommodations. When we reached our cabins, we saw the porters had indeed delivered our luggage. We first entered the cabin my brothers and I would share. There were two bunk beds and above one of the upper bunks was a small, round window where you could look out to the sea. I immediately climbed the wooden ladder to that bunk and announced in my usual loud voice, "This is my bed."

Five-year-old Leila shouted, "I want this bed; this is mine!" Mama picked her up and assured her she could have a bed just like it next door. Mama and my sisters were sharing the other cabin, which was identical to ours. Papa, who was accompanying us as far as Alexandria, was also staying in that room for the night.

After we finished checking out the cabins, Sami, Ramsey, and I hurried back to the upper deck to see how far out to sea we were. As soon as we got back out in the open, I felt the tingling of the wind blowing against my face and smelled the freshness of the sea mixed with a faint odor of fish. We stood at the railing and watched the water slapping against the side of the vessel. For the first time, I got a feel for the ship's movement. The rolling motion was similar to riding in the cable cars at the Harissa resort in Lebanon, except instead of being in the air, we were on the water.

After about a quarter hour of watching the sea and daydreaming, I looked around and realized my brothers were no longer there. I decided to go look for my parents and sisters in the lounge. As I passed some sunbathing lounge chairs, the awful smell of vomit hit my nose. A boy walking behind me said in English, "Watch out, don't step in it."

I looked down and saw someone had recently thrown up on the deck. I almost gagged, but held my nose and moved on.

As we entered the lounge, I looked at the boy who had issued the timely warning and asked his name. He told me his name was Burt and he and his family were going back to the United States after three years in Lebanon where his father had worked for Tapline, the Trans-Arabian Pipeline Company. He was very excited to see his old friends in Oklahoma City.

That first evening, we had a dinner of Italian macaroni and chocolate cake for dessert. We went to bed early, as we were going to wake up early the next morning in the port of Alexandria, Egypt.

Mama's cousin, Hilda Said, and her son, Edward, met us in Alexandria. They took us to spend the day at a beach resort. We sat on the sand and talked. We did not swim, as we had not known to bring our swimsuits, but we walked in the surf and dipped our feet in the warm Mediterranean waters.

In the evening, we said goodbye to papa as we re-boarded the ship, which would take us on to Italy. I could tell papa was sad to leave us. I could see tears in his eyes. I had never seen papa teary-eyed before and that brought tears to my eyes as all of us hugged him farewell. He stayed behind to fly back to Beirut, where he would spend the next year tying up loose ends, selling the furniture and, no doubt, my toys. For the two years after that (1961 to 1963), he would work for the United Nations in the Congo. He visited us periodically in Albany before eventually joining us permanently in the fall of 1963.

As we left Alexandria that evening, the sea was rough and the boat rocked a great deal; we all began to feel seasick. I took some Dramamine pills, had a bath and went to bed early. The next morning, we woke to a calm sea. I wasn't seasick anymore, but I did feel a cold coming on.

The cold did not stop me from exploring the *Esperia* with Burt and trying to find a girl to dance with that night. I noticed a friend of my parents, Aida Haddad, had boarded the ship in Alexandria with her three daughters. Two of them were about my age, and I decided to keep them in reserve as potential dance partners.

That business taken care of, Burt and I spent the day lounging around and playing ping-pong and various card games. We met a British man in the lounge that told us his main occupation was playing cards for money, and he showed us some amazing card tricks.

In the evening, Mama put my two younger sisters to bed, and around ten p.m. we met the Haddads on the upper deck and went into the first-class dining room together. Sami quickly joined a group of girls and boys his age; he danced a great deal all night. Ramsey spent the entire evening with the older Haddad girl, and they sat at a table with other young couples. I sat at a round table with Mama, Mrs. Haddad, and her two younger daughters.

The band was loud and there was lots of dancing. I kept staring at one of the Haddad girls; she had long black hair, full lips, gentle-looking eyes and a very pretty face. When I finally worked up the nerve to ask her to dance with me, she acted shy and refused. Embarrassed, I immediately asked her sister to dance, but she also turned me down.

Mama, who knew I had been looking forward to dancing, looked at my dejected face and said, "Nasib, let's dance." I ended up dancing with Mama and Mrs. Haddad a great deal that night. The two girls danced with each other. I was disappointed in my efforts with the girls, but still had a lot of fun dancing with the ladies.

Two days later, when we arrived in Naples, I wrote a postcard to Papa and told him, "I have a secret to tell you; nobody knows about it yet. On the next ship, I'm going to look for a girlfriend who will dance with me."

On our way from Alexandria to Naples, we stopped for a six-hour excursion in Syracuse, Sicily, and went on a tour with a large group on a bus. As it turned out, Burt and his parents were also on the tour bus.

The Teatro Greco ruins weren't particularly exciting for me, as I had seen Roman, Greek, and Phoenician ruins many times in Lebanon's Byblos, Baalbek, and Tyre. Plus, the tour guide spoke French, a language I didn't understand. I was more interested in running around and playing. Burt had also seen plenty of ruins in Lebanon and looked just as uninterested, so we passed the time by racing up and down the theater's tiers of stone seats.

Even though he only had three years of Arabic and struggled with the language, Burt spoke better Arabic than I spoke English. Because his Arabic was weak though, he preferred to speak English, and I struggled to understand his American accent and slang. Luckily, he made an effort to communicate with me, and between my small amount of spoken English and his broken Arabic, we did fine.

However, this made me realize this wasn't likely to happen in Albany with my new American friends. It made me anxious, but I decided to deal with it when the time came.

We arrived in Naples at seven the next morning, and within half an hour, our luggage was gathered outside the cabins in the corridor. I stood guard over the twenty-four pieces, while the rest of the family went in search of porters. At long last, Mama returned with the porters who started moving our luggage.

We were spending the night at the Hotel Sirena, where the Adriatica, the company that owned the *Esperia*, was putting us up until our next ship was ready to sail.

When we reached the hotel, Mama looked disgusted. She complained the hotel was dirty and we didn't have enough towels in our rooms. In one of the rooms, the lights wouldn't work. In a letter to Papa from Naples, Mama wrote, "Hotel Sirena is a very sorry kind of hotel, quite third-class. But for one night, we can stand it."

We went sightseeing in a horse-drawn carriage that had been parked in front of the hotel. The carriage took us through narrow streets filled with many people and motorcycles. The clamor of the city was exciting. I noticed many of the women wore sandals, and because the streets were dirty, their feet were filthy.

Most of the buildings in Naples had balconies, some with flowers and others with laundry hanging from the railings. I saw one woman standing at the railing of her veranda, shouting down at a vegetable street vendor below and using a rope to lower a basket.

In the evening, Mama and I took a stroll around Piazza Garibaldi, which faced our hotel. We stopped at a *tabacchi* store where I bought some stamps so I could mail postcards and at a toy store where Mama bought some things for Leila and Maria.

We got up very early the next morning and took a taxi to the port. We were the first family to board the *Augustus*, a truly luxurious ship far superior to the *Esperia*. I was amazed and kept loudly exclaiming, "It's like a palace!"

In a letter to Papa, Ramsey described the new vessel:

> The tourist class in the *Augustus* is better than the first class in the *Esperia*. The food in the *Augustus*'s tourist class is as good as the food in the *Esperia*'s first class. Here we have two big sitting rooms, two decks, a swimming pool, air conditioning, even in the cabins and bathrooms. We have a library, a ping-pong table, and another game, the name of which I don't know.

Exploring our "palace" on the way to our two cabins, I noticed a game room for playing cards, a chapel and a cinema. When we reached the tourist-class lounge, there was a group of musicians playing classical music.

We stopped to listen, and when they finished a short piece, I asked the piano player if they played every morning. "No," he said, "we're playing in the morning today to welcome the passengers; our regular times are every afternoon for an hour, and for two hours in the evening."

There was also a writing room and a library next to the lounge and a swimming pool on the upper deck. We would swim every day, even when the seas were stormy.

We arrived at our cabins and were surprised to find two very spacious air-conditioned rooms, with wider beds than we had aboard the *Esperia*. This voyage was truly going to be luxurious.

By the time we had finished settling in, the *Augustus*'s horn sounded its reverberating blasts. We were on our way to America.

On our third day, we arrived at Gibraltar, but we were not allowed to get off the ship. Instead, merchants, mostly teenage boys, came up to the side of the ship in their small boats and offered souvenirs for sale. When passengers wanted something, they lowered a basket with money, and the merchant then placed the purchased item in the basket. I thought this was a clever way for boys my age to make money, even better than what I did when I ran a lottery in Dhour Schweir. It was during the last summer before we left Lebanon. Shortly after working at Ammo Jamil's clothing store, I went to him and asked if he knew of a way I could make extra money.

"You should start your own business," Ammo Jamil advised.

"But how? I don't have any money to start my own business."

"Why don't you run a lottery? All you'll need to buy upfront is a lottery sheet and a prize for the winner. I'll lend you the money to get started. After I'm paid back for the cost of the lottery sheet and the prize, I'll keep one-third of the profits, and you'll get the other two-thirds."

It sounded like a great idea to me. I was very excited and suggested, "What about getting an alarm clock for the prize?"

He agreed, and the next day, he came into the store with a lottery sheet and the clock. After work, I set out to sell the tickets at fifty *piasters* each. I went to everyone I knew, which was mostly relatives. Some bought one ticket, while others bought multiple tickets. Ammo Anis bought the most: twenty tickets for a total of ten Lebanese pounds. I strongly suspected that Ammo Anis, who was always very pleasant and kind to us children, did so more to help me sell the tickets than because he was interested in the prize.

The next day, we drew the winning ticket, and Auntie Wadad, who had bought only one, was the winner. As I handed Auntie Wadad the alarm clock, I also felt like a winner. I said to her, "We're both winners; you won the lottery, and I won Papa's approval to figure out ways to make money."

While watching the baskets go up and down the side of the ship, I met an American boy from New Orleans. He was my age and went to a Catholic school, so I asked him to tell me all about it; I was trying to make up my mind between a Catholic school and a public school in Albany. My mother's priest in Beirut had contacts in Albany, including his sister, and she recommended my mother consider sending me to a Catholic school with a stellar reputation as an alternative to a public school.

My new friend explained the teachers at his school were priests, called "Brothers" or "Fathers," and they were very strict with the students, often beating them if they misbehaved. In ninth grade, the grade

I would enter, they studied five subjects every day: religion, English, general science, algebra and civics. When I asked him about history and geography, he told me—to my disappointment—they took those subjects in elementary school. I also learned that, unlike schools in Lebanon, the lunch period was very short, only half an hour, and the school day ended at two-thirty. Most of what he told me sounded very different from my experiences in Lebanon, but I was fine with that.

I was a little worried about the "Brothers" and "Fathers" who beat the students though, so I went directly to Mama and told her what the American boy had said. She advised me not to worry, as schools in the South were very different from those in the North in how they treated and taught students. She promised me she would find the right school for me when we got to Albany.

On the fifth day of our voyage, I made friends with an Italian boy my age, and we decided to explore the ship together. We first went from the tourist class up to the first-class swimming pool. Unlike "our" pool, this one had a waterslide. I told my new friend, "I'm going to come here tomorrow and slide and swim."

He looked at me sideways. "You can't do that; it's against the rules to come to first class."

"I know, but we're here now, and nobody stopped us."

No sooner had I said that than a voice behind us said, "Boys, what are you doing here?" It was a steward. He continued, "I'm very sorry, very . . . very sorry, but you're not allowed here."

I looked up at him and responded, "You don't have to be sorry; you didn't do anything wrong." We explained we had wanted to see what the rest of the ship looked like and ended up convincing him to give us a tour of the ship. Later that night, the steward officially announced the tour, and the next day, many more people from all over the ship joined us on it. I never did get to go back to the first-class pool to slide and swim as I had told my Italian friend I would, though.

Nine days after leaving Naples, we woke up at dawn on a hazy, foggy morning, to find the ship entering the New York harbor. I could see only the top of the Statue of Liberty as the bottom was covered by the fog, but it was still an awesome sight and one I will never forget. This was the symbol of the America we had learned about, the symbol of what America stood for: liberty, equality, and the pursuit of boundless opportunities and happiness. Gazing at it, I thought to myself, What a greeting by our adopted country!

My feelings of excitement and anticipation overwhelmed all other emotions. As we approached Manhattan, the city's skyline began to take shape. It was absolutely awesome; never in my wildest dreams had I imagined such tall, giant buildings. I was now absolutely convinced America was the country where I wanted to grow up and live. I wanted to be an American.

9. The City of Giants

THE *AUGUSTUS* ENTERED NEW YORK HARBOR ON FRIDAY, July 29, and docked at the port at one in the afternoon. It was still cloudy and foggy, so I asked a ship's officer standing next to me, "Where exactly are we?"

He pointed and said, "We've arrived at the New York City Passenger Ship Terminal; we're at Pier 85." I looked down at the pier, then back up; I simply couldn't get over the city skyline with all its incredibly tall buildings rising above the fog and clouds. We were truly in a new world, a metropolis like the one in the Superman films I used to watch.

I kept thinking, this is like science fiction! It's unreal, except I can see it with my own two eyes. I couldn't wait to stand beside those giant buildings and look up. It never even occurred to me the city streets were crowded with people and shops and restaurants and street vendors and newspaper stands and all the other things that come with wide, crowded city streets. I was totally focused on those magnificent buildings reaching up to the sky. At that very moment, I made up my mind New York was the city I wanted to live in.

As we waited on the ship's deck to be processed by passport control before disembarking, we heard a voice from the pier below shouting Mama's name: "Lily! Lily!" I looked down, and there was Auntie Rosa Lee, Mama's cousin, waving at us along with Auntie Eva and my cousin, Habib. The Maliks were currently living in Hanover, New Hampshire, where Ammo Sharl was a visiting faculty member at Dartmouth College. Also standing and waving on the pier was Auntie Nora, Papa's sister; our cousins Aida and Nabil; Aida's fiancé, Roy; and Nabil's wife, Pat. I had no idea all these people were going to meet us upon our arrival.

While my family waited to be processed aboard the ship, we shouted back and forth to our relatives on the pier, describing our trip. We hardly noticed the ninety-minute wait to clear passport control.

When we finally disembarked, Auntie Rosa Lee immediately took charge of us. "Lily, let's go get the customs officer to clear your luggage. You children wait over there with the others," she said, pointing to an area with chairs and tables where the rest of our relatives had gathered. I had only met Auntie Rosa Lee once before, when she visited the family in Lebanon, and I had been completely fascinated by this small woman with her take-charge style and good-natured enthusiasm.

I anxiously waited for the porter to arrive and help us with our six steamer trunks, two boxes, two dish barrels, and four suitcases that would be shipped on to Albany. The rest, we would take with us on the train. I desperately wanted to be done with the logistics so I could go see the city and all those giant buildings.

When Auntie Rosa Lee's husband, Uncle E.J., a Lebanese immigrant and a very successful New York businessman, showed up, things really got rolling. I watched this short, muscular man take charge, telling the porters what to do with each item.

Before I knew it, our luggage was stowed in the trunks of Nabil's and Uncle E.J.'s cars. Sami, Ramsey, and I rode with Uncle E.J. and Auntie Rosa Lee, while Mama and the girls rode with Nabil. I sat in the middle of the front seat and stared out the windshield. I could see the buildings much more closely now, but I could no longer see all the way to the top.

I thought of our five-story building back in Beirut and how I used to climb the stairs to the roof to look out across the city. How much more awesome would it be to go up to the roof of one of these giants? I could probably see all of New York, plus the ocean.

I looked up at Uncle E.J. and gently hinted, "I'd love to go to the top of one of these tall buildings."

E.J. looked down at me and fondly reminded me, "Young man, all we have time for today is this short ride to the station so you can catch your train to Albany. Soon though, you'll come back to New York, and you'll go up to the top of the tallest building in the world, the Empire State Building."

Auntie Rosa Lee chimed in, "I want you boys to come visit us in Brooklyn Heights very soon. We'll go up the Empire State Building, see the Statue of Liberty, and visit lots of other places like Greenwich Village and Coney Island."

At that, my disappointment about not getting to explore New York City immediately abated somewhat. I already knew all about Coney Island and other amusement parks from various Arabic magazines my friends and I had read, and I couldn't wait to go on some of the rides I had read about.

I wished we were going to live in this wonderland that was New York City. I knew why Mama had chosen Albany for our new home in America: Auntie Arpené lived just outside Albany, and she and her husband, August, had offered to help us get settled. In addition, Mama's priest back in Beirut had offered to put her in touch with a parish in Albany and help us find schools and introduce us to people in the community.

I could not contain my excitement as we arrived at Penn Station. It was filled with people, shops and restaurants and was huge compared to my previous experiences with train stations, namely Bab Idriss, which only served Beirut's trolleys. But even more exciting than the station was the train itself; after all, this was going to be my very first train ride.

The three-hour ride to Albany flew by. I had wanted to gaze out the window to see what America looked like, but it was already dark, and I saw little. Instead, I enjoyed walking up and down the aisles and between the cars without anyone telling me to sit down, and I spent a good portion of the trip doing just that.

Two cars from ours, I discovered a restaurant, complete with seats, tables, and a little shop selling sandwiches and drinks. I informed Mama of this amazing discovery. She explained this was called a "snack bar" and gave my brothers and me money to go buy something. We each had a ham sandwich, orange juice, and cake, and lounged around at one of the tables eating and playing cards.

10. A Flimsy Wooden House

ARPENÉ, HER HUSBAND, AUGUST, AND ONE OF THEIR FRIENDS met us at the station when we arrived in Albany later that evening. We piled into their two cars and headed to the apartment Arpené had found for us.

Our new home was on the second floor of a house; the landlord and his family lived below us on the first floor. The apartment was on a bus route and convenient to many schools, churches, and shopping. Unfortunately, when we tried to turn on the lights so we could actually see what the apartment looked like, we discovered the electricity had not yet been connected.

In addition, the apartment only had two beds at that point, so my older brothers slept there by themselves that first night, while Mama, my sisters and I stayed at Arpené's house in Loudonville, a town just outside of Albany. We didn't get to bed until after midnight, and I was so tired, I didn't mind I was spending my first night in America in a sleeping bag on the floor.

I awoke the next morning refreshed and anxious to continue my American adventure. August drove Mama, my sister Maria, and me to our apartment; Leila had a bad cold and stayed behind. We also picked up Auntie Eva and Habib from their hotel on the way.

As we drove, I looked for more of the giant buildings I had seen in New York City, but there weren't any. What I saw instead was long, wide streets with trees everywhere and houses with yards blanketed with green grass and flowerbeds. How very different from the stone and concrete buildings of Beirut and what I saw in New York City! I thought.

The streets were wide and clean, cars stayed within the lines that ran down the middle of the road, and drivers actually stopped when the countless traffic lights turned red. In Beirut, the streets were narrow and crowded with cars, and drivers paid little attention to the handful of traffic lights. Policemen often directed traffic at large intersections.

When we reached our apartment, I noticed even the sidewalks were wide, and I was amazed at how clean they were.

I also noticed—to my astonishment—most of the houses were made out of wood. I was used to Ras Beirut's stone and concrete buildings and felt a bit dejected over the prospect of having to live in what seemed to me like a flimsy wooden house.

I became even more nostalgic for our house in Beirut as we climbed the outside stairwell and entered the second floor of this "house of wood." The floor creaked, squeaked, and popped under my feet. I suddenly keenly missed the Persian rug-covered stone-and-marble tiled floors and wondered how those rugs would feel on a wood floor.

This house was much smaller than our house in Beirut. A corridor separated the three bedrooms on one side of the apartment and the living room, dining room, and kitchen on the other. There was also another large bedroom in the attic. As we inspected the bedrooms, Mama noticed the dejected look on my face and informed me I would be getting my own bedroom, as would my brothers.

I greeted this news with a grin; I had never had my own room before. As I entered the room Mama said would be mine, I immediately began thinking about how to furnish it. Where would I put my new bookcase, my most important piece of furniture? I pictured myself alone in the quiet of the night, surrounded by my books. Books had always inspired me, and through them, I could see my new American future unfolding.

The next day, as I sat on the outside stairs, a short, husky man approached me. It was Tony, the man we were renting our apartment from. He introduced himself and asked my name.

I was able to handle this level of small talk in English and said simply, "My name is Nasib."

He looked at me, confused. "Nay-sib?"

"No, Nas-eeb."

"Nas-yeb?"

"No. Say 'nas,' then 'eeb.'"

With my coaching, he eventually got it right, but it was a discouraging first encounter with the locals.

Afterward, I went to Mama. "People are going to have trouble with my name," I said, telling her the story of my encounter with Tony.

In response, she said thoughtfully, "In Lebanon, people usually don't have middle names, but if they do, it's generally their father's name. That's what we did with your immigration paperwork. In this country, your official name is Nasib Albert Badre. Why don't you use your new middle name, 'Albert,' when you introduce yourself?"

"Do people in America often go by their middle name?" I asked, curious about this new concept.

"Yes, they do, and 'Albert' is familiar to Americans. It will be easier."

From that moment on, I started going by "Albert" in school and, later, professionally, reserving "Nasib" for family and close friends.

The name incident didn't dampen my spirits though because everything was still so new and exciting. I was literally having a new experience every day.

It was raining on our second day in Albany, but we had to go shopping for basic necessities, so we headed to a big-box store called King's, which seemed to sell just about everything imaginable. I was flabbergasted, never having seen a store the size of a football field before. For the first time in my life, I had the experience of "shopping," of walking through the aisles and looking at things, without necessarily purchasing anything.

Back in Beirut, we had whole shopping districts, with individual stores all along the streets, and *souks*, which were like very long alleys with dozens and dozens of shops, one next to another. My friends and I often walked along the cobblestone alleys of the *souks*, but we never went into any of the shops to look at their wares. Vendors would shout at passersby, trying to sell them things as they walked along. This American store was one building, with all kinds of goods under one roof, and you could walk around and look at the various goods with no merchant bothering you. It seemed extraordinary.

Of course, Mama bought a great many things for our apartment, including items for our kitchen and dining room and cleaning supplies.

From King's, we went to Whitney's department store to buy some furniture. This was the first time I had ever been in a department store, where you could find everything from furniture and pillows to clothes and toys, all in one place. We also purchased our first television there. While at Whitney's, we had lunch at the store cafeteria, another first for me. There, I tasted my first tuna salad sandwich and fell in love with it.

The television was delivered and installed the next day. My introduction to American popular culture during our first month in Albany came predominantly through watching television. Shows like *I Love Lucy, Bonanza, Candid Camera,* and *The Ed Sullivan Show,* along with a daily dose of the CBS news helped me learn English and pick up some slang.

My brothers and I also learned about America by meeting neighbors, store vendors, and people at Mama's new church. We also went shopping, read product labels and saw how business was done in our new country.

My younger sisters were too young to learn from TV or from such outings, though. Maria was three and a half and didn't like meeting new people. She stayed close to my mother most of the time, and when Mama started working, the lady downstairs took care of her during the day. Thus, she learned about America simply be being surrounded by it.

Leila, who turned six shortly after we arrived, learned about her new country by playing with kids her own age. Mama didn't have to try very hard to find friends for her, as there were four girls Leila's age in the neighborhood, and they often played on the sidewalk in front of our house. When they first asked Leila to go out and play with them, she refused, saying she didn't know any English. After fifteen minutes of prodding, she finally went out to play, and when she came back half an hour later, she said she wanted to go back out again after lunch. By the time she started school a month later, she was able to express herself in English a little.

Mama's priest in Beirut had put us in touch with a Catholic priest in Albany, Monsignor Ryan. He and his sister came to visit us on our third day in Albany, and they invited us to dinner at their mother's house.

At dinner, the mother and sister offered to help us acclimate to daily life in Albany. They informed us, in America, teenage boys often made some pocket money during the summer by mowing peoples' lawns, and they had a large front lawn that needed to be mowed. They suggested it would be a good experience for us and offered Sami, Ramsey, and me $1.25 an hour each to mow their lawn. Ramsey wasn't interested, but Sami and I agreed, and the next day, we spent two hours mowing.

We had never mown a lawn before, though we had seen it done on the American University of Beirut's football field. The novelty made it fun, and the only unpleasant part was raking up the cut grass afterward, which fell to me. Sami did most of the actual mowing.

Afterward, the priest's mother and sister invited us into their kitchen for a glass of lemonade. They asked me where I was planning to go to school in September, and I told them I was trying to decide between Vincentian Institute (V.I.) and Albany High School. They both insisted V.I., which was a Catholic school, was the better institution with a fine reputation.

They told me more about the school and answered many of my questions. I was particularly curious as to whether V.I. was coeducational. They assured me it was, though the boys and girls took classes separately, with the girls being taught by the Sisters of Mercy and the boys by the Brothers of the Holy Cross.

I wrote to Papa to tell him what I had learned about V.I. from Monsignor Ryan's sister and what the neighbors had told us about Albany High School, hoping that putting my thoughts down on paper would help me clarify things in my own mind. It turned out V.I. was a very good school with an outstanding academic reputation and very high standards in teaching. In thinking about my American future and my goal to one day work in "the realm of the mind," this appealed to me greatly.

There was only one month left before school started, and we needed to make some decisions. Sami and Ramsey were both considering their options for college. Sami ultimately decided to finish his bachelor's degree at Siena College, a Catholic university, while Ramsey chose Rensselaer Polytechnic Institute, but had to wait a year before starting at RPI while he took advanced math and science courses at Albany High School. Both RPI and Siena were near Albany. Mama had already decided to send Leila to V.I.'s elementary school. Maria was still too young for school, and because Mama was going to work as a secretary at St. Rose College, our downstairs neighbor, Antoinette, agreed to take care of Maria during the day.

That left me. I was going to start ninth grade and was still struggling to decide between public school and the private Catholic school. I visited both schools and was very impressed by V.I. The building was huge, and they offered summer school to those who wanted or needed it. V.I. also had a huge auditorium with a large stage, and I was delighted by the prospect of joining the dramatic club. In addition, the organization that ran V.I. had schools all over the world, and they were planning to open a school in Beirut soon. That connection was comforting somehow. I decided to attend V.I., and Mama set about trying to make an appointment with the director.

V.I.'s vice principal, Brother Lucas, finally called Mama back, and we went over to the school to see him. It was only a five-minute walk from our house to the school, which was nice; I wouldn't have to ride a school bus! Brother Lucas, a small man with glasses who wore a black suit with a white collar like the one our minister in Beirut wore, met us in his office.

After we said our hellos and introduced ourselves, Mama asked Brother Lucas what courses I would be taking and whether we could get the textbooks in advance, since I was going to have a bit of a language barrier to break through. He told us ninth graders took math, history, a language, science, English, citizen education, and religion, but I didn't have to take religion because I was not Catholic. For the language course, I could choose between French, Spanish, or Latin, but he strongly recommended I take Latin. He only had the math, history, and religion textbooks on-hand to offer me, saying I could get the rest of the textbooks once classes started in September. I took only the math and history books, since I wouldn't be taking religion.

11. Adaptation and Isolation in America

MAMA FELT A GOOD WAY TO INTRODUCE ME TO AMERICAN culture and language was for me to find a friend my age before school started, ideally someone who would also be a student at V.I. in the fall. St. Vincent de Paul was the church associated with V.I., and Mama spoke with the pastor, Rev. James Toole, asking if he could introduce us to a family with a boy my age that would be going to V.I.

He was very obliging, and the next day, a fellow teenage boy knocked on our door. Mama let him in, and he introduced himself as Bill, explaining Father James had asked him to introduce himself to the Badre family and meet me.

I heard the conversation from the other room and came to join them. "Bill, this is Albert," Mama said, introducing me.

I still wasn't completely comfortable with going by "Albert," so I said, "Hi, Bill. My friends and family call me 'Nasib'; you can call me that, too, if you want." He responded with, "Hi, Nasib," pronouncing it perfectly.

Bill invited me to take a walk around the neighborhood, and he would show me around. I accepted his offer, and we set out.

I was a boy of few words throughout this encounter, because conversing in English didn't come naturally to me yet. It took me a while to express myself, as I was always trying to translate what I wanted to say from Arabic, and I often couldn't remember the English words.

Bill first took me to his house—only five blocks from ours—to introduce me to his parents and younger brother. His parents were waiting for us in the hallway; they were clearly expecting my visit.

"Mom, Dad, this is Nasib," Bill introduced me.

His mother greeted me in a very loud voice and then asked, "Have you ever had ice cream?"

"Yes, of course," I said, a bit confused.

"Come into the kitchen; we'll have vanilla and chocolate on a cone."

We followed Bill's mother into the kitchen, and I noticed the rooms' arrangement was identical to our house. Bill's house was also made out of wood, like mine. I was now convinced all houses in America looked the same.

In the kitchen, I was so absorbed in enjoying my ice cream I didn't notice it melting and dripping all over my shirt, the table, and the kitchen floor until Bill's mom burst out laughing, pointing at the wet floor. Bill noticed my red-faced embarrassment and immediately said, "Let's go to the basement. I want to show you the bookcase I'm building."

"Can't you buy a bookcase from the store?" I asked, confused by this activity. Surely, one could buy anything and everything in America!

"Yes, but I like carpentry; it's my hobby."

I wasn't familiar with these words. "Car-what?"

"Carpentry," he explained patiently. "Building furniture out of wood is one of the things I like to do. I also like to help my dad fix things around the house. Here's my tool box." He proudly showed me a metal box full of unfamiliar items.

"Your what?" I asked.

"These are the tools—the screw driver, the saw, the hammer—I use to do things like tighten screws, cut wood, and hammer nails."

I was surprised; it had never occurred to me a fifteen-year-old boy would be expected to fix things around the house. In Beirut, when something broke, we either asked the maid to fix it or we hired an out-side service. It suddenly dawned on me in America, "do it yourself" was not just a saying; it was a way of life. I realized I was at an even greater disadvantage than I had expected; my upbringing in Lebanon truly had not prepared me for the life of an average American teenager.

This became even more clear when I asked Bill how much pocket money his parents gave him every week, so I could tell my mother what was normal for a boy my age.

"*Give* me?" he said incredulously. "Nothing is free here, buddy."

I was perplexed. "What do you mean?"

"You have to work for your pocket money here. When I was younger, I did chores around the house, like taking out the garbage or washing the dishes after dinner; in return, I was paid $2.50 a week. Then I got a paper route, and that's how I make my pocket money now."

"What's a 'paper route'?" I asked.

"*The Albany Knickerbocker* newspaper pays me ten dollars a week to deliver the morning paper to all the houses in the neighborhood."

When I went home that night, I told Mama about Bill's carpentry talent. I also told her how amazed I was that, in America, you had to work for your pocket money. To my chagrin, she responded by starting a similar system, in which we had to earn our pocket money through housework. She assigned us all chores such as washing the dishes, sweeping the floors, cleaning the bathroom, putting up and taking down the washing from the line and ironing the clean clothes.

Mama handled the cooking, and she actually had to learn how to cook using the Betty Crocker cookbook. In Beirut, our kitchen maid, Shafia, did all the cooking.

The next day, I went back over to Bill's house; he was going to show me the school, the movie theater, and other places where teenagers "hang out," another word I didn't really understand.

As I walked along the sidewalk toward his house, I passed two teen-age girls, both of whom were looking at me and smiling. Just as I passed them, they started giggling, and as I put more distance between us, they began laughing loudly. I felt very awkward and uncomfortable, certain they were laughing at me. I wondered if I were walking funny; perhaps Americans walk differently, and I looked like a foreigner.

When I arrived at Bill's house, I told him about the two girls. He grinned and said, "They weren't laughing at you; they were trying to get your attention. They were interested in you. That's what American girls often do when they're too shy to come up to you and introduce themselves."

Bill took me to the school and told me that even though boys and girls are separated in the classrooms, all social events and school clubs are coeducational. Coming from an all-boys school in Beirut, "social events" with girls would be a new experience.

On our way back to my house, he asked if I would like to play softball with him the next day. When I looked perplexed, he asked, "Do you know what softball is?"

I responded, "No," nodding my head up and down, as we did in Lebanon when we wanted to express the negative.

He grinned. "You said 'no,' but still moved your head up and down; in Lebanon, when you want to say 'yes,' do you shake your head sideways?"

I realized in America, moving the head down and up means "yes," while moving it sideways means "no"—the opposite of what I had grown up with. The difference was yet another thing I would have to get used to and learn.

I went home frustrated and told Mama, "Not only do I have trouble speaking in English, but even my gestures are out of place in America."

A couple of weeks before school started, we were still busy learning how to take care of ourselves without maids. The daily routines of making our beds every morning, cleaning our rooms, and taking turns washing the dishes were still foreign. With every passing day of having to do chores, I missed our maids, Shafia and Josephine, more and more. I had never done housework before or had even given it much thought.

A few days after "the America announcement" earlier that year, I had gone to Mama and asked her whether the maids would be coming with us to America.

"No, they won't. We can't get visas for them, and besides, it would be hard for them to leave their families in Lebanon," Mama answered. She had added we wouldn't be able to afford help in America that was as good as Shafia and Josephine. I had accepted Mama's explanation and didn't really give it another thought until we were in Albany and my chores started to pile up.

I sat on my bed one day, thinking about our maids back in Lebanon and how much I missed them. Unlike my brothers, I had spent a great deal of time with our maids; they had been my companions, especially when no one else was around. Throughout my childhood, Shafia and Josephine—and Nabiha, Suzanna, and Wasima before them—had always been there for me. They prepared and served our daily meals. They were the first ones to greet me with smiles and afternoon snacks when I came home from school. They were my playmates when none of my friends or cousins were around. At bedtime, they told me old stories, like the one about the ghoul who scared all the children in the village, the sleeping princess who was awakened with a kiss, the girl who fell into a well and discovered a world of beautiful wonder and many others, which I loved to hear over and over again.

Of course, Shafia and Josephine didn't always agree with everything our family did. After my parents came back from their New York trip in 1958, they decided to embark on a new lunch experiment. As we entered the dining room for lunch one day, we were surprised to see a mound of baguette sandwiches piled on a platter in the middle of the dining room table. There must have been at least ten sandwiches, each a foot in length.

As we sat down, Mama informed us, "From now on, we will have lunch and dinner American style because it is healthier. This means instead of having a heavy lunch, we will have light sandwiches and then an early cooked dinner around six p.m." Mama failed to explain that a "light sandwich lunch" could be anything from a single hamburger to a light tuna salad spread between two pieces of bread. I suspect because we were used to having a heavy lunch, Mama felt that we ought to have huge filling sandwiches as part of our American experiment.

I loved baguette sandwiches, so I thought it was an excellent idea. In my head, I thanked the Americans for coming up with the idea of sandwiches, even though, as I learned after we immigrated, a baguette is not a popular sandwich bread in America.

I consumed two whole ham sandwiches at the first "light sandwich" lunch. As I was finishing my second sandwich, I noticed Shafia's face held a look of strong disapproval. In fact, she looked downright annoyed.

After lunch, I followed Shafia to the kitchen. "What's the matter?" I asked her. "Don't you like baguette sandwiches?"

As though she had been holding it in, Shafia blurted out, "It's more work to prepare all these sandwiches—and different ones every day!— then to prepare a cooked meal. Everybody in this country eats a cooked lunch, so why should we change something that's healthy and good?" Shafia was an excellent cook and justly proud of what she prepared for us. I suspect she took the American sandwich experiment as an insult to her skills.

To her delight, the experiment lasted only two weeks. Perhaps my parents got tired of having sandwiches every day.

I was particularly fond of our Dakoun maids, Shafia and Wasima. Dakoun is a small Maronite Catholic village in the Chouf district of Mount Lebanon near Abay, my paternal grandmother's ancestral village.

The day after my parents announced their decision to immigrate and told me the maids would not be coming with us, I asked Shafia what she would do after we left for America. She told me she would go back to Dakoun and help her cousin Wasima raise her boys.

Wasima had been our maid when I was born, and she was with us until I was five years old, when she got married. I was very attached to her and missed her a great deal after she left.

After we immigrated to America, I didn't have any contact with the Dakoun maids until my first trip back to Lebanon in 1974. Later, during the Lebanese civil war in the 1980s, many of Dakoun's Christians were viciously massacred. It's possible that Wasima and Shafia and their families escaped to Abay, but we have never been able to find out for sure.

The days passed, and the novelty of my American experience began to wear off. Routine and sometimes even drudgery and boredom began to set in. My friend Bill informed me teenagers in America learned to be independent from an early age, but I hadn't realized that, at least in my case, "independent" meant being alone most of the time.

It slowly dawned on me I knew absolutely no one around me. I felt nostalgic for my daily life in Beirut, where I lived so close to my friends and relatives. Every morning, I would walk out of my building and run into many familiar faces, all greeting me, "*Sabah al kheir*" (Good morning). Here, people went about their business without so much as that simple greeting.

After a short walk along the streets of my new neighborhood one day, I keenly felt the emptiness of my immediate surroundings. I was alone and bored. Whenever I got bored in Beirut, I would go visit my grandmother to play a card game called *Basra* or walk over to one of my cousins' or friends' houses to play, or talk to Shafia and Josephine.

Alone on the streets of Albany, with strangers all around me, and no place to go and no one to visit, I turned back home. As I was about to climb the stairs up to our apartment, I saw Mama talking with our downstairs neighbor, the landlord's wife, Antoinette, who was hanging her laundry in the backyard. Mama offered, "I can help you hang those sheets."

The lady looked insulted and said with an annoyed frown and a raised voice, "Of course not! I can do it myself; I don't need you to help me." I was starting to realize the "do it yourself" approach to life was very prevalent in America, unlike in Lebanon, where you expected others to help you and you helped others in turn.

We learned that, in the United States, your neighbors only came to your aid when you were in serious need, like when Sami got stuck while driving in the snow during our first snowstorm.

A policeman on the corner kept shouting "Sand, sand," at him, pointing in the direction of a nearby sand pile. Sami couldn't figure out that "Sand, sand," was shorthand for "Go get some sand from that pile and put it under your tires to get some traction." Fortunately, another driver got out of his car and came over to explain.

The day after the "hanging sheets" incident, we were all busy with our chores. After spending most of the day washing, ironing, and folding our clothes, Mama decided the last chore of the day would be to wash and mop the kitchen floor. Just like Shafia had done on the marble kitchen floor back in Beirut, she dumped a bucket of hot soapy water on the linoleum floor. Within a few minutes, Antoinette came running up to our apartment, shouting, "Dirty water, dirty water!"

With a confused, perturbed expression, Mama asked, "What dirty water, where is it?"

"Down in my kitchen," the lady screamed. The water Mama had dumped all over our kitchen floor had leaked through the landlady's ceiling and was now dripping on her counters and floor.

We ended up spending the remainder of the evening helping Antoinette clean her kitchen, but by the end, she was all understanding and smiles, even offering to cook one of her delicious pasta dishes for us.

After that long, exhausting evening, I went to bed still feeling somewhat alone, despondent, and nostalgic. Homesickness had set in badly.

I woke up the next morning to the sound of laughter and voices speaking in a familiar mix of English and Arabic coming from the living room. It sounded like I was in Beirut again.

Feeling a surge of excitement, I pulled on my clothes quickly and hopped, skipped, and jumped into the living room. And what a delightful surprise awaited me! There was the Hadawi family—Papa's sister Auntie Nora, tall, beautiful and, as always, smiling; my cousins Nabil and Aida; Nabil's pregnant wife, Pat; and Aida's fiancé, Roy—all gathered in our living room, sitting on our new sofa and chairs. In doing so, they made it feel like home.

The day was full of laughter, Lebanese food that Auntie Nora brought up from Brooklyn, and talk about Nabil and Pat's firstborn due in November and Aida and Roy's wedding in September. Antoinette brought up a tray of her delicious homemade pizza, and we played cards. At the end of their visit, we took the Hadawis on a tour of Albany before they had to head back home to New York. At the end of the day, we were all happily exhausted.

After the visitors left, Mama suggested we have something light for dinner and asked me to go to the grocery store and buy a couple cans of tuna so she could make tuna salad sandwiches. In the store, I found a shelf filled with stacks of cans that said "tuna" and had pictures of tuna on them. Not paying much attention beyond those details, I chose a couple and brought them home. Sami opened the cans and poured the contents into a bowl, and Mama then quickly mixed the tuna with mayonnaise and made sandwiches.

We ate sitting in front of the television—as had become our habit—instead of at the dining room table. I immediately noticed the sandwich didn't taste like the tuna salad we got in the restaurant, and as I chewed, I felt something crunchy. Just as I was about to say something, Sami blurted out, "I think this tuna has bones in it."

Mama went to look at the discarded can and gasped, "This is cat food!" We all laughed at my misunderstanding, and Mama told me to be more careful in the future before she turned to making butter and jelly sandwiches.

I learned that day reading the labels was just as important as looking at the pictures. I thought to myself, I've been learning American slang by watching TV; now, I had better start learning written English by going to grocery stores and reading the labels.

After the fun, relaxing day with relatives, the cat food incident plunged me right back into the mentally and emotionally demanding process of learning about and coping with my new life.

Mama tried to keep as much continuity in our lives as she could. We regularly went to the movies, and when the circus was in town for a week in mid-August, we attended that as well.

12. School in America

*I*WAS EXCITED TO BEGIN THE SCHOOL YEAR AND WAS ANTICI-
pating all the new friends and activities it would bring. If nothing
else, I was looking forward to having something to do and not being
bored anymore.

I was also looking forward to making more new friends. Even though
Bill was nice, he was one grade ahead of me in school and surely would
rather hang out with his own classmates and friends. I was now looking
forward to meeting guys like Bill, but who were in my own grade.

In addition, I was excited to see what kind of sports I could play
at V.I. In Beirut, I had been quite good at football—called 'soccer' in
America—as well as track-and-field events such as sprinting and the
high- and long-jump.

I was also still very interested in international affairs and looking
forward to having discussions with my classmates about such issues as
my English got better.

Bill had informed me V.I. had a dress code and all the boys had to
wear a navy-blue jacket and a tie to school everyday. When I asked him
why this rule was in place, he simply said it was required and did not
explain further. As I was to soon discover, V.I. had many unexplained
requirements, such as when walking in the building's hallways, one
always had to walk on the right in a single-file line and remain quiet.
Thanks to Bill's warning, Mama and I purchased a blue blazer.

Shortly before school started, I received two letters. One was from
Papa, wishing me a happy birthday and promising to send a gift to me
very soon. He then turned to my education, reminding me my studies
should be my only preoccupation:

> I understand from your mother's letter that your school starts
> on September 6th. I am expecting you will take your schoolwork

with great enthusiasm and you will make a good showing at school. You must start in from the very first day with no distractions and forget everything, absolutely everything except your studies.

The other letter was from V.I.'s vice principal, Brother Lucas, welcoming me to the new school year at Vincentian Institute. It included my schedule and assigned classrooms with a map of the school. Classes would start on Tuesday, September 6, at seven forty-five a.m. in a "homeroom" on the second floor. I had never heard of homeroom before and assumed it meant the first class after arriving at school from home.

Our lives were changing yet again as we all excitedly prepared for the coming school year. Sami had enrolled in Siena College and would be going there for the next three years, even though he only had one year left to go at the American University of Beirut. He and my parents had gone back and forth many times, trying to decide whether Sami should finish his degree in Beirut or go to Albany with us. Ultimately, they all agreed he should go to Albany and get acclimated to the American way of life before trying to get a job and building a career here, even though it meant several more years of school. It was truly an agonizing decision.

Ramsey had enrolled at Albany High School as a special student in preparation for entering *Rensselaer Polytechnic Institute,* where he would spend four years and receive an engineering degree. Leila started first grade at V.I.'s elementary school, which was in a different location than the high school, where I was enrolled.

The V.I. high school was around the corner from our house, and for me that had been the best reason to go there. It reminded me of Beirut, where I had always walked to school.

At long last, my first day of school arrived. I woke up feeling nervous, anxiously anticipating all the new classes, new friends, new teachers, new rules, and new experiences I was going to have. Unfortunately, having to put on a jacket and tie made me feel even more uptight. Up until then, the only times I had ever been required to wear a jacket and tie were when we went to church and for the family Christmas Eve party.

When I got to school, I climbed a stone stairwell to the second floor, looking for the classroom Brother Lucas had mentioned in his letter. I entered my "homeroom" and saw several boys were already there, all sitting quietly. They all turned and looked at me for a moment, then turned back toward the front of the room and stared silently ahead at an empty teacher's desk.

I sat down near the left side of the room and was now one of those silent boys turning and staring at every new student that entered the room. I wondered why everyone was so quiet. I knew why I was silent: I couldn't find the right English words to start a conversation. I was thinking in Arabic and had difficulty translating my thoughts into English.

There was no such thing as an English as a Second Language (ESL) program in the schools in the early sixties, which I would have benefited from greatly. Everyone around me, including my parents, teachers, and school administrators, simply assumed I would learn English by living with it and coping.

I had the math and history textbooks Brother Lucas had given me earlier, but noticed everyone else had several other textbooks on their desks. I wondered where and how they got them, but didn't know how to ask.

Eventually, the classroom door flew open, and a tall man dressed in black with a white collar just like Brother Lucas's came in pushing a cart full of books. He stopped in front of the teacher's desk and introduced himself as Brother Tadius, then asked all thirty of us to stand and mumbled a long string of words. I didn't understand what he was saying, but after several mornings of the same thing, discovered that these words were the morning prayer.

After the prayer, we all sat down again. Brother Tadius said something I couldn't understand about the books on the cart he had brought in. Everyone else got up, went to the cart and started taking books, so I assumed this must be where I could get the rest of my textbooks. But when I reached the cart, I found none of the books I needed were there; it only contained the books I had and the religion book, which I didn't need.

Brother Tadius glanced over at me; I think he knew I hadn't understood what he said earlier, because he said very slowly, "Room 2 on first floor, to get books." Then he addressed the rest of the class again. "Now everyone back to your seats, and let's start by introducing ourselves."

When my turn came, I stated my new American name: "Albert Badre." It sounded really weird to me; I was giving Papa's name as my own.

"Al, you have an accent," Brother Tadius said very slowly. "Where are you from?"

As I would soon discover, Americans like to abbreviate names. I liked the sound of "Al"; I had never heard anyone call Papa "Al." The name belonged to me alone. From then on, I always introduced myself as "Al."

Fortunately, this time I understood what Brother Tadius was asking and responded, "Lebanon."

When the bell rang at the end of homeroom, we all hurried off to our next class. I tried to push past other students in the hallway to get to my next classroom early so I could get a seat in the front, but one of the Brothers stopped me and said, "Single file on the right."

I didn't know what he meant by a "single file." I clearly looked confused, and by the time the Brother had explained what he was talking about, I was one of the last students to arrive in the classroom. I ended up having to sit at the very back of the room.

At lunchtime, I walked home, where I had a tuna salad sandwich and a glass of chocolate milk. This was my routine for my entire three years at V.I.

Three weeks into the school year, Brother Tadius announced in homeroom that we each had to choose an advisor from among one of our teachers. The advisor was supposed to check in with each of his students regularly to find out how we were doing in our schoolwork and if we had any difficulties.

I chose Brother Tadius because, as I wrote to Papa, "[He] is very kind to me." He often asked me if I was making friends and even helped me decide on which extracurricular activities to join.

I had problems understanding class lectures and discussions throughout the first trimester. As a result, I spent the first two months of school struggling with my classes, the English language, and my school life in general. Part of the problem was that many of the words and slang terms my teachers used in their questions and the students used in their answers were ones they had grown up with and knew the meanings of without thinking about it. It took me a while to figure out that "bread" meant "money," that a "Five and Dime" was a retail store of inexpensive items, and that "Sears" was a department store.

After three weeks of Latin and two failed quizzes, I told Mama I was never going to do well in Latin because I had no one at home to help me. She agreed with my logic and advised me to switch to French; she could speak and read it and would be able to help me with my lessons.

I seemed to be struggling with everything. After school each day, I would go home and study from three in the afternoon until eleven at night. The next day, I would go to school still tired from my late night.

Mama understood my difficulty with spoken English was affecting how I did in all my coursework, and she decided to hire a tutor for me, whom I met with three times a week. A few days later, Papa made a surprise visit from Lebanon, and he became my tutor for the next two weeks. I did much better with his help, but after Papa left, I went back to struggling.

I persevered though, and after three months at V.I., I no longer struggled to express myself in English and understand what the teachers and students were saying. By spending several hours each day doing homework and reading ahead in the textbooks—as Papa had always insisted I do—my grades actually improved to above average by the end of the first trimester.

Even as my grades and my English improved, I was still very much alone socially. Although I occasionally hung out with a few classmates from school, we were not close. They were not like the friends I had had in Beirut, and I shared very few interests with them. With my Beirut friends, I played football, talked about Lebanese and Middle Eastern politics, went to the movies, and went just about anywhere and everywhere in Beirut. My new classmates in Albany had no interest in politics and knew next to nothing about football, which they called 'soccer.' Our interactions were mostly limited to class assignments and chatting about the next school holiday, movies, and Hollywood celebrities. They were shockingly uninformed about the rest of the world and had no interest in learning about the world beyond their school, classroom, and sports team.

I increasingly and painfully realized that, to my new American classmates, my history was completely invisible. No one knew or cared about Lebanon's history, cultures and politics, or my life there.

I missed the big family gatherings we had back home, with all the generations spending time together. In America, everyone seemed to be divided by age; teenagers mingled with teenagers, and adults with other adults. In Lebanon, we gathered in family groups. Sometimes we were playful and noisy; sometimes, we simply sat and listened to parents, aunts and uncles discuss politics, current events, and day-to-day experiences. The older generation was highly regarded, and we listened to their wisdom and learned from their experiences.

<hr>

A few days before the Christmas holiday started, Sami, who always got up before anyone else, came into my room one morning and shouted, "Wake up! Look out the window!"

I rushed to the window. "Wow! It's snowing!"

The streets and sidewalks were totally covered by a heavy blanket of snow. It covered the roofs, the windowsills, the lampposts and even the electric wires. Swirls of snow fell soundlessly onto the leafless trees. I couldn't wait to go out to touch and feel it.

I hurried into my coat, hat, boots, and gloves and raced outside. My boots sank into the cold, wet stuff up to my knees. This was the closest I had ever been to snow. In Beirut, snow was always something that existed somewhere else, up in the mountain villages. While many of my friends had often gone skiing, I never had. In fact, I had never gone to any of the Lebanese mountains when they had snow.

Two kids about my own age came running over, both bundled up like packages; one's face was almost completely covered with a knit hat with holes for his eyes. "Let's build a snowman," the boy shouted. He pulled his mask off and said, "You guys move the snow here; I'll start building. We need to pack three big balls, starting with the largest first." Without questioning his orders, we all got busy.

No sooner had we finished building the snowman than Sami came out with two shovels. He handed one to me and said, "We have to clear the snow from the sidewalk in front of the house."

At that moment, my bubble burst, and I realized with snow comes work. It was another chore, not just fun.

13. Visiting the City

AROUND THAT SAME TIME, MAMA SUGGESTED WE TAKE advantage of the long Christmas holiday to go down to New York City. Auntie Rosa Lee had been calling almost every week, insisting we come stay with her in Brooklyn Heights. My brothers and Maria didn't want to go, so they stayed behind while Mama, Leila, and I made the trek down to New York City.

I didn't know much about Auntie Rosa Lee. I had met her for the first time when she visited Lebanon in the mid-1950s and then again when our ship docked in New York City. As Mama, Leila, and I got on an early morning Greyhound bus to the city, I asked Mama, "How is Auntie Rosa Lee related to us? And what does she do in New York?"

"Auntie Rosa Lee is my first cousin on my mother's side and a well-respected doctor—a pulmonary and pediatrics specialist."

"I don't know what that means," I said, "but it sounds pretty important." After I got to know Auntie Rosa Lee better, I found out she had achieved the height of her profession when she became the President of the American Medical Women's Association.

Mama went on to tell me, "Auntie Rosa Lee loves family and insists whenever any of her relatives visit New York, they must stay with her and Uncle E.J. at their home in Brooklyn Heights."

After a surprisingly comfortable three-hour bus ride, we arrived in New York City, my favorite city, the city I had promised myself I would someday live in. We took a cab to Uncle E.J.'s furniture store in Manhattan, left our luggage there, and set out to become acquainted with New York City.

After shopping at Macy's and having lunch at the store's restaurant, we began our exploration of the city's streets. I loved the hustle and bustle of New York, loved walking the wide sidewalks and feeling totally anonymous in that vast sea of people. Because no one knew me, I felt completely comfortable watching people and staring at their faces. The way people acted, talked, and looked fascinated me.

That night, after leaving Leila with Auntie Rosa Lee and Uncle E.J., Mama and I took the subway to Radio City. It was my first subway ride, and I thought it was awesome.

As we entered the subway car, Mama took my hand and said, "Let's sit right here. Don't move until we get to our station."

The only thing I could hear above the deafening noise was "Sit here," and so I sat where she pointed. As we rode, I looked around the over-crowded train car and was struck by the colorful drawings that covered the train's walls.

After about twenty minutes, we reached Times Square. Mama reached for my hand, and we walked out—or, more precisely, were shoved out—the door to the station platform.

We attended the *Christmas Spectacular* show at Radio City Music Hall and saw *The Sundowners*, a movie about an Australian family's conflict between a father who wants to continue his nomadic way of life and his wife and son's desire to settle down. I enjoyed the evening thoroughly and was particularly excited to see the Radio City Rockettes dance.

After the show, we returned to Brooklyn Heights, where Auntie Rosa Lee was waiting up for us. I excitedly told her all about the movie and the Rockettes. Eventually, Mama said, "You ought to get to bed; we have a big day tomorrow touring and doing Christmas shopping."

Auntie Rosa Lee told me my bedroom was on the top floor and Mary, the family's Irish maid, would have breakfast ready at eight in the morning.

When I responded I didn't eat breakfast, she said, "Nasib, breakfast is the most important meal of the day. I'll see you in the morning at eight."

The next morning, I had an enormous breakfast of fried eggs, bacon, toast with butter and jelly, coffee, and orange juice, all of which I enjoyed thoroughly. When I first woke up, I hadn't been very hungry, but when

I got to the breakfast table and saw all the food, my appetite soared. I loved the eggs and the butter and jelly on toast. I had not had orange juice in a very long time, and it was delicious. I found myself wishing I had a "Mary" to prepare a breakfast like this for me every day.

After breakfast, Mama, Leila and I took the subway to Times Square. We spent the entire day Christmas shopping and ate dinner at Gimbels Department Store restaurant. Then, it was time for the event I had been waiting for since we first arrived at New York harbor: we went to the Empire State Building and took the elevator up to the 102nd floor. The view from the top of the highest building in New York was spectacular. We could see the streets sparkling with the dazzling red, white, and green lights of Christmas far below us. It was a truly awesome experience, and the images and atmosphere of New York City during the Christmas season were forever planted in my brain.

The next morning, I took the bus back to Albany by myself, as Mama and Leila were spending an extra day in New York. My independent streak was starting to show itself, and I wanted to do things on my own. I was now thoroughly convinced I would one day live in New York City. I was also now more determined than ever to build my social life and get involved in school activities in the new year. I wanted to get to know my classmates and make real friends among them. Participating in activities with them would help me learn more about them and at the same time, improve my conversational English. All of this would help me learn more about the American culture, and eventually make it easier for me to work toward my ultimate goal of a future career in "the realm of the mind."

14. Basketball, Tennis, High Jump, and Reading

ETERMINED TO PARTICIPATE IN SCHOOL ACTIVITIES, I decided to try out for the freshman basketball team at the start of the winter session.

Forty-five students showed up for the tryouts; only eleven would make the team. Many of them had played on their school's eighth-grade basketball teams the previous year; my only experience with the game was playing street basketball in Beirut. They were all very good, certainly better than me.

The coach had us play in teams of five to see how well we could dribble, pass, and shoot the ball into the hoop. We also did drills like jumping to touch the hoop and shooting free throws. With that last exercise, none of mine went in. I left the gym discouraged and certain I would not make the team.

As I expected, the next morning, my name wasn't on the posted list of those who had made the team. I went to homeroom thinking about what other activities I could try out for.

As I sat down, getting ready to start the day with the morning prayer, Brother Tadius came over and said, "They want you in the front office."

My stomach turned over. In my school in Beirut, being called to the front office meant one of two things: something serious happened within my family or I was in trouble.

When I arrived, the secretary, Ms. Irvin, an older lady with white hair and a kind face, greeted me with a smile. When I saw her smiling, I thought to myself, it can't be bad.

"The coach would like to see you right away before classes start," she said. "Go to his office next to the gym."

When I got to the coach's office, he wasn't there, but I heard the dribble of a basketball coming from the gym. Peeking in, I saw the coach showing a couple of student-players how to attack ball screens and recover on dribble penetration.

I stood at the gym entrance watching for what felt like forever. Finally, the coach saw me and waved me over. "I wanted to talk to you about yesterday's basketball tryouts. You did the best of anyone trying out at jumping for the hoop. You're a very good jumper, and in the spring, you should go out for the high jump. I think you could have a very good future in basketball, but you need more practice. I've arranged for you to practice with the team, but not play in the games."

I was very excited, because I now had an activity where I might be able to make friends. My mother was also pleased, because she had always wanted me to get involved in school activities.

Ultimately, I sat on the bench during all the home games and some of the away games. I got to know and hang out with a few of my teammates, who were also in my classes. We became good friends, but only hung out in school and during basketball practice. Unlike my friends in Beirut, I never saw them or played with them outside school. Other than Bill, I still had no friends outside of school, and even he was a bit distant, as he was a grade ahead of me and generally wanted to hang out with his own friends.

As the basketball season came to an end, so did the winter cold. The warmth of spring melted away the mounds of ugly, dirty, chunky snow. I felt the urge to participate in outdoor sports and wanted to play soccer, which we called football in Beirut, but our school didn't have a team.

Instead, I went out for tennis, which I did well in, playing doubles. I had learned to play tennis during our summers in Brummana, where I had participated in a few tournaments.

My tennis friends became my friends outside of school as well, and I became close with one teammate in particular. Danny was short and wore thick glasses on his round face. When not playing tennis, he always had a book in his hands. He was very fast on the court and could return a ball more often than not. He and I continued to play tennis after the school season was over, and he was unique among my American acquaintances in that we often discussed politics and history. Later that summer, when my family moved to a big three-story house on Madison Avenue, Danny and I would go to the tennis courts across the street from my house, play a few sets, and then go to the store two blocks away for a soda pop.

In late spring, after tennis was over, I joined the track and field team, hoping to compete in the fifty- or one-hundred-yard sprint. In Beirut, the fifty-meter sprint had been my strongest event; once, in third grade, I even broke the school's record.

Unfortunately, my V.I. track and field coach didn't want me to sprint, insisting I had a great future in the high jump and should focus solely on that. I did okay that season, but not exceptionally well. Even with lots of practice, I had not improved; by the end of the season, I could not jump any higher than I had the previous year in Beirut.

The coach tried to encourage me, saying, "Sometimes you have to practice for months before you see improvement. You must not give up. You should practice every day, all year long. You don't see it now, but you have a very bright future in high jumping, and if you do well, you could easily get scholarships to more than one college for it." If nothing else, that coach taught me one thing: the importance of perseverance.

I initially took the coach's advice and spent the entire summer practicing the high jump under his supervision. But by the end of the summer, I still was not seeing any improvement. I became discouraged and spent more and more time playing tennis and reading books I had ordered through the Great Books Club.

As a result of all my athletic activities and extracurricular reading that spring, I wasn't focusing on my schoolwork as much anymore. Toward the end of my first school year in America, I wrote to Papa and confessed I was not doing as well in school as I had the previous fall. I told him about all my activities, as well as the ones I planned to join in the next year: the dramatic club, the stage club, and the choir. I also wanted to learn judo and how to bowl.

With all my activities, I was thinking less and less about how much I missed Lebanon and how different my life in America was. In fact, I became increasingly certain I never wanted to permanently leave my new country. I wrote to Papa to specifically tell him about my feelings on this matter in case he was entertaining any thoughts of moving us back to Lebanon.

15. Lorraine and the Molineauxs

OVER THE NEXT COUPLE OF YEARS, MY CONVERSATIONAL
English improved and I made friends, but my social life was still limited to hanging out with my sports buddies. I occasionally went to a "sock hop" dance at school, where you take your shoes off so as to not scratch the floor, but I never really danced, just watched the girls dance with each other.

Sami, on the other hand, was very active socially and seemed to have many friends with whom he hung out, went dancing, went on overnight camping trips, or went to events like the Tanglewood Music Festival. He would occasionally invite Ramsey and me to join him, like the time when a group of us climbed Mount Marcy in the Adirondacks, or when we went square dancing with a bunch of his friends.

Sami was always dating different girls from the College of St. Rose, but then, in the spring of 1962, when I was a sophomore in high school, I came home from school one day and found Sami sitting on the living room couch next to this tall, thin blond girl. She looked like she had popped right out of a magazine that showcased the quintessence of the beautiful American girl.

"Nasib, this is Janet," Sami said seriously.

From that day forward, Janet was a member of our family. She fit right in with our musical family, and she often joined in singing songs like "Church in the Wildwood" and "My Bonnie Lies over the Ocean" with her lovely voice. She was a lot of fun, always ready with a witty comeback. Most important to me, though, was her willingness to discuss big ideas with me. We had read some of the same books, and she was interested in talking about them.

Then, late in the spring of my sophomore year, I met Lorraine Molineaux and her large family, and things were never the same for me again.

One day, I was looking out the window of our Madison Avenue house, which was across the street from the Washington Park tennis courts, watching for Danny, who was supposed to meet me for some tennis. He was always late, so I figured I would just head over once I saw him.

Suddenly, movement on the sidewalk caught my eye. A pretty girl with blond hair and a determined look was pushing a baby carriage. The two younger Molineaux twins, who often played with Leila and Maria, were walking beside her. This was clearly the older Molineaux sister Leila had mentioned when she told me the Molineaux family had eleven children. They lived right around the corner from us on South Lake Avenue.

I ran to Mama and told her who I had seen walking by. "I want to meet her; Leila told me her name is Lorraine. Can you invite the family over for tea and cake? Leila said they love to drink tea."

Mama looked at me suspiciously for a moment, and then grinned. "You want to invite the entire family over so you can meet Lorraine? Why not just invite Lorraine?"

"No way, I don't even know her," I protested. "Please Mama, I really want to meet her."

"Okay; I suppose it would be nice to get to know this family since Leila and Maria play with their children almost every day."

It was quite a gathering, with six of us—Papa was still in the Congo—and thirteen of them. Lorraine was the second child and the eldest daughter in that huge family.

When I finally worked up the nerve to talk to her, I realized Lorraine had never heard a Lebanese accent before. When I casually asked her, "You a suffa-more?" in my quick Lebanese accent, her lovely blue eyes appeared startled.

"Excuse me?" she said in a very soft and polite voice.

"You are a suffa-more?" I repeated in the same quick syllables.

Lorraine and her mother, Teresa, a very attractive lady with a young-ish face and a clear, crisp British accent, exchanged confused glances.

I didn't understand what was so odd about my question. After a brief quizzical look at both of them, I realized my mistake: they thought

I was asking if Lorraine was "suffering more." I laughed and clarified: "In school—you go to Vee-Eye?"

"Yes," she answered.

"Your class, tenth?" I rephrased.

"Oh, yes! Tenth grade—I'm a soph-more."

The next day, I went over to Lorraine's house to ask if she would like to go to the ice cream shop on Madison Avenue with me. Her home was a lovely three-story house with brick steps leading up to a bright-red front door. Lorraine answered the door with a big smile and invited me in. I entered a large, bright entrance hall and noticed a wide staircase leading to the upper floors. It seemed like an enormous house.

As I stood in the entrance hall, I saw a baby grand piano just inside the living room. "Do you play the piano?" I asked Lorraine.

A door swung open just then, and Mr. and Mrs. Molineaux emerged from what looked like a hallway to the kitchen. "Hello, Nasib! Good to see you. Yes, Lorraine plays the piano very well," Mr. Molineaux said. I was thrilled, now knowing we had something in common. "What brings you here?"

"I came to ask Lorraine if she would like to go get some ice cream," I said politely.

"Yes, may I?" Lorraine chimed in. "I've finished all my homework."

"Of course, go ahead," Mr. Molineaux said, "but Lorraine has to be back in time for dinner."

Lorraine gradually became accustomed to my Lebanese accent, but I realized I would have to slow down my speech somewhat if she were to understand everything I said. In general, I often spoke quickly and my accent was very heavy, so I frequently had to repeat myself, which irritated me. This particularly happened when I was tired.

In the fall of my junior year, I decided to ask Lorraine to the Halloween dance at school. I went over to her house, confident the moment I asked her, she would enthusiastically agree before I could even finish my question. But when the moment finally came, there was a quiet pause before she responded, "I'll have to ask my father."

I was crushed, but didn't want to show it. "That's fine. Why don't you go ask him right now?"

"He's at work. I'll ask him when he comes home."

I went back home feeling rejected, thinking she didn't actually want to go out with me and the "I need to ask my father" thing was just an excuse. However, the next day, Lorraine called me and said, "Dad said it was okay! I can go to the dance!" I immediately felt embarrassed for doubting her. Later, when I got to know Lorraine even better, I learned her father's answer had in fact been, "I can't think of a nicer young man for your first date."

Only seniors had the privilege of dressing up in costumes for the dance, but we both planned to enjoy it anyway. The night of the dance, we nervously walked the few blocks from Lorraine's house to the school and entered the dimly lit and ghoulishly decorated auditorium where I began to introduce Lorraine to anyone and everyone I knew.

"You've only been here for two years, and you have so many friends," she said. I felt like a big guy, impressing her.

My relationship with Lorraine deepened very quickly. I wrote to Papa about her without mentioning her name or that she was my steady girlfriend. I wasn't sure what his reaction would be to my spending time with a steady girlfriend rather than focusing on my studies. He never commented on it, so perhaps this was indeed the best tactic to take.

Lorraine was my steady girlfriend for the next year, and I saw her almost every day after school. Mrs. Molineaux often invited me to stay for one of her delicious dinners. She was a great cook, and her lasagna was a special treat. By the end of the fall trimester, I was practically living at their house. I felt I was going steady, not just with Lorraine, but with the entire Molineaux family.

The Molineauxs included me in many of their family events, such as picnics and Sunday trips to Snyders Lake and, once, to Lake George. They would pack a huge basket of sandwiches and a large jug of juice, usually a mixture of Kool-Aid and pineapple juice or lemonade, and all fourteen of us would squeeze into their black stretch limo. I never saw another car like it on the road—a car that looked like a car, but when you rode in it, it felt like a bus. Later, I learned Mr. Molineaux's clever solution to transporting such a large family was to purchase this black limousine secondhand from a funeral home.

Mr. Molineaux, who looked stern and administered no-nonsense discipline, actually had a wonderful, loving heart. He was completely devoted to his family. Auntie Rosa Lee met the entire Molineaux family in the spring of 1963 when she came to visit and was so impressed with Mr. Molineaux and how he managed eleven children with such tender efficiency that when she was invited to appear on NBC's *Today* to talk about her role as the president of the American Medical Women's Association, she recommended they invite him on sometime. Her recommendation panned out, and Mr. Molineaux was soon a guest as well, talking about how he managed his family, organized and conducted the children's orchestra—The Molineaux Ensemble, composed of the older Molineaux children—and prepared and served tea to everyone each morning.

One day early in the spring of my junior year, when the snow had finally melted away and the leaves were starting to bud, I went over to Lorraine's house and found her practicing a Bach minuet on the piano for a rehearsal of The Molineaux Ensemble later that day. Seeing her at the piano made me want to listen to classical music again, especially my favorite, Beethoven. We had left all our classical music record albums in Beirut. We had some Arabic music—mostly by Fayrouz and Wadih Al Safi—Papa had brought with him from Lebanon before heading to the Congo to take up his U.N. post, but that was it.

"Do you know of a record shop around here where I can get some classical music? One not far; one we can walk to?" I asked.

"Yes," Lorraine said. "It's called The Blue Note, and it's about half an hour's walk."

"Okay, lets go!"

It was a long walk to The Blue Note Record Shop on State Street, but it was worth it. After half an hour of browsing, I purchased two Beethoven and two Mozart albums, including Beethoven's Third, also known as the *Sinfonia Eroica*, conducted by Otto Klemperer. We walked back to my house, and I immediately put the *Eroica* on.

As we listened, Lorraine started going through my family's record collection. She picked an Arabic 45 RPM record and asked if I could put it on. It was Fayrouz's "Atnee Naya Wa Ghani." After listening to it, she asked, "Do you understand what she's singing?"

"Yes, of course," I said, and I translated some of the lyrics for her.

She looked at the Arabic words on the record's cover and said shyly, "I'd like to learn Arabic."

"Okay! Wait a second; I'll be right back." Excited, I raced up to my room on the second floor and grabbed a textbook I had used when I was first learning English. It contained Arabic phrases with the English translations beside them. I hurried back down to Lorraine, handed the book to her, and said, "Here, you can have this. You can use it to learn some Arabic."

The next day, she greeted me with, "*Marhaba*"—"Hello" in Arabic. I was absolutely delighted and told her if she were to commit to learning five words or phrases per day, I would try to practice conversational Lebanese Arabic with her, though I still needed to practice my conversational American English and wanted to do that most of the time.

I was also close with Lorraine's older brother, Ian, who also attended V.I., and the three of us often hung out together. On May 1st of my junior year, all three of us marched in the May Day parade Vincentian Institute students were required to participate in.

We had rehearsed for weeks, practicing marching in the auditorium. We all had to know what to do when we passed the reviewing stand and how to keep our lines straight when we turned corners or went around curves. Of course, our uniforms—complete with beanies, white gloves, and a rosary on our belts—also had to be perfect.

After the parade, the three of us walked home together. It was a long walk after an already exhausting day. We talked and laughed about the failed trip to Mount Marcy Ian and I had taken in August of 1962 with my brother Sami and his friends, several months after I met Lorraine and her family.

Mount Marcy is the highest peak in the Adirondacks Mountains of upstate New York. On the morning of our trek, Sami had said, "Guys, be prepared for a long hike—it's about seven miles. The first part will be a couple miles on a trail to the foot of the mountain. Then, it gets really rough."

Eight of us squeezed into Sami's Datsun and drove two hours to the site. As we began our hike, the group decided since several of us wanted to walk at different paces, we should divide into groups of two and meet at the foot of the mountain in two miles. If it got late before we got to the foot, then we should stop for the night, make camp, and continue the next morning.

Ian and I paired up, and we took our time walking, exploring and looking for trail markers. We had to retrace our steps a few times, because we missed the trail markers and went down an unmarked path.

At one point, two hikers coming back down the trail told us to watch out because they had seen a couple of black bears on the trail. After that, we weren't just looking for trail markers—we were now also anxiously watching for bears.

Around six in the evening, we saw a lean-to just off the trail and decided it was a good place to stop for the night, since we clearly weren't going to make it to the foot of the mountain before dark. We gathered some wood and lit a fire to keep the bears away. Fortunately, we had some potatoes in our backpacks, so we grabbed a few, poked holes in each one, smeared them with butter and placed them under the burning wood to cook. After about forty minutes, we opened a couple cans of beans and grabbed two potatoes from the fire, leaving the rest to simmer some more. We ate, drank Pepsi and had a surprisingly nice evening.

By eight o'clock, we were tired and decided it was time to get some sleep. No sooner had we gotten into our sleeping bags in the lean-to and turned off our flashlights than we started hearing the buzzing of what must have been hundreds of mosquitoes. We buried our heads inside our knapsacks, but sleep was impossible.

A few hours later, I heard the sound of scratching. "Stop scratching," I told Ian, "I can't sleep with all that noise."

"I'm not scratching; it's on top of the lean-to."

Alarmed and scared, I whispered, "It must be the bears the hikers told us about; let's get out of here and fight them in the open."

We slowly crawled out of the lean-to, Ian with an ax and me with a flashlight. I pointed the flashlight at the campfire, and there, looking right back at us, was a pack of seven raccoons standing in a circle around our still-smoking campfire, trying to get the potatoes we had left there. After a moment of surprise when the flashlight illuminated their faces, they ran away with a great deal of hooting and shouting.

We couldn't get back to sleep that night, and the next morning we decided to just hike back to the parking lot and wait for everyone else to show up a couple of hours later. We never made it to the foothills of Mount Marcy.

Ian had a great talent for fixing things and for carpentry. Having previously encountered the same skills in my friend Bill, I was now more convinced than ever being able to build and fix things was a requirement for growing up as an American boy.

One day, Lorraine took me down to her family's previously unfinished basement, which Ian had turned into a rec room. The now-finished rec room had unusually high ceilings, a spacious area where the floor had been tiled with linoleum and paneled walls. The room's main feature was an entertainment counter with a record player and records. Bookshelves and cabinets surrounded it. The wall space above the counter was decorated with musical symbols and a pegboard, where 45-RPM records were hung by their center holes on the pegs that extended from the wall. Several cushions were scattered about the floor for seating.

"Wow, Ian did all this?" I asked, extremely impressed.

Soon after, I gave Lorraine my varsity letter and pins, a symbol of serious courtship at the time, and we promised we would always be for each other and we would not go out with anyone else. We even talked about getting married in the future, but for me, it was more like a distant hope, given how young we were.

After that, we spent even more time together, often going on long walks. Sometimes we walked to the religious art shop on Central Avenue to browse. More often, we would walk to Jake's Market for soda or The Dairy on Madison Avenue for ice cream cones. Lorraine jokingly complained I was trying to make her fat with so much ice cream, but then she would turn around and bake cookies for us the next day.

We went to Lyons Lake with Sami and Janet several times. Lorraine and I would rent a rowboat and row to the middle of the lake to enjoy the quiet of the calm water.

When Sami and Janet got engaged, Lorraine and I wanted to get them a wedding gift from the both of us. We selected a wall plaque containing the poem "Desiderata" we found at a religious goods store on Delaware Avenue.

16. Moving on from Albany

A FEW DAYS BEFORE THE END OF MY JUNIOR YEAR AT V.I., Mama came into my room to tell me some important news. "Papa has accepted a position as a professor at the University of Iowa. We'll be moving to Iowa City in August."

My first thought was of my father's long-awaited reunion with our family. I jumped off the bed excitedly. "When will he be arriving from the Congo?"

"Early July," Mama answered. "We'll leave Albany in early August." I understood "we" meant me along with my sisters, Leila and Maria. Ramsey would remain in Troy, as he had a couple more years to go at RPI, and Sami was getting married and moving to California, where he had a job with the United California Bank.

This would be another major transition in our lives and one that initially gave me great relief; ever since Papa had related the story of his "close call" in the Congo, I had been wishing and hoping he would soon leave the Congo and join us in America.

Papa had been working with Dag Hammarskjöld, the U.N. Secretary General, who had been negotiating a deal between the Congolese government and the Katangan separatists. My father was the top economic advisor to both Hammarskjöld and the president of the Congo. As such, he was a member of the Secretary General's inner circle and often traveled with him on official U.N. business.

As part of the negotiations, Hammarskjöld had to fly from the Congolese capital of Léopoldville (now Kinshasa), to the southern province of Katanga. My father was initially supposed to be on that flight, but when the U.N. party arrived in Léopoldville, there were some difficulties with the language barrier. Hammarskjöld had a very important document the president of the Congo needed to read and sign off on before Hammarskjöld returned from his negotiations in Katanga. Unfortunately, it was written in English, and the Congo's president did not read English—though he was fluent in French. My father was the only member of Hammarskjöld's entourage who was exceptionally fluent in both English and French, so they made a last-minute decision Papa would stay behind in Léopoldville to translate the document, while the rest of the entourage went on to Katanga.

Unfortunately, Hammarskjöld's plane mysteriously crashed on the way to Katanga. Everyone aboard was killed; only my father survived, having been saved by a document.

After telling me about Papa's impending return and our move, Mama left the room. I sat back on my bed, thinking. "I can't leave my adopted city, my school and my friends! Above all, can't leave Lorraine." I was comfortable at V.I. and in Albany and did not want to move again.

I was adamant I would remain in Albany for my senior year, and I tried to convince my parents this was a good plan. Mama was supportive at first and tried to find ways to help me realize what I so desperately wanted. She even went so far as to get her friend, Barbara Seminick, a Lebanese-American woman she had met on the city bus a year after we arrived in Albany, to agree to let me rent a room in her house.

Papa, on the other hand, was much less sympathetic and wanted me to go with them to Iowa City, where he could direct and monitor my schoolwork. Still, I tried my best to convince him in a letter, explaining my staying wouldn't even be much of a financial burden:

> I hope to be working at Myers, and making about 400 dollars, which will surely pay my room rental next year in Albany. The other day I went especially and ate dinner at a restaurant to see how much it would cost me. It turned out it will cost all together, with a whole dish, a beverage, and a desert, one dollar. I was completely satisfied with my meal. I did not have to eat till next day at noon. At lunch in school it costs 30 cents to eat a whole meal. Then let us put 20 cents more for other food expenditures. The sum will come out to be one dollar and fifty cents a day for 300 days. This is 450 dollars of food a year. I will be paying 400

for the room. We will put 150 more just to be on the safe side. This will make it 1,000 dollars all together 400 of which I will be paying from my own work money.

Unfortunately, by this point, my grades had dropped to the point of being dismal. I rarely studied and spent most of my time on my social life, Lorraine, sports, and extracurricular reading. One month before our move to Iowa, Papa sat down next to me on the living room couch, looked me in the face and very seriously said, "If your grades don't improve drastically during your senior year, you won't be able to get into college, and you'll end up washing dishes in some restaurant for the rest of your life."

Coming from a family of academics and professionals, the thought I could potentially spend the rest of my life working in a restaurant hit me hard; it made me feel very uncomfortable, like a traitor to my family's tradition and status.

But then, the strong, almost uncontrollable desire to stay in Albany overwhelmed me. I turned to Papa. "I could still stay here, study hard, ace every course, improve my GPA, and get into a college somewhere."

"You have too many distractions here; you won't be able to focus on your studies. In Iowa, you'll be a new student in a new school; you can spend all your time studying there."

Mama, who had previously supported my desire to stay in Albany, now strongly agreed with Papa on this issue. She entered the room just then and added, "Nasib, your father's right: you need to spend your last year of high school studying to improve your GPA. Besides, Papa will be in the academic community in Iowa City. Our family will 'be somebody' again; you'll make new friends and move on to better things."

Papa followed up. "Remember what you told us back in Beirut about working in 'the realm of the mind' and writing books? Well, you can't do that if you don't go to college and then continue on to postgraduate study. And you can't go to college if you don't spend all your time next year studying and improving your grades."

After several such conversations with my parents, I slowly became convinced I had to go to Iowa with my family and get serious about my future, despite my deep desire to stay in Albany.

Almost three years to the day after our arrival in Albany from Beirut, we were once again moving. We all helped pack and load a rented truck Sami and a classmate of his from Siena College would drive to Iowa City. Then, my parents, sisters, and I climbed into the Datsun, and off we went.

I sat in the back seat as Mama drove, and it suddenly hit me: I felt like I had been plucked from the fertile ground where I had finally grown some roots and now had to start all over again. I desperately wanted to stop the car and go back. I felt utterly helpless, not because I knew I couldn't, but because of the bitter realization that if I wanted to build a successful future, I ought to forget about Albany and look forward to what was ahead.

We took our time getting to Iowa City, stopping first for a couple of hours at Niagara Falls, which I had already visited several months earlier with my brothers, Janet, and her two sisters. Despite that, I was just as mesmerized by the loud tumbling waters as I had been during my first visit. I stood gazing at the falls for half an hour, hypnotized by the sheer force of the water falling into a swirling pool below, totally oblivious to my emotional distress at having left Albany for good.

Two hours later, we got back into the car and continued on our trip. Mama said, "Let's sing," as we always did on family car trips. I didn't feel like it, but it didn't really matter whether I felt like it or not. Mama started singing "I've Been Working on the Railroad," and Papa joined in, harmonizing slightly out of key. After a while, I found myself drawn to the singing as well, singing along to songs like "Red River Valley," "The Isle of Capris," and "Michael, Row the Boat Ashore."

That night, we stopped at a hotel just outside of Cleveland, Ohio, where I got my own room. After checking in, we walked to a restaurant next to the hotel for dinner. I noticed a pay phone beside the restaurant's entrance and immediately asked Mama for a quarter. I was surprised when Lorraine was the one who answered the phone; usually, one of her parents did.

"Hi, this is Nasib. What'chu doin'?"

Lorraine answered very softly, "I miss you; I feel blue."

"I miss you, too. I'll call you when I get to Iowa City. I'll try to talk every day. Bye now."

Her voice cracked as she said, "Bye."

I joined my parents and sisters in the restaurant. Mama looked at my grim face and said, "Nasib misses Lorraine." The moment she uttered those words of sympathy, tears came to my eyes; that night, I couldn't stop crying in my hotel room until I fell asleep.

Strangely, the next morning, I awoke refreshed and excited about getting to Iowa.

We arrived in Iowa City late in the afternoon the next day. My parents had purchased a two-story house halfway between the University of Iowa campus and my new school, Iowa City High School. Iowa City did have a Catholic high school, but the public high school, City High, had a stellar reputation. In addition, almost all of the children of University of Iowa professors my father knew were going to or had attended Iowa City High School.

Sami had already unloaded our furniture and set up all the beds in the four bedrooms, two on each floor. He and his friend were halfway back to Albany by the time we arrived.

The next day, I asked my parents, "Can we go see how I'll get to school?"

"Sure, let's all go," Mama answered, "then afterward we can go to 'see-da-rabbits.' You want to come with us for that, too?"

"No, I'm not interested in seeing any rabbits," I said, somewhat confused as to why my parents wanted to go see some bunny rabbits.

Mama laughed and enunciated more clearly: "'Cedar Rapids' is a city not far from here."

"Oh, what's in Cedar Rapids?"

Papa, getting his jacket on, answered, "We're going to a Lebanese grocery store there."

"Sure, I'll come; I want to see what the rest of Iowa looks like."

We got in the car and drove down Summit to East Court Street, turned left on Morningside, and were at the school in just five minutes. "This is great," I told my parents. "It will be an easy twenty-minute walk from the house."

The road to Cedar Rapids was surrounded by farmland that stretched all the way to the horizon. Some farms were flat, while others gently rolled into the distance. It was different from what I had seen in New

York, which was filled with forests. The Iowa landscape impressed me and made me feel happy and refreshed. It seemed everytime I changed geographic location, the novelty impressed me and had a positive impact on me. In fact, I still feel that way today whenever I travel.

At the Lebanese store, my parents bought groceries and lots of pita bread and *manaeesh*, the oven-baked flatbread covered with a spread of olive oil, thyme, sesame seeds, and sumac we loved as a special treat. Browsing through the aisles, smelling the aromas of Lebanese food, and listening to spoken Arabic not only reminded me of Beirut; it also made me hungry for home-cooked Lebanese food.

Back in the car, Papa said, "Those Lebanese, you find them everywhere—even in the middle of Iowa farm country." Sitting in the back seat, Leila, Maria and I gorged ourselves on *manaeesh* and Pepsi.

After five minutes on the road, Papa, sitting in the front passenger seat, turned back to look at me. "Nasib, tomorrow let's go to your school and pick up your textbooks." I had about two weeks before school started, and he wanted to help me get a head start on my physics, chemistry and math courses. As far as Papa was concerned, these were the important prep courses for college.

He and I—well, he more than I—had decided I needed to have a solid foundation in the sciences for my pre-med major. We had agreed on pre-med, though my real passion lay in philosophy and religion, both of which had increasingly become the focus of my extracurricular reading. When I had told him this, he responded, "Philosophy and religion would make a good hobby, but they're not for serious careers."

17. Another New School

WITH PAPA'S HELP, I SPENT THE WEEKS BEFORE MY SENIOR year of high school reading and studying all my new textbooks. Since I didn't know anyone, I was determined to do well in my last year of high school and focus on my studies.

I walked to school on my first day with confidence and excitement. I was not as anxious about going to a new school as I had been for my first day at V.I. in Albany. It did feel slightly odd to not wear a jacket and tie to school and to have girls in my classes. The atmosphere at City High felt freer than what I had experienced at V.I. and there were fewer rules.

My first day was a short one. It started with homeroom, where Mr. Gore, my homeroom teacher who also taught my chemistry class, assigned us our lockers and told us we had to purchase our own locks. No one spoke to me that first day or even seemed to notice me, and we were dismissed before noon.

The next day, at the end of physics class and just before the lunch period, I asked the student sitting next to me where the cafeteria was.

"I'm going there now; let's walk together," he said, and as we walked to the cafeteria, he introduced himself. Dan was a tall, slim, handsome boy who walked at a good pace. He had a pleasant smile and a kind voice, though he was quiet most of the time. He didn't say much as we walked to the cafeteria.

Having lunch at school was a new experience for me, so I watched how Dan got in line and got his food; then I did the same, copying him. We sat with a few other guys Dan knew. Three of them—Bill, Randy and John—were in my physics class. I later discovered these guys were among the brightest kids in the school, and they often hung out together.

It only took me a few weeks to realize my classmates belonged to various different cliques and groups, which hadn't really existed at V.I. My lunch companions were in the "bright kids" clique. These were the people I hung out with at school and, later in the semester, outside of school as well. There were other groups, the most prominent of which were the "sports stars" and the "socially cool" groups. All of these cliques were already in place before I moved to Iowa City, so I felt free to roam among them, ignoring clique boundaries and trying to be friendly to all. As a result, I felt accepted by most of my classmates.

~~~

Friday, November 22, 1963, began as a normal, end-of-the-week day. As my first afternoon class, English, was about to begin, a classmate charged in and said in a low voice, almost a whisper, "Did you hear the news? President Kennedy was shot."

I wasn't sure whether to believe my classmate or not, but I figured if it were true, someone with authority would come tell us soon. Sure enough, just as class began, the principal's voice came over the loud-speaker, announcing President Kennedy had died from a gunshot wound. School was canceled for the rest of the day, and the principal said we should all go home.

I hurried home teary-eyed, finding it hard to believe this sort of thing could happen in America. Assassinations took place in other countries, in places like Algeria and Iraq and in South America. Not in the United States.

My first actual awareness of an asssaination was during the Lebanese civil war of 1958. Around midsummer, the BBC reported a coup d'état in Iraq against the pro-Western government and the assassination of Iraq's King Faisal II and Prime Minister Nuri al-Said. Al-Said was captured trying to flee Baghdad disguised in women's clothing and was then killed and dragged naked through the streets. The horrific mental image—thankfully, I never saw actual photographs—of al-Said's assassination made a permanent distasteful impression on my mind. The adults around me often spoke of Nuri al-Said as a very shrewd politician—someone to be admired.

When I got home from school, no one was there. I turned on the news, which was showing a repeat of Walter Cronkite's teary announcement President Kennedy was dead.

For the next three days, I was glued to the news. The only exception was for the half-hour when I walked to the corner of Gilbert and East Burlington to call Lorraine later that day.

"Did you hear the news?" I asked in an alarmed voice.

"Yes," her voice cracked. "We were dismissed early from school; how about you?"

"Yes, we were, too."

By the next day, the news coverage was focused on a man named Oswald whom the police said was the perpetrator. On Sunday, I was still watching when Oswald was escorted through the police station by two plainclothes police officers on his way to a Dallas jail. I watched as a man in the crowd shot him and as Oswald clutched his stomach with a painful grimace before falling to the floor. The Monday after the assassination, school was canceled, and I spent the day with Leila, Maria, and Mama, watching Kennedy's funeral on TV.

18. Becoming American

JUST BEFORE THE START OF MY FRESHMAN YEAR OF COLLEGE, I decided to make a trip to Troy, New York, to visit Ramsey at RPI, where he was about to start his senior year, and then go on to my favorite city, New York City, to visit Auntie Rosa Lee, Uncle E.J., my cousin Aida and her husband, Roy.

The day after I arrived in Troy, Ramsey said, "A few of my friends are going to the Saratoga racetrack. Do you want to go, too? It would be a nice way to spend your day here, before going on to New York."

I was thrilled. "Sure, I'd love to. I've never been to a horse race before."

We had a great time. Ramsey's friends were very funny, and we laughed a great deal. We bet and we lost, but we had fun watching the races.

I could tell Ramsey's transition to American life, and his assimilation, was complete. His knowledge of conversational English before immigrating served him well. He seemed very comfortable with his life at RPI and with his American friends. He was finishing his senior year at RPI and working at the hospital as an X-ray technician to pay his expenses. In addition to college friends, many I met were his coworkers, medical residents, doctors and nurses. His X-ray job inspired his Engineering brain to come up with an invention that would help the X-ray technician constrain children during an X-ray procedure. He won an award for the invention and was offered a fellowship by General Electric to develop his gadget.

Auntie Rosa Lee called that evening to confirm my arrival time at Penn Station in New York the next day. After we went over the logistics, she added, "E.J. and I plan to head to our house in Central Valley over the weekend. We'd like you and Ramsey to join us."

I agreed instantly, thinking it sounded wonderful. Ramsey had to work during the day on Saturday, but he would drive down on Saturday night. Auntie Rosa Lee also invited my cousin Aida and her husband Roy, with whom I was planning on staying for a night while I was in town.

The next day, I took the train down to New York City, and Auntie Rosa Lee—with her bubbly, energetic personality and big warm smile—met me at the train station. With her take-charge attitude, she directed me, "Follow me. We'll take the subway."

Auntie Rosa Lee always walked at a very rapid pace, and I struggled to keep up while carrying my suitcase. Almost running behind her, I followed her to the subway station where we took the Seventh Avenue Express to Brooklyn Heights.

As we shoved our way onto the crowded subway car, she said, "Tomorrow evening, we'll go to the opera at the Met."

I had never seen an opera before, though I had listened to records with opera overtures and arias. I was very excited at the prospect of seeing one live.

The next day, I got up early to find Auntie Rosa Lee and Uncle E.J. at the breakfast table, with Mary, the Irish maid, serving eggs. During the last year, I had gotten back out of the habit of eating breakfast. In addition to eggs, Mary had prepared oatmeal, toast with butter and jelly, and freshly squeezed orange juice.

As we finished eating, I announced I was going to spend the day in Greenwich Village and the bookstores Brentano's and Barnes and Noble, as I planned to buy several new books, but would be back in time for the opera.

That night, we went to see Gounod's *Romeo and Juliet*, and that experience had a lasting effect on my life. For the rest of my life, whenever I traveled, the first thing I did was find out if any operas were performed while I was in town.

The next day, Auntie Rosa Lee took me to the Statue of Liberty and Chinatown. When we got to the Statue of Liberty, I was reminded of my arrival in this country, which felt so long ago, though it was only four years. I thought back on my feelings that day and how, after being awed by the majestic statue, all I could focus on in New York City were the skyscrapers.

In Chinatown, I was amazed to see streets that didn't look like they were in America at all. None of the signs were in English, and everything was written in Chinese characters.

I indicated my amazement at this to Auntie Rosa Lee. In response, she said, "This is a country of immigrants, and when immigrants come here, they often tend to live and work in close proximity to those who share their culture and language. For example, Little Italy is just a few blocks from here. In the early 1900s, it was the neighborhood where many Italian immigrants lived. Today, it's almost exclusively Italian shops and eateries. Atlantic Avenue in Brooklyn is where you'll find all the Lebanese shops and restaurants. You're just not used to seeing this because your parents took you to Albany and Iowa City—places with a very small Lebanese population, so there aren't immigrant neighborhoods like these."

As Auntie Rosa Lee was describing immigrant life in America, it dawned on me that indeed I had not been associating with Lebanese or Lebanese-Americans since I left Lebanon. My entire life in America so far consisted of making American friends and immersing myself in American culture such as learning slang and eating hamburgers and tuna salad sandwiches. I sometimes did miss the food I would get from the Beirut grocery stores and street vendors. American stores did not have grocery items such as hummus or the Lebanese flat bread we call pita today. While I was aware occasionally you could find a Lebanese grocery store, such as the one we visited in Cedar Rapids, Iowa, I was surprised to learn from Auntie Rosa Lee Lebanese-American immigrant neighborhoods such as the one in Brooklyn had many stores that carried Lebanese food items, as well as other goods imported from Lebanon. In those neighborhoods, people spoke Arabic and listened to Lebanese music.

Auntie Rosa Lee also told me those same immigrant communities would often organize music, dancing, and food festivals, called *Hafli* in Arabic. I now realized our intentional immersion into American culture in order to assimilate and be successful Americans cost us the benefits of the Lebanese experience in America. But even with this realization, I was confident the choice my parents made was the right one— the choice of total assimilation into life in America.

In later years, I made it a point of looking for Lebanese-American immigrant communities wherever I traveled in the country. When I moved with my wife to Ann Arbor, Michigan, for my graduate studies, it didn't take us long to discover the Middle Eastern groceries and restaurants of the large immigrant community in nearby Dearborn.

After spending a couple of days with the Audis, I went over to Aida and Roy's place to spend the night with them before driving to Central Valley the next day. We went out to dinner and had a long conversation about the current situation in the Middle East.

Aida; her brother, Nabil; my Aunt Nora; and Uncle Sami had left Palestine in 1948 after the nation of Israel was established in 1947. Like many Palestinians, they fled, fearing for their lives in the wake of the news of the Deir Yassin massacre by the extremist paramilitary Jewish group, Irgun. As a result, the Hadawis left in a hurry, leaving behind their two houses in Jerusalem and all of the houses' contents. European Jews who were immigrating into Israel soon occupied their houses.

Talking about all of this and the current situation in Israel drove home for me for the first time just how awful it must have been for them to lose everything so suddenly.

The next day, Aida, Roy and I drove to Central Valley, about fifty miles north of New York City, near Bear Mountain. The Audis had a beautiful house on the slope of a hill, with a view of another tree-covered hill. We spent the entire day visiting and conversing in the large, heavily wooded backyard. Ramsey had a car accident on his way to Central Valley. Because of the injuries he sustained in the accident, he came to stay with the family in Iowa City for a long recovery period. As a result, he was not able to follow through with the fellowship offer from General Electric. He eventually went back to Troy and finished his senior year at RPI.

Six years after Mama, my siblings, and I first arrived in America, I decided it was time for me to become an American. I took and passed the immigration exam in the Davenport courthouse, where I had to answer questions such as, "Who is the President of the United States?" and "What is the name of the state where you currently live?" My swearing-in as a U.S. citizen was scheduled for November 9, 1966.

I asked my best friend, Doug, to come with me to the swearing-in ceremony at the Davenport Courthouse as my witness, to which he enthusiastically agreed.

The day of the ceremony, as we entered the courtroom, I was immediately surrounded by a group of about ten older women who took hold of my hands and sang "America, the Beautiful." I was the only one being naturalized that day and was a little embarrassed by the attention. I could barely look at Doug, who couldn't stand up straight from laughing.

I was curious though, and after they finished their song, I asked the ladies, "Who are you?"

"We're the Daughters of the American Revolution," the woman on my left said.

"But the American Revolution took place almost two hundred years ago!" Trying to be funny, I added, "You couldn't possibly be the daughters. You don't look that old."

Several of them smiled at my joke. The lady on my right chimed in, "We're the direct descendants of those who fought in the Revolution."

Soon, the judge entered, and the Daughters all sat down. I remained standing, with Doug standing behind me, for the swearing-in ceremony. It was a short ceremony, and I had already memorized the swearing-in oath. Then, the U.S. District Clerk asked me to sign the naturalization certificate, which also involved officially changing my name from "Nasib Badre" to "Albert Nasib Badre."

Immediately afterward, I was swarmed by a group of local Iowa reporters. "Are you the nephew of Charles Malik?" one asked, before another reporter, this one from the Davenport paper, took me aside and conducted an in-depth interview with me, asking about my family, why we immigrated, my major at the University of Iowa, and my career ambitions.

When I saw the article in the next day's paper, I was surprised by how short it was, given how many questions the reporter had asked. My first interview as an American citizen was underwhelming, but I didn't mind: I was officially an American!

Photos

Christmas Eve, 1959. *Left to right:* Ramsey, my father, my mother, me, Sami.

Leila on left and Maria on right, at ages three and five, in Beirut

American University of Beirut Campus, showing the athletic field and the Mediterranean Sea.

My parents wedding at Ain El Assis, August
1938.

Uncle Charles Malik, Rabieh, Lebanon, 1974.

My family's Schweir rented mountain house, 1956–1959.

Auntie Eva and Auntie Rosa Lee in
Central Valley, New York.

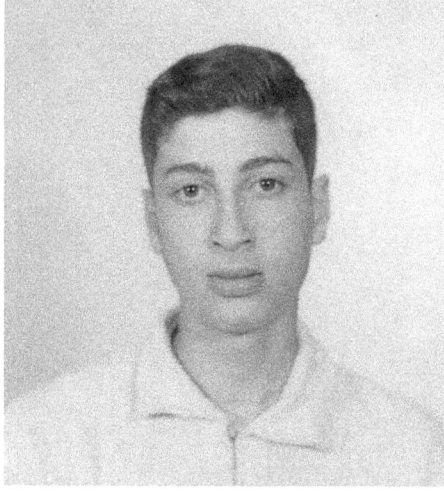

Me at the age of fourteen.

Becharre: Lebanese mountain village of Jibran Khalil Jibran.

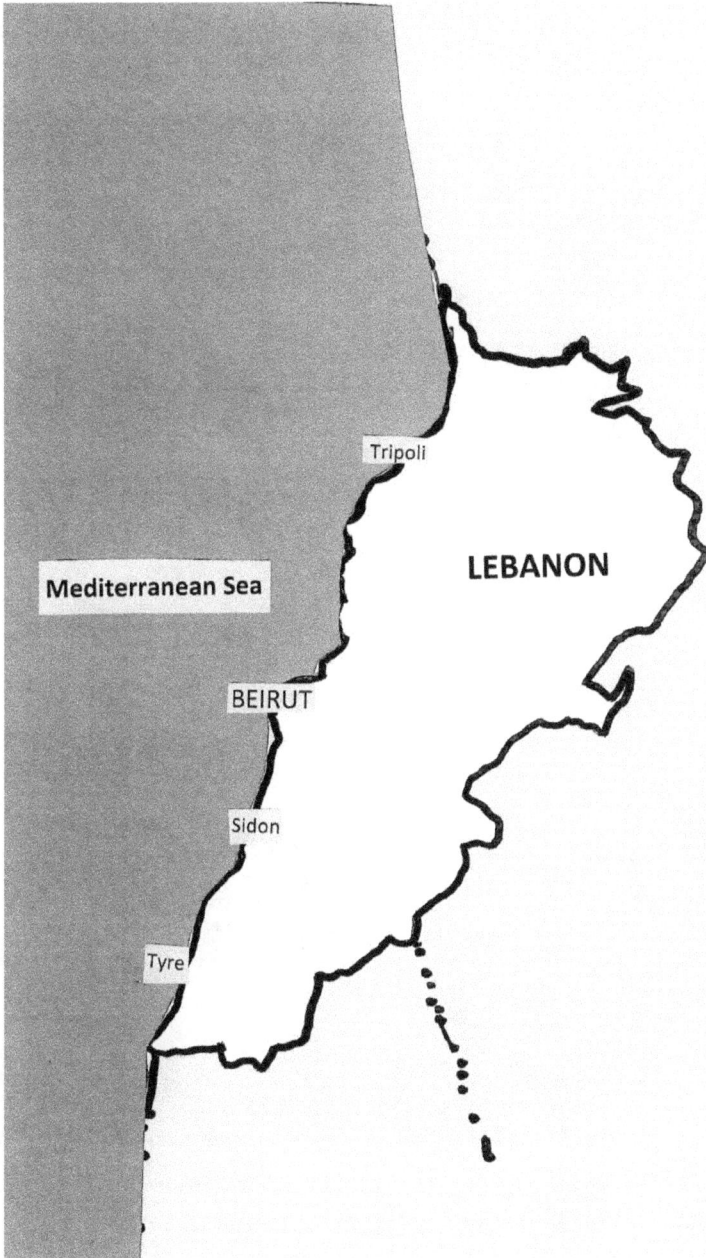

My elementary school map of Lebanon with the four coastal cities and Mediterranean Sea.

My mother and the three boys, circa 1948. *Left to right:* Ramsey, me, Sami.

I am sitting on bumper of our first car, the Humber Hawk, in front of the entrance to our building, 1952.

My mother and Aunt Ellen on the balcony of
our residence in Ras Beirut, 1953.

Leila chasing me
with rug beater.

Falling down laughing after
she tags me.

My father, with Aunt Nora and my mother, on balcony of our residence in Beirut, 1951.

Relatives at San Michelle Beach cabin party, spring, 1960. *Sitting, left to right:* Aunt Wadad, Aunt Nida, Kahlo Fuad, Aunt Ellen. *Standing left to right:* Aunt Salwa, Nelly Korban, my mother, Ammo Jamil.

Badr-Sabra double wedding. *Left to right:* Fuad and Wadad Sabra's parents, Uncle Fuad Sabra, Aunt Ellen, Aunt Wadad, Uncle (Kahlo) Fuad Badr, my maternal grandparents, Hana and Habib.

Left to right: Maternal grandmother, Teta Hana, with me sitting on her lap, my uncle Fuad Badr, my mother, Ramsey, my maternal grandfather, Jiddo Habib, Sami, Aunt Ellen.

Aunt Eva, 1974, at the Malik's home in Rabieh, Lebanon.

The *Esperia* stopped for an excursion in Syracuse, Sicily. With Burt, a friend I met on ship at the Greek theater.

Family on the *Esperia. On the left, from front to back:* Ramsey, my mother, Maria. *Front to back on the right:* Sami, Leila, and me.

Leila on bicycle with friends in Albany, 1962.

My mother and children, Christmas, 1961. *Left to right:* Sami, my mother, Maria, me, Ramsey, and Leila.

Our Albany house on Madison Avenue, 1963.
Standing left to right: Janet, Sami, Ramsey, my
mother, and me. *Sitting:* Leila and my father.

Madison Avenue house, Albany, 1962, with
Leila and friend on the walkway, Maria in front
of the stairs, my mother and me at the entrance.

My father tutoring me in Albany, late September, 1960.

Lorraine and me, 1963.

My friend Doug, 1965.

Barbara's sister Maggie and husband Tom.

Barbara's sisters, Pat and Ruby, at our wedding.

Barbara and me, our wedding.

At our wedding, Barbara with her mother, Mrs. Harbison on her right, and my mother on her left.

Our apartment in New York.

My mother and father in Big Canoe, Georgia, mountain house.

My mother, Lily Badre, at one hundred.

Family, 2014. *Left to right:* Me, David, Shawn, James, Sejal, and Barbara.

Barbara and me on the Saratoga Express.

Part III
On Exploring Religion and Spirituality

19. Socrates, Plato, Aristotle, and the Bible

SHORTLY BEFORE MY FIRST YEAR AT V.I. BEGAN, MY FAMILY started watching the summer Olympics on TV. My keen interest in many of the Olympic events, particularly in track and field and swimming, were due to my very active participation in school athletics. Ramsey and I were glued to the TV, keen to not miss our favorite events. Two days later, Mama announced, "We'll be going to visit Auntie Eva, Ammo Sharl and their son, Habib, in Hanover, New Hampshire, before you start school."

My only response was, "Do they have a TV?"

I was excited about seeing Ammo Sharl because he was not at the port when we arrived in New York. My brother and I bonded with Ammo Sharl during the Lebanese parliamentary elections of 1957.

A few days before Election Day, we accompanied him from Dhour Schweir, where we were spending the summer, to the village of Bterram in the Koura district. He was running for a seat in parliament from Koura. Bterram was Ammo Sharl's birthplace, and it was a quiet village nestled among ancient groves of olive trees and surrounded by beautiful mountains. Ammo Sharl's brother, Gabriel the Jesuit priest, came as well. When we reached the village, there was already a large gathering of supporters waiting for Ammo Sharl to address them. He mounted the platform set up for his speech as the crowd applauded and cheered. The noise was deafening, and that day I realized Sharl Malik was a truly charismatic speaker. Still, this particular episode was mostly memorable because of a car accident we had in the middle of the night on our way back to Dhour Schweir. From Koura, we drove to Beirut, where we dropped off Gabriel. I distinctly remember Gabriel telling Ammo Sharl, "Pay attention to your driving. Don't doze off; you have three children with you," as he got out of the car. From Beirut, we continued on our way, and sure enough, Ammo Sharl fell asleep at the wheel as he drove up the winding mountain road. The car went off the road into a steep ditch. Amazingly, no one was hurt.

As soon as he had ascertained we were okay, Ammo Sharl got out of the car, knelt, and kissed the ground over and over again, thanking God no one had been hurt.

A driver in a passing car stopped and offered to give us a lift to Dhour. It was a small car, and Ammo Sharl sat in the front passenger seat, while we three boys and another passenger sat on top of each other in the back. I was squashed, with someone sitting on my lap the entire trip. In truth, that hurt more than the accident itself had.

The next day, Ammo Sharl called and spoke with each one of us, asking our forgiveness and inquiring over and over again whether we were truly unharmed.

For many days after the accident, I kept thinking about how Ammo Sharl—this very important man who, together with Mrs. Eleanor Roosevelt, had helped draft the United Nations Universal Declaration of Human Rights—showed complete humility as he knelt and kissed the ground in front of children. His conduct at the scene of the accident and his later gesture of calling us to apologize and ask our forgiveness made a deep and lasting impression on me.

We took the bus to Hanover, and Ammo Sharl met us at the Hanover bus station and drove us to their house, which they were renting from a Dartmouth professor who was on a one-year leave. When we arrived, we walked through a small gate into a yard full of flowerbeds, trees, and dense shrubbery; it was a veritable jungle. Nestled in the middle of all that greenery was a huge old house.

As soon as we entered the house, Auntie Eva greeted each of us with a huge hug. Suddenly, I heard an announcer on TV narrating the events of a swimming heat. In response to my no-doubt excited expression, Auntie Eva said, "I heard you were following the Olympics." Sami, Ramsey, and I rushed into the living room to watch.

After a while, Ammo Sharl joined us. He looked over at me and said, "Those athletes worked very hard to get to the Olympics. You can do that too, Nasib, if you practice." Always the teacher, he continued, asking,

"Do you boys know anything about the origins of the Olympics?" We shook our heads in the negative, and he told us how the Olympics had started in ancient Greece. He said the ancient Greeks loved to compete in all sorts of things, including athletics, and the Olympics were an athletic competition between different Greek city-states.

Ammo Sharl's story about the origins of the Olympics sparked my curiosity in Greek culture; little did I know this would be the beginning of my interest in philosophy and theology. As Ammo Sharl left the living room to go to his office, I followed him. "I'd like to read something about the ancient Greeks."

"Have you ever heard of Socrates, Plato, or Aristotle?"

When I confessed I had not, he told me Plato and Aristotle were the greatest philosophers to ever live and suggested I read some of their writings. He explained if Aristotle had lived after the coming of Jesus Christ, he would have been considered a philosopher of the Judeo-Christian tradition, because he argued for the existence of one God instead of many gods, as was prevalent in ancient Greece. He recommended I read Aristotle's philosophy, especially his theory about the Prime Mover, and gave me copies of Aristotle's books *Physics, Metaphysics,* and *The Nicomachean Ethics,* as well as Plato's *The Republic.*

Over the next few years, when I wasn't studying, socializing or playing sports, I spent many hours alone reading the philosophy books Ammo Sharl had given me and many others that these readings had sparked my interest in. I was especially interested in coming up with cogent arguments for Aristotle's Prime Mover and the existence of God, which led me to delve into the theology of Thomas Aquinas.

⌒

At the start of the winter session of my freshman year at V.I., some of my friends encouraged me to join their religion course, insisting the teacher, Brother Davies, was "a cool guy" who was always telling jokes and making the class fun. But, most importantly, they told me, "The grade you get doesn't count in your overall GPA for college."

It didn't take me long to decide to join, especially since I already knew Brother Davies, who taught my history class. I had initially opted out of the religion class simply because I could as a non-Catholic. But with all the religion and philosophy books I was reading on my own, I was curious as to what they were covering; besides, I was getting bored in study hall. It helped I wasn't worried about being behind in the coursework, given how much philosophy and theology I was reading. In fact, I knew more than most of the students in the class.

My new religion class was the first period after homeroom. As I entered the room on my first day, Brother Davies was standing by the door with a big smile on his face. He looked straight at me through his frameless eyeglasses and greeted me. "Hello, Al. I'm glad to see you in this course. Go ahead and sit right here," he said, pointing to a seat at the very front of the room.

Brother Davies started the class by explaining he would spend the first two weeks talking about the origins of the Catholic Church—which he said was established by Jesus Christ himself—as well as Christ's divine and human natures.

After about a week, I had a great many questions, but was hesitant to ask them because I noticed no one else was asking questions. Then, one day, Brother Davies observed, "I've been lecturing all this time, yet you haven't been asking any questions." Looking right at me, he continued, "Let's have some discussion today."

I felt encouraged and raised my hand to ask a question about the divinity of Christ. He answered this and many other questions I had by reading and explaining verses from the Bible. I was satisfied with many of his answers and decided to pursue learning about the Catholic Church and the Bible on my own.

At that, I realized I had never actually read the Bible. Except for my mother, my immediate family was not very religious and was more Protestant in name than in devoted practice. I knew various stories from the Bible because when we were young, Mama used a Biblical picture book to tell us stories like those of Samson and Delilah, Noah's ark, the birth of Jesus, the visit of the Magi, and His crucifixion and resurrection. I decided to add the Bible to my reading list. I borrowed Mama's copy and started with the New Testament.

Shortly after this, I wrote to Papa, listing the books I had read and was reading, but purposefully did not mention the Bible. I strongly

suspected he would want me to stay away from reading religious material, especially about Catholicism, due to lingering sensitivities surrounding Mama's conversion. I often wondered, but never asked, how
he felt about my going to a Catholic school. I told him:

> I am very interested in world affairs and intend to make it a
> hobby. This you may not believe, [but] I am also interested in
> Philosophy, and I believe Aristotle is the greatest whoever wrote.
> I have already read some of his *Metaphysics, Ethics, Politics,* and
> *Poetics.* I also read Plato's five dialogues: *Apology, Crito, Pha-
> edo, Symposium,* and *The Republic.* I also read Marcus Aurelius'
> *Meditations.* I am reading now Epictetus's *Discourses.* I have read
> *Introduction to St. Thomas Aquinas.* I also read *The Red Badge of
> Courage* by Crane; it is a great novel; *Kim* by Kipling, *Kidnapped*
> by Stevenson, and *Julius Caesar* by Shakespeare. *The Pearl* is one
> novel I liked very much. I am reading now, *Theology and Sanity*
> by Frank Sheed, and also *Epictetus* and Twain's *Huckleberry Finn.*
> Next week I will finish with *Theology and Sanity* and I will begin
> Homer's *Iliad.* So as you can see I am reading more than one
> book at a time. I found out that "the world is in books."

20. World Affairs and Culture, Past and Present

*H*ISTORICAL AND POLITICAL ISSUES AND RELIGIOUS CON-
flicts already occupied my mind by the time I was thirteen. I
absorbed ideas about politics and religion by eagerly listening to the
adults around me. Whenever family and friends gathered for a social
occasion, talk often revolved around issues of the day. I almost always
chose to sit inside with the adults instead of going outside to play with
friends. I listened and I learned.

With the return of Ammo Sharl Malik, Auntie Eva, and my cousin
Habib to Lebanon in 1956, politics and history further consumed my
interest. Ammo Sharl had just served as Lebanon's ambassador to the
United States, and he was about to join the Lebanese Cabinet as the
Minister of Foreign Affairs.

One of my favorite pastimes was to sit quietly in their living room
when they had visitors and listen to discussions about current events.
These conversations often focused on the ongoing conflict between the
United States and the Soviet Union and, closer to home, the schemes of
neighboring Syria and the United Arab Republic (UAR) under Gamal
Abdel Nasser. Nasser wanted to unite all Arab countries into one nation,
and Syria, which was part of the UAR, had plans to appropriate Lebanon as part of Greater Syria.

Papa was a regular participant in these discussions. Whenever he
spoke about a topic, it was difficult to refute his logic. He was highly
skilled at explaining very complex concepts in very simple ways. He
was a natural-born teacher and in fact had spent his entire life, from
when he was a teenager, in the teaching profession.

My interest in domestic politics intensified during the Lebanese parliamentary elections in May and June 1957, because Ammo Sharl was
running for parliament in the Koura region.

I brought my interests in political issues, history and world affairs with me to America. My religion class at V.I. further spurred my interest in Western civilization, history, and philosophy, and this continued into my second and third years. I wanted to know more about the history of the Roman Empire and all the key players in Rome, such as Julius Caesar, Marcus Aurelius, and Augustus. I also began reading about the history of the Catholic Church and the European Middle Ages.

In my second-year history class, we used a textbook called *The World in Our Day*, which was about recent history and covered the current conflict between the Soviet Union and the West. However, I lost all faith in the author's accuracy when I discovered a major mistake about Ammo Sharl; the author had confused him with Jacob Malik, a Soviet delegate to the U.N. during the Korean War. After pointing out the error to the teacher, I immediately wrote to Papa about it:

> I raised this point [to the teacher], and showed the error in the book. The teacher was really upset about the mistake, since he [k]new Ammo Sharl, and heard him talk once. He started talking how outstanding a man was Sharl Malik and how he raises the name of Lebanon all over the world. It is really a shame, for imagine, thousands and thousands and thousands of high school students in the U.S. shall receive this same publication with the name "Sharl Malik" as a Soviet delegate to the U.N. during the [K]orean war, when he is extremely anti-communist.

During this time, I got to know Ammo Sharl as an ardent anti-communist, a man who saw the world as a battlefield between the Soviet Union and the West, between "Marxist–Leninist dialectical materialism," and Western civilization and traditions. I was particularly inspired by his speeches, "Will the Future Redeem the Past?" and "Some Urgent Tasks," which he gave me copies of when my family spent Christmas of 1961 with the Maliks in Washington, D.C. These speeches were largely commentaries on world affairs as informed by Judeo-Christian values.

I read and reread both documents, memorizing many phrases, such as, "He who sees and knows only history can never understand history"; "While living in history, one must have roots outside history"; and "One's living roots must extend to God." I was captivated by the way Ammo Sharl articulated his ideas, using expressions such as, "superficiality and paralysis, mediocrity and inaction," to criticize the West vis-à-vis communism.

As a result, I developed a very active interest in international politics. Wanting to listen to the news from Europe and the Middle East, I saved my pocket money and purchased a transistor radio with a short-wave band for $47.80. On it, I could listen to the BBC, the Voice of America in Arabic and in English, the Canadian Broadcasting Corporation, the Voice of Russia in English, and the United Arabic Republic's radio, which came directly from Cairo. As a result, I was able to get more news about the Middle East.

In October 1962, we were all glued to the television for a couple of weeks, waiting to see if war would break out between the United States and the Soviet Union over the Soviet missiles in Cuba. I watched President Kennedy issue an ultimatum to Nikita Khrushchev and the Soviet Union and Adlai Stevenson ask the Soviet representative on the U.N. Security Council, Valerian Zorin, whether his country was installing missiles in Cuba.

Stevenson boldly added, "Don't wait for the translation; answer 'Yes' or 'No.'" When Zorin said he didn't have to answer because he wasn't in an American court of law, Stevenson fired back, "I am prepared to wait for my answer until hell freezes over." Then he proceeded to show the Security Council aerial photos of the missiles.

Though most of my friends weren't interested in international politics, everyone was following these events, fearing the United States might be attacked. I was adamant America should immediately go into Cuba and remove both the missiles and the Castro regime once and for all. None of my school friends agreed with me. They were concerned if the United States attacked Cuba, the Soviets would retaliate and attack us. I countered the Soviets would see it as us defending our neighborhood against hostile action. Plus, the Soviets knew if they attacked us, Moscow could be a target. They weren't going to risk being directly attacked for the sake of Cuba.

I was hooked on international politics, and thanks to Ammo Sharl's speeches, I became increasingly interested in learning about the "Western civilization" he said we needed to defend from the spread of "Marxist–Leninist materialism." In my third-year history class, we used a book called *Men and Nations: A World History,* which helped me delve more deeply into the history of Western civilization. My interests in Plato, Aristotle, and the ancient Greeks that had begun with Ammo Sharl's Greek Olympics discussion only grew deeper as a result of this class. I could see how the dots connected the story of Western civilization from the Greeks to the Romans, to Christianity. I was also particularly interested in Greek and Roman history because both Greece and Rome dominated the Mediterranean world from which I had come.

We also covered the tumultuous history of the Catholic Church, especially the Protestant–Catholic schism, which had never been resolved to my satisfaction in religion class. I understood at the time of the Protestant Reformation, Catholics believed Protestantism was nothing more than a revolt against true Christian beliefs and values. In turn, the Protestants, led by Martin Luther, were unhappy with the church, the clergy and their practices, particularly the selling of indulgences, whereby parishioners would make a monetary payment to the church in exchange for absolution from certain lesser sins, such as lying.

As I read further on my own, I started to grow in the conviction the Protestant churches started by the likes of Martin Luther, John Calvin and, later, Henry VIII, could not really trace their beliefs and practices to the original, historical church established by Christ.

21. Mind Matters

M Y BURGEONING FOCUS ON MATTERS OF THE MIND AND intellectual discourse intensified in my sophomore and junior years of high school. With my growing interests in history, religion and world affairs, I began writing down my ideas, which were often simply a rehash of what I was reading. After reading Ammo Sharl's speeches about the threat of communism to Western civilization and Christianity, I decided to write an essay on that subject and show it to my English teacher. I told Papa about it:

> The next day when I saw him, he told me the paper is an excellent one, and the faculty has decided to publish it in a literary magazine the school publishes and distributes at the end of the year. I called the essay, "An Urgent Need." It is about Christianity and communism.

"An Urgent Need" was the first of many essays I wrote for the school's literary paper, *The Vincentian*. In it, I focused on the conflict between communism and Western Christian civilization. I was adamant there was only one conflict in the world and it was the pivotal battle between Christianity and communism. In referring to the communist threat, I argued it sought to dominate everything and everyone and set humanity back to the time before Christ bought our salvation with his death and resurrection.

I also asserted communism's spread was due to the zeal and dedication of its proponents, something they had learned from the spread of early Christianity. They had adopted the traits of fervor and dedication that had characterized the early Christian fathers' efforts to spread their message.

As I wrote more essays for *The Vincentian*, my tone evolved from one of being in the midst of a battle, to a stance of searching for a way out of the trenches. In my second piece, "The Way Out," I asked whether there was actually a way to establish and maintain peace among peoples and nations. Citing Dostoevsky, whose novels I was reading at the time, I continued, "Dostoevsky knew that man can accomplish nothing if he does not have peace in his own soul." This, I maintained, could only be done when humans recognize and admit there is something beyond the world we see and experience and Jesus Christ is our God and Savior.

I followed this up with a piece called, "The Final Goal of Progress," in which I explored the questions, "To what end does progress lead? Does it ultimately lead to man's happiness?" I suggested social and scientific progress will lead nowhere without making an effort to uplift the individual and embrace the simple principles of love and understanding.

The Vincentian's editor asked me to write an editorial for the paper's Christmas 1962 edition. In response, I wrote a piece called "The Reality of Christmas." By then, I was reading and rereading St. Matthew's "The Sermon on the Mount" over and over again. It was becoming increasingly clear to me Christ came not to endorse the existing ways of the world, but in fact to rebel against them.

This was the first time I had ever embraced an anti-establishment stance, and I felt empowered by the idea I could—and perhaps even should—reject the establishment, particularly where there was social injustice and corruption. The notion Christ was born in a stable encouraged me to reject this world's values, such as money, greed and power.

Thanks to all of my reading, thinking and writing, by my third year at V.I., I was a Catholic in spirit. I had come to believe Christ was divine and the Catholic Church was the authentic historical church established by Jesus Christ, with the apostle Peter as its first pope. I kept my beliefs to myself, telling only Mama. Because I did not wish to hurt Papa, whom I never told about my beliefs, I vowed to join the Catholic Church only after I was no longer living at home.

One morning in the spring of my junior year, Father Thomas Maloney, the school's principal, stopped me in the hallway as I was walking to class. He greeted me with his famous wide smile, saying, "Al, I've read the articles you've been writing for *The Vincentian* and thought you might be interested in entering a speech competition I'm organizing. You could speak about what you wrote."

I was flattered he had asked me and agreed immediately.

"Great! Students will submit drafts of their speeches, and then four will be selected to give their speeches in a school assembly," he explained. "The winner will go on to a competition among all the Catholic schools in Albany."

I almost immediately decided to speak about Christ's divinity, titling my speech "The Son of God." I wrote it in one week, showed it to Mama, who made a few edits, and then submitted it to Father Maloney.

The very next day, Father Maloney informed me my speech had been selected. When he handed it back to me, I saw he had written, "Excellent & will make a fine speech," on it.

I delivered my speech before the entire student body—approximately 1,000 students—and all the teachers. After I finished, I looked down onto the podium to gather my papers. When I looked up again, I was surprised to see the audience standing and applauding. I was elated.

I ended up coming in second place to a girl named Karen, but I didn't mind. The judge, who was a speech coach from outside our school, came up to me afterward and said, "Even though you had a standing ovation and the content of your speech was excellent, your delivery was not as good as Karen's."

"I was simply happy with the way the audience applauded for me," I told him. On my way down from the stage, Brother Davies stopped me and said, "Excellent speech and very impressive for a young man who's been in this country for only three years." Many of my classmates later told me I should have won first place, but as I said to the judge, I was pleased with how my speech had been received.

⌐⌐

The following year at Iowa City High School, my goal for the year was to focus on getting the best grades I could, especially in my science classes. I was taking AP Physics and AP Chemistry and needed to do well in both to prove I was ready for college and for a pre-med major.

What intrigued me about chemistry was the scientific method and the process of conducting experiments to test hypotheses. One day, while we were conducting an experiment on hot and cold reactions, a student photographer from the yearbook came in and snapped a surprise photo. When the yearbook came out at the end of the year, there I was in the middle of the photo, holding the clamp that controlled the fluid's flow into the reaction vessel.

My favorite subject was physics. Mr. Campbell, the physics teacher, made the subject interesting and exciting. When we got to the chapter on light, I was intrigued by the question of whether light behaved like particles or waves. Mr. Campbell conducted an experiment, showing, in the context of quantum mechanics, both theories could be possible.

We also covered topics like Newton's laws of motion, the second law of thermodynamics, electricity and magnetism. The universe, its laws, and its mysteries fascinated me, especially the Big Bang Theory. It prompted me to think about how the universe formed and what had caused it to form in the first place.

These thoughts brought me back yet again to my passions: philosophy and theology. I re-read Aristotle's theory on the Prime Mover and dove into the first volume of Thomas Aquinas's *Summa Theologica*, which examines the proof for the existence of God for the first time. The *Summa* was among the books in my now substantial library, but I had only skimmed parts of it before.

Aquinas posited five arguments for the existence of God, starting from ideas about motion, causation, contingency, degrees of perfection, and design. The arguments about motion and causation captivated my attention the most, as they allowed me to consider the question, "Was God the first cause, the spark that set off the Big Bang and created our universe?"

I increasingly could not fathom how people could live their lives, day-in and day-out, without thinking deeply about questions like, "How did the universe begin?" or "What is the purpose of life?" But none of my friends showed any interest in discussing these questions.

22. A Christmas Visit to the Molineauxs'

*A*T THE END OF THE FALL SEMESTER OF MY SENIOR YEAR IN Iowa City High School, my report card showed a stellar performance in my science classes, the subjects that really mattered to me—and my father.

Two weeks later, I took a train to Albany to spend Christmas with the Molineaux family. I arrived the day before Christmas Eve, and Lorraine and Mr. and Mrs. Molineaux met me at the station.

I shared a bedroom with Ian on the top floor of their enormous house while I was visiting. I felt quite welcomed and like a privileged member of the family to be invited to the upper levels of the house. I had never been upstairs, and I was sure only family was allowed above the first floor.

Early on the morning of Christmas Eve, Ian's and my bedroom door opened, and Mr. Molineaux entered holding two cups of tea, one for Ian and another for me. Mr. Molineaux brought tea to everyone in the family every morning as a wake-up call. When he handed me a cup, I felt more accepted as a member of the Molineaux family than ever before—more than when I was invited to the dozens of dinners I shared with them, more than when I joined the Molineaux family for outings.

The rest of the day passed slowly. Lorraine and I took a long walk along the snow-covered sidewalk of Madison Avenue, oblivious to the frigid Albany air, totally absorbed in our conversation about the real meaning of Christmas and how it had been distorted by commercialization and consumerism.

Later, Lorraine, Ian and I attended midnight mass at St. Vincent De Paul, and the entire experience was marvelous. We went a little early to listen to the choir sing Christmas carols before the mass, and as a result, we were able to sit close to the front of the church. This proved to be a good idea because, by the time mass began, there was not a single empty seat left, even though it was a very large church.

Even more special was the fact that this was my very first high mass. The entire mass was sung with the accompaniment of a fabulous-sounding organ. The choir was magnificent, and the uplifting music and some Gregorian chanting combined with the smell of incense to make me feel I was truly in the house of God, celebrating the birth of His Son, Jesus Christ. I felt a holy presence that made me want to become a Catholic right then and there. My only frustration with the whole experience was I could not receive communion because I was not formally a Catholic yet.

On Christmas morning, there was no tea delivery. Instead, we all rushed—still in our pajamas—down to the living room, where Mr. Molineaux had our tea waiting for us. The younger children quickly dug into their red-and-white flannel boot-shaped stockings, which were hung along the fireplace mantle and stuffed with small gifts.

After that, I assumed we would open the gifts under the tree, so I was surprised when Mr. Molineaux said, "Everybody get dressed for mass." This was different from my family, where gift-opening came right after the stockings. Even though Ian, Lorraine, and I had gone to mass the night before, we now went again with the entire family. After mass, we came back to the house for a delicious brunch and then opened the gifts.

I gave books to Lorraine and Ian and a house-shaped Christmas ornament to Mr. and Mrs. Molineaux, which Mama had helped me select. I received two gifts: a decorative red necktie from "Santa" and a very nice book about praying the rosary from Lorraine.

After two more enjoyable days with Lorraine, I took the train back to Iowa City. I loved Lorraine and the Molineaux family in general, and I missed being with them, so my departure was a sad one for me. Still, when I said goodbye to them, I was already looking forward to and thinking about getting back to school and the second semester of my senior year of high school.

One lazy Saturday a few months later, as the Iowa winter was slowly drawing to an end, Mama called from the front door, "You have a letter from Lorraine!"

Our letter writing had dwindled to about once a month by the middle of the second semester. We were both busy with schoolwork and new friends.

Lorraine started her letter by telling me how much she valued our friendship and loved my family, especially Mama. She went on to say she didn't want to hurt me, but had decided to end our relationship. She felt we should both be free to develop new relationships with others and needed to experience more in life before she could make a lifelong commitment to me or to anyone. She was certain it wouldn't be fair to either of us to continue any longer, hiding our plans and promises of future marriage from our families, not dating as normal teenagers did, and pretending everything was fine and would work out.

Her letter didn't anger me; Lorraine was very realistic and reasonable, and what she said made sense. We were both young and had to go on with our lives. What really saddened me was her returning the varsity letter, pins, and Arabic book I had given her.

23. Meeting Doug

A WEEK AFTER THE BEGINNING OF THE SECOND SEMESTER, I was walking home from calling Lorraine when I saw a boy coming toward me along East Court Street I had seen in school earlier that day. He walked with a distinct bounce and a cheerful smile, and when our paths crossed, I stopped and greeted him, "Hi, you go to City High, right?"

He looked at me with wide eyes through his thick black-rimmed eyeglasses. "Yes, I do. You, too?"

"Yes, my name is Al."

"I'm Doug."

I looked at him closely, noticing his round smiling face and disheveled blond hair. "I never saw you last semester," I said.

He grinned. "That's because I spent the semester in France."

"Oh, what were you doing in France?"

"Learning French and about French culture and history."

"Do you know any other languages?"

"Yes, I grew up speaking German; my mother is German."

Doug's father was a surgeon at the University of Iowa hospital. His parents were divorced, and his mother lived in Davenport, Iowa, with her new husband. Doug, along with his two sisters, lived with his father and stepmother in Iowa City.

"Do you plan to go back to France to continue your studies?"

"No, not right away, but I am going to spend two months in Mexico this summer to learn Spanish." He already knew a little Spanish, but he did not speak it as fluently as he spoke German and French.

We talked animatedly as we walked, and when we reached my house, I stopped and asked, "Do you live far from here?"

"Just twenty minutes' walk away, on Lower Muscatine Road. I always pass your house on my way home from school."

"Would you like to come in for a Coke?"

"Sure."

I introduced Doug to Mama and my sisters, who were on their way out, as we went into the kitchen.

"So were you in school in France?" I asked.

"No, I was staying with a French family in Paris, learning French by speaking with them. I was also picking up the language on my own just by living daily life."

"What do you mean?" I asked, curious as to how his experiences learning French differed from my experiences learning English.

"I learned French phrases and vocabulary by reading all the store-front signs, posters, billboard ads, banners, displays, and road signs, writing them down in my notebook and memorizing them."

"Were you able to converse well in French?"

"Well, beside practicing with the people I lived with, I would go out to restaurants to order food, talk to shopkeepers, and ask directions to places."

I saw Doug at school the next day, and he asked if I would like to come over to his house after school, get a sandwich, and then go for a walk around the University of Iowa campus.

I was delighted. "Sure! I'll just need to drop my bag at my house on the way."

"I noticed you have an accent, Al; where are you from?"

"Lebanon."

"Oh, then you probably know French! France ruled Lebanon for a long time."

"I only know a few words in French because the elementary school I went to didn't have French classes. We spoke Arabic at home."

"Where did you learn English?"

"In Albany, New York, where we lived when we first came to America. In Beirut, we only had English class once a week. I learned to read, but couldn't converse in English very well."

When we reached Doug's house, we entered a brightly lit kitchen, made and ate our peanut butter and jelly sandwiches, and continued talking about France. I asked Doug whether he had followed the French–Algerian crisis and De Gaulle's decision to give Algeria its independence while he was in Paris.

"Yes," he said, "but the French people didn't pay much attention to it, even though it was always in the news."

This was the first time in my three-and-a-half years of high school in America I met a classmate who actually knew something about Lebanon, followed international affairs, and wanted to talk about current events in Europe. Doug's interest in French culture, history, and language dovetailed with my focus on Western civilization and international affairs.

I had just finished reading a book by Christopher Dawson on European history and the Catholic Church and wanted to talk to Doug about my deep interest in Catholicism and how I believed European history was grounded in church history. I was a little hesitant to bring the subject up because I was afraid he would have a negative reaction but plowed ahead all the same and told him about my thoughts on the subject.

He smiled, then said, "Yes, in Europe, especially during the Middle Ages, European history and church history are practically the same thing."

I was surprised and delighted. "You know, in his book, *The Making of Europe*, Christopher Dawson says religion and, more specifically, Catholic Christianity, is at the roots of Western culture."

"Are you interested in the Catholic Church and church history?" he asked.

"Yes, very much."

"Are you a Catholic?"

"No, but I'm considering becoming one."

He jumped excitedly. "Just two weeks ago, before I left Paris, I visited the Cathedral of Notre Dame de Paris."

"Oh, did you meet the hunchback?" I joked.

He laughed and went on, "I went there on the first Friday of the month and saw the Crown of Thorns relic, the one said to have been placed on Jesus's head before the crucifixion."

I could see Doug had at least a cultural interest in the church and felt encouraged enough to tell him more about my interests.

"I've been reading the writings of some of the early Church Fathers."

"Oh, who?"

"Augustine, Gregory of Nazianzus, Jerome; I'm currently reading about Clement and Tertullian, who lived at about the same time. Clement, a Greek convert to Christianity, ran a Christian school in Alexandria and adapted the Gospel to Greek philosophy and culture. On the other hand, Tertullian, whose writings were considered heretical by the church hierarchy of the time, found no meaningful relationship between the Gospel and Greek philosophy; he asked, 'What has Jerusalem to do with Athens?'"

Doug looked at me. "Good question; what do you think?"

"I'm absolutely convinced they have everything to do with each other. As Thomas Aquinas convincingly argued, Reason, which is the basis for Aristotle's philosophy, and Faith, which comes from Divine Revelation, are the two pillars of Christianity."

Doug seemed interested and asked if I could recommend some books. I enthusiastically offered, "One of the best books I've read on Catholicism is Frank Sheed's *Theology and Sanity*." I lent it to him, and we had many great discussions about it as he read it.

One day, as we were strolling alongside the Iowa River in the middle of the University of Iowa campus, Doug stopped and looked at me. "If someone were to ask you to give one good reason why you want to become Catholic, what would you say?"

I paused, then replied, "The one passage in the Gospels that convinced me the Catholic Church is the church Christ established and Peter was the first pope of is Matthew 16:13–19. Let me read it to you." I opened the little New Testament I carried with me and read:

> He [Jesus] said to them, "But who do you say that I am?"[16] Simon Peter replied, "You are the Christ, the Son of the living God."[17] And Jesus answered him, "Blessed are you, Simon Bar-Jona, for flesh and blood has not revealed this to you, but my Father who is in heaven.[18] And I tell you, you are Peter, and on this rock I will build my church, and the powers of death shall not prevail against it.[19] I will give you the keys of the kingdom of heaven, and whatever you bind on earth shall be bound in heaven, and whatever you loose on earth shall be loosed in heaven."[20] Then he strictly charged the disciples to tell no one that he was the Christ.

Doug took the Bible from me. As his eyes seemed glued to the passage, I continued, "You see, I already believed in Jesus Christ. When I read this passage, I became a convert to the Catholic Church. As a Christian believer, I looked around me and saw dozens and dozens of denominations and churches, and I went on a quest to determine which one was the church Christ had established. This passage convinced me it was the Catholic Church. The debate between Catholics and Protestants is over whether 'the rock' on which Christ will build His church is Peter himself or simply anyone who professes—as Peter did to Jesus—He is 'the Christ, the Son of the Living God' as we read in Matthew 16:16."

Doug asked, "So what do Protestants believe?"

Having been brought up in the Presbyterian church, I explained, "Protestants believe Jesus's statement to Peter that 'You are Peter, and on this rock, I will build my church,' is intended for any Christian professing the divinity of Christ as Peter did; Catholics believe Peter is The Rock. The fact is many of the apostles, like Philip, Nathaniel, Andrew, even John the Baptist, made similar proclamations, but Christ didn't say to them, 'You are the rock.' He only said that to Peter."

Doug looked up at me. "That's really powerful, convincing."

I continued, "Also, it's very clear in John 20:21–23 that Christ gave the Apostles—the first priests, in my opinion—the power to forgive sins in his name. Let me read to you what he said:

> As the Father has sent me, even so I send you . . . Receive the
> Holy Spirit. If you forgive the sins of any, they are forgiven; if you
> retain the sins of any, they are retained.

That's why in the Catholic Church, and only in the Catholic Church, we have confession, the sacrament of penance."

Doug thought for a few minutes, then asked, "So how is it your family comes from a Lebanese Protestant background? How did there come to be a Protestant church in Lebanon?"

"Good question. For centuries, Lebanese Christians belonged to the eastern churches: the Maronites, the Melkites, and the Greek Orthodox. The Protestants are only a recent addition within the last two centuries."

"Well how did your family become Protestant?"

"To make a long story short, Protestant missionaries came to Lebanon in the nineteenth century. I read once they came to convert Muslims but ended up only converting eastern Christians. Anyway, my great-grandfather, Yousef, met the missionaries and became a Presbyterian in the mid-nineteenth century. And that's what we've been ever since."

"What was he before he became Protestant?" Doug asked.

"We were Greek Catholics, also known as Melkites." I paused, then added, "Actually, just like the Maronites, the Greek Catholics are an eastern rite of the Catholic Church and are in communion with the pope. They trace their origins to the first Christian community in Antioch in the first century."

Doug said, "That's interesting, especially since the Greek Catholics are in communion with the pope. It means you're on your way back to your original family religious heritage by joining the Catholic Church."

"I suppose you could say that; it does feel like continuity."

24. Exploring Catholicism in College

D OUG AND I DECIDED TO ATTEND THE UNIVERSITY OF IOWA, registering for the same courses, as we were both pre-med majors. The semester flew by, and I did well enough to make the honor roll. However, by the end of the first semester, I knew pre-med was not the right major for me; my heart was elsewhere.

I had taken a course on the history of Western civilization and was now thinking about changing my major to history. Though my parents had encouraged my original pre-med major, I was now largely independent and didn't feel the need to inform them of this change.

Browsing through the course listing for the spring semester, I noticed a course on Catholicism. "Doug, did you see this course, Introduction to Catholicism? I think I'll take it, along with another course on Western civilization."

Doug was interested, but had not yet decided to change his major and wanted to take another course offered at the same time. Looking ahead in the course catalogue, he said, "I see there's a course on the History of the Catholic Church offered in the fall; lets take that together, instead."

I looked at the listing. "Welsh is the professor; the same guy teaching this semester's Intro to Catholicism; sure, I'll take that with you, too. I want to take both."

Welsh, a short, husky man with a round face and a Roman nose, entered the classroom, walking with confidence. He deposited a stack of books on the instructor's desk and then stepped over to the podium where he placed an open notebook. "Good morning, I'm Father Welsh, and this is Introduction to Catholicism. If you're in the wrong class, this is your chance to escape."

His first lecture was about the origins of the Catholic Church, and he gave a cogent explanation of the continuity of the church from the Apostle Peter to the current papacy. He impressed me immediately as a clear, articulate, and logical lecturer very comfortable with the material he was presenting.

After several classes, I decided to meet him and tell him about my interest in Catholicism. I went up to him after class one day, introduced myself, and asked for an appointment during his office hours. He was very obliging and, in a very friendly manner, asked me to walk with him to his office where we could talk.

As we entered his office, I saw books everywhere: in built-in bookcases on all four walls, in stacks on the floor and on a table in the corner. In contrast, his desk was very neat and contained only one open book.

As we sat, he asked me where I was from, about my family and parents, and how I became interested in the Catholic Church. I told him about my family's Protestant origins in Lebanon, Mama's conversion to Catholicism, and my three years at V.I. in Albany.

He seemed very pleased and wanted to confirm, "So you would like to become a Catholic?"

"Yes, I would, but I have to wait until I no longer live at home."

"Do your parents know of your religious conversion?"

"My mother does. We've had many discussions about Catholicism and spiritual issues. I haven't told my father yet; I suspect he wouldn't take it well. I get the impression even though he respected my mother's decision to become a Catholic, he was never happy about her conversion. I'm positive he would be even less so with mine."

"Why do you think he would be against it?"

"Well, our family's history is steeped in the Protestant traditions of Lebanon and Syria. My great-grandfather was the first Lebanese-born Presbyterian minister."

"I see. I agree you should take your time and for now, continue reading and learning about the Catholic Church." With that, he handed me a book about the teachings of the church. "After you finish reading it, let's meet again," he said.

A few weeks later, we met again to discuss the book, and he answered my many questions about the sacraments. After our conversation, he paused and then asked me if I would like to work as his student assistant. "I have so many books," he explained, "and as you can see, I really don't know where things are or how to find what I need. All my books need to be catalogued, and I think you would be the perfect person to do it."

I excitedly jumped at the offer; it meant I would spend lots of time reading books I would never have been able to buy. Plus, I welcomed the small income, which I saved so I could get my own apartment in a year or two. I spent the rest of the fall semester working twenty hours every week cataloguing Father Welch's books. For the next two years, Father Welch became my mentor and spiritual advisor.

One day, late in November of my first semester as his student assistant, Father Welch came into the office with a big box of envelopes. He pointed to a stack of prayer books, letters and a Rolodex on a table across the room and said, "You see that Rolodex over there? It contains the names and addresses of all my friends. Every Christmas season, I send letters to all those friends and enclose a prayer book. I've already addressed the envelopes; would you be kind enough to place a letter and a prayer book in each envelope and then seal them for me?"

I agreed, of course, and spent the rest of the day stuffing and sealing hundreds of envelopes. I didn't fully appreciate the value of those Christmas letters until several years later, when my wife, Barbara, and I joined the ranks of the letters' recipients. I knew then we were among the hundreds of names in his most prized possession, that fat Rolodex. We continued to receive annual Christmas letters from Father Welch until his death in 1989.

When I had declared a "religious studies" major and philosophy minor, I was taking many courses and reading many more books in both areas. I continued to immerse myself in Catholic theology and church history but was developing a new interest in studying the development of religion in America. I took courses on the subject with Sydney Mead and Stow Persons, both of whom were fascinating and engaging lecturers.

In Mead's class, we used his seminal book, *The Lively Experiment*, as the primary textbook. I became fascinated with the idea of "the West" in American religious history. I learned the idea of "the West" was often conflated with ideas of religious utopia and the invitation to "go West" was met with mixed responses by conservative New Englanders in the nineteenth century. In fact, conservative New Englanders and Eastern-ers in general tended to view westward migration negatively.

For example, Ralph Waldo Emerson said, "The wise man stays home." John Greenleaf Whittier often emphasized the noble simplic-ity of life in New England in his poems. Even some religious leaders suggested western migration might result in a barbaric society. On the other hand, there were those, such as Nathaniel Hawthorne, who saw the nation's ongoing westward migration as advantageous.

I wrote a paper in Mead's course on the idea of "the West" being equated with religious utopianism. In the nineteenth century, westward migration was infused with a sense of utopianism when it was asso-ciated with Biblical imagery and phrases. The West became the "new Promised Land." The Mississippi River took on another name: "the new Jordan." The western-bound Americans became the "new chosen people."

Mead gave me an A on the paper, but in his comments, he reminded me of the severe anti-Catholic sentiments associated with Western migration. This led me to delve into the New England religious leaders' attitudes toward Catholics, which were extremely negative.

This strong anti-Catholic sentiment reminded me of what Mama had experienced among the Protestants of Beirut when she converted to Catholicism. Learning about the Protestants of New England and their sentiments toward Catholics finally explained the Beirut Protes-tants' attitudes toward Catholics; after all, many of the Protestant mis-sionaries that came to Lebanon in the nineteenth century were from New England, and they likely brought their anti-Catholic prejudices with them. It also explained why Beirut Protestant roots inspired us to constantly look to the West for cultural and religious sustenance. For us in Beirut, the West was our new Promised Land.

In Persons' class on the history of ideas in America, we used his book, *American Minds*, which introduced me to many early Ameri-can religious intellectuals. I learned about Roger Williams, a Protestant religious leader, who was an early champion of religious liberty, the abolition of slavery and the separation of church and state. These concepts were new to me, as I had not encountered them in my studies of Catholic theology and church history. I realized these ideas were unique to American religious culture. Williams' doctrines did not conform to the established ecclesiastical order at the time. In fact, they were directed against the established order and, as a result, Williams was expelled from the Massachusetts Bay Colony.

The other early American religious intellectual giant we covered was Jonathan Edwards, who played an important role in the Great Awakening, a revivalist movement that emphasized pietism and personal experience with and knowledge of God. Persons explained while the Great Awakening was a specifically American occurrence, it was also merely the American variant of a larger movement in Western culture. As Persons lectured, I kept thinking to myself, this is nothing new; how is the 'revivalist experience' different from Catholic spirituality, as exemplified in the lives of saints such as Francis of Assisi and Catherine of Siena?

25. On My Own

*A*T THE END OF OUR FRESHMAN YEAR, DOUG AND I WANTED a restful break after an exhausting semester of intense studying and exams. We came up with the idea of spending several days secluded in the wilderness with our theology books, where we could read, talk, and meditate. Iowa City was surrounded by farmland—not exactly our idea of wilderness—so we did some research, trying to find an area within driving distance where we could camp in forested seclusion.

We decided to go to northern Minnesota, close to the Canadian border. This being the days before GPS and Google, this was the extent of our plan. We checked out a tent from the University of Iowa recreational department and bought two sleeping bags, two knapsacks and some canned food. Borrowing my parents' secondhand Chevrolet, we set out around eleven a.m., driving north from Iowa City.

We stopped briefly near Minneapolis for a hamburger and some gas. We reached Duluth about seven that evening and then continued north toward the Canadian border. Ninety minutes later, we decided it was time to get off the main road and take one of the many unpaved dirt tracks into the surrounding wilderness. It was pitch dark by then and we could barely see the outline of the trees around us. Half an hour later, exhausted from a long day of driving, we stopped and looked for a clearing where we could pitch our tent. It only took a few minutes to find a nice flat area for the tent and our sleeping bags. We were delighted with the spot we found, not only because it was a flat surface, but also conveniently near where we parked the car. After pitching the tent, we thought about building a fire to keep the wild animals away, but we were too tired to do that, and went right to sleep.

We woke up early the next morning to the sounds of chirping and whistling birds, ready to soak up the wilderness's fresh air, to read, and to meditate. We poked our heads through the tent's opening to get a better look at our surroundings and, to our great surprise, discovered we had pitched our tent in somebody's driveway. No wonder the ground was so nice and smooth! There went our dream of being in the uninhabited wilderness.

We could tell the homeowners were in the house because at the end of the driveway there was an open garage with a parked car. We were now desperate to get out of there before the owners woke up. As we hastily and nervously packed the tent and our sleeping bags back into the car, we realized we forgot to get anything for breakfast. At that point, hungry and frustrated, Doug whispered, "Let's just get out of here and go visit my mother in Davenport."

I thought it was a great idea. "Yeah! We can stay on a comfortable couch, read, and talk there. Besides, Davenport has a large Catholic bookstore."

On our way, we stopped at a coffee shop where we had coffee and toast with jelly, and laughing about our great adventure into the wilderness. To think we thought we had found a gorgeous clearing in the middle of the woods.

Eight hours later, we reached Davenport, Iowa. Doug's mother, a tall, vivacious woman, greeted us with her heavy German accent: "Haallo, see you look very tired; come, I show you room with two beds." We had some sandwiches and then crashed, grateful for beds and a shelter we wouldn't have to pack up in the morning.

Throughout my sophomore year, Doug and I continued taking our required courses together and reading theology and philosophy books on our own. We frequently went to Davenport to purchase these from the Catholic bookstore there.

At the end of my sophomore year, Doug and I began looking for an apartment to share during our junior year. My parents were moving to Carbondale, Illinois, where Papa had accepted a more senior position as a professor of economics at Southern Illinois University, and Doug and his father were in serious conflict over Doug's interest in Catholicism. They quarreled continuously and Doug wanted to get out of the house.

We looked for a place within walking distance of the School of Religion (now the Department of Religious Studies), where we had most of our classes, and also close to the Catholic Students' Newman Center, where we went for social activities and to pursue our interest in the Catholic Church. We found a furnished room on the second floor of a house three blocks from campus. We shared a kitchen with another student rooming on our floor. The owners lived downstairs on the first floor.

Having a kitchen with a refrigerator meant we now needed to decide what to put in it. We were on our own and for the first time in our lives needed to decide what foods we should buy and prepare. As we sat on our beds pondering this question, Doug, who had just started working at MacDonald's, suddenly jumped up and exclaimed excitedly, "Nasib, at MacDonald's, we have lots of food left over at end of each day we throw away. Maybe I can get some of that for us to eat for dinner."

The next day, Doug came home empty-handed. "All the unused food has to be thrown away and employees aren't allowed to take any leftovers home." The manager was concerned if he allowed employees to take leftovers home, they would over-prepare to make sure there were always leftovers. It made sense, but that didn't help us any.

We sat back down on our beds and started planning again. We needed to eat healthy, but also keep our expenses down, as we had very little income. After a while, Doug said, "My dad once told me cream of wheat and apple butter can provide all the daily nutrition we need and also satisfy hunger."

"Great idea! Let's go buy some." I had never had either apple butter or cream of wheat, but once I tried them, I found them delicious. They were easy to prepare, and we didn't have to spend a lot of time worrying about what to eat. That entire year, our diet consisted of apple butter on toast and cream of wheat with milk. We'd occasionally get a salad and chocolate cake at the Student Union cafeteria to mix things up a bit.

~

I had to make an income to support my independent living, and that's when I met the Armaly's. Mansour and Aida Armaly were friends of my parents from Lebanon; Aida's family had attended the same Protestant church in Beirut they had, and Mansour had gotten his medical degree at AUB. Mansour Armaly was an internationally renowned ophthalmologist who studied glaucoma; he directed a national study that found glaucoma occurs at an unusually high rate among family members.

Dr. Armaly offered me a job in his research lab at the University of Iowa hospital, and I accepted it purely to make some money; I had no interest in ophthalmology. Still, he was always trying to convince me to go back into the sciences, and I often speculated Papa had asked him to talk to me about the benefits of a science degree.

However, my work with monkeys and cats in his lab made me less interested in pursuing a science major than ever. I was responsible for sedating the animals and then bringing them to the operating room where Dr. Armaly operated on their eyes.

In order to sedate the monkeys, I had to don a very thick glove on one hand, put that gloved hand into the cage and shove the monkey up against the cage's wired wall. Then, with the other hand, I would inject the monkey with a sedative. The problem was that every time I put my hand into the four-sided wire cage, the monkey would bite my gloved hand before I was able to get ahold it. Even though the heavy glove protected my hand from puncture wounds, it was a very painful pressure bite.

With cats, I would take them out of their cage and carry them to the lab before we sedated them. I had to be careful about some aggressive cats scratching me.

For me, the pain of these bites and scratches was the practical side of science, and as a result, I developed an utter distaste for it. I was much more comfortable with thinking and writing about ideas. In essence, I was introduced to the process of doing science in the wrong way; it was not until much later in graduate school I came to appreciate the challenges and joys of scientific inquiry and analytic thinking.

My focus on philosophical and theological questions kept me totally uninterested in practical issues. When I had to do a chore, I always tried to find the shortest, easiest path to accomplishing it.

For example, one spring day, Dr. Armaly came up to me and said, "Nasib, we're going out of town for spring break. Would you be willing to feed the fish in the fish tank in our living room? They were a birthday present for my son, Fareed."

"Sure, I'll be happy to."

Dr. Armaly knew me well by this point; he looked at me cautiously and said, "Now listen carefully. You have to sprinkle a spoonful of food into the tank every other day for the next two weeks. It's very important you do not forget."

The first two times I went over to their house to feed the fish, I did exactly as Dr. Armaly told me to. But then, the next time I went over there, I thought to myself, Why do I need to keep coming here every two days to feed the stupid fish? I could just drop enough food for the remainder of the two weeks into the tank, and the fish can eat when they get hungry.

A week and a half later, Dr. Armaly and his family returned. Their first day back, I went to work at the lab as usual. As I was about to bring a couple of cats into the lab, Dr. Armaly came into the assistants' office looking very upset. "Do you know what you did?"

I looked up at him, confused. "No, what did I do?"

"You killed the fish by dumping a large amount of food into the tank."

I was genuinely puzzled. "They had enough food to last them a long time; they couldn't have starved."

He gave me a really irritated look, frowning like I was stupid. "If you overfeed the fish, they'll die from overeating."

"I didn't know that. I'm really sorry." I felt really bad for the rest of the day, but I suspect he forgave me, because he didn't say anything more about the incident.

My work with Dr. Armaly continued until the beginning of my senior year. I was making good money, and by the time I graduated, I had accumulated over $1,000 in savings—quite a small fortune at that time—but I just didn't want to deal with the cats and monkeys anymore. I quit on good terms though, and continued to visit the Armaly family at their home.

26. Converting

ON WEEKENDS, DOUG AND I WOULD GO TO DAVENPORT TO visit his mother, and while there, we would often go to the Catholic bookstore. On one such weekend in mid-November of 1965, after visiting Doug's mother for lunch, we went to the bookstore, and as we entered, I saw a display for a book called *The Way* by Josemaría Escrivá.

Curious, I opened it and began to read. I stood there for twenty minutes, totally oblivious to everything around me and completely immersed in the writer's deep spirituality. As I stood there reading, I suddenly felt a strong desire well up within me.

"It's time for me to join the church," I said to Doug. "I'm ready, so what am I waiting for? What are *we* waiting for, now we're on our own? Let's get baptized as Catholics."

Doug instantly agreed. "Sure, let's go back to Iowa City and get ahold of Father Welch."

I bought the book and we left the store.

We got to St. Thomas Moore Church rectory, next to the Newman Center in Iowa City, in the evening, but we rang the bell anyway, hoping Father Welch would answer. Instead, Father McEleney, the pastor, an old man with an ancient-looking face, white hair, and a permanent smile, opened the door.

"Hello young men, what can I do for you at this late hour?"

"Is Father Welch available?" I asked. "If not, we can come back tomorrow."

"Let me see," he said, inviting us inside.

A few minutes later, Father Welch appeared with a surprised look on his face. "What are you doing here this late?"

Almost in one voice, we said, "We want to talk to you about getting baptized."

With a grin and a red face, almost as though he was embarrassed, he said, "Is it so urgent you couldn't have waited until tomorrow? Well, now you're here, let's go ahead and schedule it. I'll get my appointment book." He left and a few minutes later, returned with his black leather appointment book. "How about we schedule the baptism for December 4th? There's no home football game that day." Father Welch was an avid Iowa Hawkeyes fan.

A little perplexed, I said, "But Father, don't we need to take some kind of preparation lessons before we become Catholics?"

"No need to; both of you have taken all my courses on Catholicism, and you know more about the Catholic faith than most people who were raised Catholic do."

We were elated, and three weeks later, Father Welch baptized us and heard our confessions.

At first, the idea of confessing my deepest, most intimate faults to another person who knew me to be honest and faithful made me uncomfortable, but I understood and believed in the theology behind it. After all, the Apostle John tells us on the day of His resurrection, Christ said to the Apostles, "Receive the Holy Spirit; whose sins you shall forgive, they are forgiven; and whose sins you shall retain, they are retained." I was intellectually convinced of the sacrament of penance and believed it was how I would achieve reconciliation with God. It was just the reality of having to confess before a person who knew me well, but did not know my faults, that made me feel uncomfortable. Still, I went through with it, and from then on, it was never an issue for me again.

Both Doug and I were confirmed a year later.

27. War, Anti-war, and Peace

"D O YOU WANT TO GO TO AN ANTI-VIETNAM WAR RALLY ON campus in about an hour?" Doug asked me one day.

I had not thought about the Vietnam War very much at the time, but said, "Sure, I'll go and see what it's all about."

The rally itself was partially a teach-in, educating people about the Vietnam War, and partially a festive student party. We sang folk songs and listened to anti-war speeches intermingled with chants against the war, the Johnson administration, and the police. Among the literature distributed was an article by Senator George McGovern from the May 1967 issue of *The Progressive*, titled "The Lessons of Vietnam." I read it as we stood there, and it quickly convinced me the war in Vietnam must end.

I already had a distaste for conflict as a result of my experience with the short Lebanese civil war of 1958. Early in 1958, pro-Western President Chamoun had announced he planned to run for another six-year term. This did not sit well with the Muslim community. Chamoun had become the second president of the Lebanese Republic in 1952, and the six years that followed were a time of heightened discord between Christians and Muslims, precisely because of the Chamoun administration's pro-Western policies. Eventually violent conflict broke out between Muslims and Christians.

The Muslims wanted Lebanon to ally itself with the United Arab Republic and join the Arabs in belligerency against Israel. There was no active war between Israel and the Arab nations at the time, but a state of cold war existed, and many felt hostilities could commence at any time. Eventually, a six-day war did break out in 1967, involving Israel, Egypt, Syria and Jordan.

On the other hand, the Christians, led by President Chamoun and Minister of Foreign Affairs Charles Malik, "Ammo Sharl," wanted an alliance with the West, which would involve direct American military intervention to counter Syrian troops who were starting to enter Lebanon from the east.

An alliance with Western Europe and America would also mean Lebanese neutrality toward Israel, and it would keep Lebanon in the Western sphere of influence, away from Soviet domination. The United Arab Republic, composed of Egypt and Syria, was considered to be within the Soviet sphere of influence.

President Chamoun's appointment of the pro-West Malik in 1957 and his endorsement of the Eisenhower Doctrine for the Middle East, which stated any country in the Middle East could request U.S. economic or military aid if it were threatened by another country, only heightened the discord between the Christian and Muslim communities. This discord developed into full civil strife, with violent demonstrations by Muslims, during the summer of 1958.

Shortly thereafter, we heard Syrian troops had crossed the border into Lebanon, ready to occupy our country in support of the Muslims and Arab unity. I was frightened by this news and asked Mama whether the Syrian soldiers would come to our village in the mountains. She assured me they would not because they were afraid of the men in Schweir. In my child's mind, I thought that men like our school principal, with his weightlifting slides and The Rimmani, were well known, even to the Syrians.

Fortunately, President Chamoun and my uncle, Ammo Sharl requested American assistance under the Eisenhower Doctrine, and the Americans responded. United States Marines landed on the Lebanese shores. Our friends who were on the beach told us many Lebanese greeted the Marines with Pepsi and ice cream. The Marines were expecting hostility but were instead met by sunbathers enjoying a day at the beach and vendors offering summer treats. The Syrians, having heard of the U.S. forces coming in, had already pulled back to their side of the border.

Within hours, a line of U.S. jeeps and military trucks drove along the narrow road in front of our house in Schweir. One of the Marines shouted out in Lebanese Arabic, "It's great to be back in Lebanon among friends! I love the smell of the pine trees in the Lebanese mountains!" This U.S. Marine was a Lebanese-American immigrant! Little did I know in just two years, I would be another such immigrant.

The next day, we heard a deafening sound above our house. We went out to the balcony, and saw an American military helicopter, so close we could almost touch it. The entire episode was very exciting for a boy like me.

The short civil war of 1958 ended with President Chamoun's resignation, rather than his running for another term; the election of Fuad Shihab as the third president of the Lebanese Republic; and the slogan, "No victor, no vanquished," referring to the fact neither side won the conflict. The events of 1958 woke me to the reality of sectarian divisions within Lebanon, Lebanon's relationship with its neighbors and the effects of Arab nationalism, whose advocates aspired to unite all the Arab countries into one nation.

Later, as Doug and I walked back to our apartment, I said, "McGovern makes lots of sense; his argument we have no business fighting in what amounts to a civil war in Vietnam is quite convincing. I also question the morality of what we're doing in Vietnam. I bet you anything if we look up what the church says about what makes a just war, we'll find this is not a just war."

"Those are my thoughts exactly," Doug replied.

I began a project to determine exactly what Catholic doctrine said made a war "just" and quickly ran into my favorite theologian, Thomas Aquinas. I found in Catholic doctrine, a war is justified only to put a stop to the activities of an aggressor who has done severe and lasting damage, other means of conflict resolution have been attempted and failed, the probability of success is high and the evil produced by engaging in war is less than that perpetrated by the aggressor. I was now convinced on at least three of these principles; our engagement in Vietnam was not a just war.

The more I read about the concept of a just war in Catholic literature, the stronger my anti-war sentiments grew. I wrote to my parents about my feelings:

> I have become vehemently weary of the Vietnamese war and war in general. With serious urgency, I question the concept of jus-tice in the nature of war. I cannot rationally accept the premise war can be just at all. I am not so sure war or violence is not the result of collective neurosis . . . I can only think of an operation as being just . . . when it is directed toward the preservation of all, and not just in the interest of two or three groups.

The Newman Center had a bookcase filled with current issues of Catholic magazines and journals. That is where I learned about the activities of Dorothy Day, a journalist, social activist and Catholic convert. After her conversion, she cofounded the Catholic Worker Movement, a pacifist organization that combines aid to the poor and homeless with nonviolent action on behalf of the marginalized. She also engaged in civil disobedience for the cause of the poor and founded the Catholic Workers newspaper. I also learned about the anti-war efforts of the Berrigan brothers and the Trappist monk, Thomas Merton. Dan-iel Berrigan, a Jesuit; his brother, Philip, a Josephite; and Merton were all active war protestors, and they had founded a coalition against the Vietnam War. They inspired me to actively engage our student Catholic community in the anti-war effort.

"Doug, we need to do something to show our church's opposition to the Vietnam War," I told my friend one day.

"How about we organize a peace vigil?" Doug suggested.

"That's a good idea," I said, "but Father McEleney will probably nix it. He wouldn't want the parish to get involved in anything political."

"What if we talk to Father Stangohr? He'll probably be sympathetic." Father Clarence Stangohr was a former Protestant minister who had converted to Catholicism. He was considered a maverick that often had his own ideas about what Catholics should practice and believe. He was always willing to do something innovative to challenge the church's current practices, and sometimes, even its authority.

Sure enough, Father Stangohr jumped at the idea of a peace vigil, suggesting, "We can make it an interfaith prayer vigil, not just for Catholics, but for Lutherans, Episcopalians, Methodists, and others."

"Oh, that'll make it really big," I said, impressed with the scope of the idea.

"Sure," he continued. "We'll also invite the Jewish rabbi."

We decided on a date, and Father Stangohr, Doug and I dove into planning and preparing for the peace vigil. Doug designed and printed brochures, which we posted at the Newman Center and in the church. Father Stangohl contacted the local Protestant churches and the Jewish Rabbi to invite them and their congregations to participate in the event. I worked on putting together the vigil program, which the parish printed for distribution to participants.

Three weeks later, hundreds of people from the local Jewish synagogue and various Christian denominations attended the vigil.

It was an hour-long event, with prayers and hymns that focused on the message of peace, and all of the attending ministers and the rabbi each gave a short homily. During the opening prayer and the hymn, Doug and I stood on opposite sides of the altar, each holding a lit candle. It was an honor, but at the time, all I could think about was how tired my arms grew in that position.

By the end of our junior year, Doug and I saw less and less of each other, as he became more involved in the broader anti-war movement, while my focus remained on the specifically Catholic peace movement. In addition, he found a girlfriend in the campus anti-war community. Charlene was a very talkative and assertive girl who knew what she wanted, and I was sure she wanted Doug. Even though Doug and I still shared an apartment, I hardly saw him because he frequently stayed with Charlene, who later became his wife.

28. Anonymous in the City

*A*FTER MY JUNIOR YEAR ENDED, I DECIDED I WANTED TO spend the summer in New York City. Ever since I had first set foot in New York I had been yearning to go live in that magical city of culture and monstrous buildings.

I decided to take one of my required general education courses at NYU and transfer the credits back to Iowa. I checked with an official at the registrar's office, and she told me as long as I got a B in the course, the credit was transferable and would apply toward my social science requirement.

I called my parents to discuss my plans. I knew Mama would likely go along with the idea, seeing it as a fun adventure. But I felt sure Papa would ask lots of questions.

Mama answered the phone, listened to my idea, and then asked, "Where would you stay?"

"I'll look for a room in the Village, close to the NYU campus."

"How about staying with Auntie Rosa Lee?"

"No, I want to be independent, on my own, and not have to answer to anybody."

"How are you going to find a room when you're still in Iowa?"

"I'll look for one when I get there; I love the idea of not knowing what's going to happen next. I really want to explore and experience being anonymous in New York."

After that, Papa got on the phone, and I knew the real interrogation was about to begin. "Why do you want to waste your time going to New York? Why not stay in Iowa and take courses you need to graduate?"

"I'll be taking a course in economics, which is a requirement at Iowa. The credits will transfer and count toward my degree." I knew by telling him I would be taking a course in economics, it would soften the blow.

I was right. "Okay, Nasib, this sounds fine," Papa said. "You know, Aida's husband, Roy, is an economist working at the U.N.; he used to be my student at AUB and got his doctorate in economics at Columbia. You should contact him if you need any help with your economics class."

"That's a good idea, Papa. Maybe I'll stay with them the first couple of nights until I find my own place."

Mama must have been listening, because she chimed in, "You should stay with Auntie Rosa Lee until you find your own place; she'll be hurt if you don't."

"Maybe I'll stay the first night with Auntie Rosa Lee and the second with Aida," I allowed.

The day after my finals were over, I took the train to New York City, arriving at Grand Central Station late in the afternoon. I took the subway to Brooklyn Heights and walked one block to 7 Monroe Place, a beautiful brick townhouse. Mary, the housekeeper, opened the door, and Auntie Rosa Lee and Uncle E.J. both came down from their comfortable second-floor combination library and family room. Hugs and air-kisses followed.

Auntie Rosa Lee offered to show me my room, and as we walked up the stairs to the top floor, she said, "You know you can stay here the entire summer."

"Thank you, but I really want to be close to NYU. I'll visit a lot."

What I really wanted was to finally experience being anonymous in this huge city, a desire I had held ever since we arrived in New York seven years earlier. I had longed to walk the streets of this city where no one knew who I was and where I knew no one, where I could watch people and look at each face without feeling self-conscious. For me, New York was a place of energy and creativity. The idea of being anonymous in the city gave me a feeling of independence, privacy, and adventure all at the same time.

Sitting in a coffee shop in the middle of this humming metropolis allowed me to think deeply about ideas, such as the meaning of life, truth, and purpose.

New York City attracted unique people who were different and individualistic. Plus, if you were a man looking for the company of women, your chances were extremely good. Rumor had it that there were seven girls to every guy in the city.

The next morning, I took the subway to Greenwich Village, where New York University was located. After registering for a course in economics, I went in search of an apartment or room to rent. I thought to myself, I'm only here temporarily; maybe I should just look for a room I can rent on a weekly basis in a nearby residential hotel.

I explored the streets around NYU and found such an establishment on Eighth Avenue. At the front desk, I asked the clerk if they had any rooms for rent.

"Yes, we do," the clerk replied. "How many nights you plan to stay?"

"Two months. The room has one bed, correct?" I asked.

"No, each room has two beds. This way, we can send you 'visitors' every once in a while."

I looked at the clerk, puzzled, then realized that this was a hotel mostly used by prostitutes. They would bring clients to any room with a vacant bed.

I was out of there within two seconds.

The best thing to do, I thought to myself, is to go to University Housing and look for off-campus places for rent.

As I started down Tenth Street toward campus, I saw a "Room for Rent" sign in front of a six-story building. I went in and asked the clerk behind a desk in the lobby to show me the available room. It was very simple, with a bed, a small table with a lamp, and a chair. There was also a small bathroom with a shower, a vanity and a toilet. Towels, soap, and bed sheets were included. I paid for the first week's rent, and, just like that, I now had a place to stay near campus.

I used a payphone a block away to call my parents and let them know I had found a room for the summer. Mama told me Ammo Sharl was going to be in New York later in the summer and I should call him when he arrives. She would let me know when he did.

Calling Ammo Sharl, an important and busy man, was not an easy thing for me to do.

Still, when the time came, I called. "Hello, Ammo Sharl. This is Nasib."

"Hello, Nasib. Your mother told me you're in New York. Why don't you come down to the Harvard Club on Saturday, and we can have lunch together? Make sure you wear a sport jacket; you don't need a tie, though."

I had never been to the Harvard Club before, and as I entered the building, a formally dressed man behind the lobby desk asked me, "How can I help you?" I gave him Ammo Sharl's name and explained I was coming to see him. The man got on the phone, and a few minutes later, Ammo Sharl and I entered a dimly lit room together. It was a combination sitting and dining room with lamps everywhere, tables, leather couches, and lounge chairs.

We sat at a table in the corner, and Ammo Sharl ordered a Coke for me, though he had nothing to drink himself. "It's good to see you, Nasib," he greeted me, breaking my anxious silence. "What are you doing in New York?"

"I'm taking a course in economics at New York University," I said, giving my standard, official answer.

"Your mother told me you are very interested in religion and philosophy."

"Yes, I'm majoring in religious studies. I hope to get into a graduate program in philosophy."

"Instead of philosophy, I really think you should go into history. You need a solid history background in order to fully understand Western civilization; you can get into philosophy later." There was a pause, and then he said, "You know, your father told me he wants you to go into something much more practical."

I knew how Papa felt because it was a recurring theme in our conversations. But I was determined to do what I felt was my calling: to become an internationally known philosopher.

I went on to tell Ammo Sharl about my interest in the Catholic Church and I wanted to work for some Catholic organization while in New York City. I mentioned I was hoping to make a job contact during the summer I could come back to after I graduated until I decided on my plans for graduate school.

"I know a priest at the Catholic Relief Services for the Middle East in Manhattan. I can put you in touch with him." He gave me the priest's phone number and added, "Call him on Monday after I've had a chance to tell him about you."

I called the priest on Monday, and we set up an appointment for Wednesday that week. He was very pleasant and kind to me, but let me know from the outset they had no available positions at the time, though he would keep me in mind if something came up. Then he asked about my family, when we came to America and my major in college. Suddenly, he said, "Since you come from Lebanon, you must know French. I need a document originally written in French translated into English."

I didn't tell him I didn't actually know French; I wanted a job with their organization so badly I thought if I got the document translated, the priest be grateful and give me a job. I took the proffered piece of paper and went looking for someone who knew French and could do the translation quickly.

My first thought was to go to NYU's language department. I loved walking in the city, so as I left my meeting with the priest in Midtown, I decided to walk to NYU in the Village. As I reached Fifth and Eighteenth, I saw the Barnes and Noble there. It occurred to me the bookstore might have a section on foreign languages and just maybe one of the people working there knew French.

I approached the reference desk and asked the girl behind the counter, "I have something I need translated from French to English. Do you know anyone who knows French and can translate?"

"I know French. Let me see what you've got." After looking at the piece of paper for a moment, she said, "I'm fluent in French. I can translate this for you."

"Oh, thanks! When can you do it?"

She paused, looking me over. I was pretty sure she was trying to decide whether I was a decent guy who could be trusted.

"I live in the East Village," she finally said. "Why don't you come over Saturday around noon and bring the document with you? My name is Cathy."

"Great!" I responded as she wrote her address on a piece of paper. "I'll do that. I'm Al."

Cathy's one-bedroom apartment was sparsely furnished. The very small sitting room contained a chair and table. We sat on cushions on the floor across from one another and she handed me a pad of papers.

"I'll translate aloud, and you can write it out."

As Cathy began translating aloud, I watched her. She struck me as very attractive, barefoot in her tight shorts. All of a sudden, I realized

I had not socialized with girls and had not been this close to one since my early high school years with Lorraine.

After half an hour, Cathy and I had finished the translation. I wanted to ask her if she would like to go get lunch somewhere and found myself wondering whether she had a boyfriend. Before I could ask her anything though, she said, "Would you like to come to Midtown with me? I'd like you to meet my cousin and friends."

Already meeting the family? I thought. Looking good! And her 'friends'? Either she doesn't have a boyfriend, or she's going to introduce me to him.

Aloud I said, "Sure."

When we reached our destination in Midtown, we entered an apartment that contained two couches, two grand pianos arranged back-to-back, and two young guys. "Al, meet my cousin and his roommate. They're piano aficionados and music students at Julliard."

She asked them to play something, but her cousin simply responded, "Not in the mood." Instead, we sat on the two couches while Cathy tried to make conversation with these two very odd guys. It didn't work.

After a while, Cathy looked over at me. "Al, how would you like to come with me to New Jersey and meet my ex and his fiancé?"

I thought, Oh, good, her boyfriend is an ex. Aloud, I said, "When? Today?"

"Yes, we can take the train to Newark and be there in half an hour. We can have dinner there and then come back."

"Okay. Let's go now so we won't get back too late." I had already moved back to Auntie Rosa Lee's place for my last two weeks in New York and wasn't sure how she would react to my coming in very late.

I was starting to think perhaps I had finally found a girlfriend. I wanted to call my parents and tell them, because I had once overheard them saying to each other I didn't know how to befriend girls like Sami did and it was going to be difficult for me to find a girl to marry. But then I decided to wait until I was certain she was The One.

When we arrived at her friends' house in New Jersey, Cathy introduced me. "Al, meet my ex-husband and his fiancé."

I was totally floored. "He's your ex-husband? And you still visit him?"

"Sure, we have a very friendly relationship."

To my mind, this was the end of our relationship; it was over before it even began. It would never sit well with my family Cathy was divorced. Furthermore, as the night wore on, I was shocked to discover she was ten years older than me.

After dinner, Cathy asked me if I would like to spend the night there, but I said I couldn't, giving the excuse Auntie Rosa Lee was expecting me. We took the train back to Manhattan, and that was the last I saw of Cathy and the end of my adventures with girls until I met the girl that would become my wife.

I spent the last few days of the summer at Auntie Rosa Lee's house, hanging out with my cousin Robert, who was a doctoral student at the University of Michigan, where he was finishing his dissertation in philosophy. He lent me a copy of it, and as I started reading, I immediately realized I would need to spend a considerable amount of time studying in order to fully understand and appreciate the content. Still, it was a pleasure reading his prose, particularly aloud. Robert truly had a gift for expression and language.

After a week in Brooklyn Heights, I was ready to go back to Iowa City, and one night, I announced at the dinner table I would be taking the train back in two days.

Robert chimed in, "I'll be driving to Ann Arbor tomorrow. Would you like to ride with me and then take the train from Ann Arbor to Iowa?"

I jumped at the invitation. "That'd be great. I've been wanting to visit the University of Michigan as a potential place for graduate school."

"Great. You can spend a couple of days with me, and I'll show you around."

I ended up loving Ann Arbor, the campus, and the university. Having lived in Iowa City, I already knew how much I enjoyed living in a university town.

29. Jobless in the Dream City

THE DAY AFTER THE SPRING SEMESTER OF MY SENIOR YEAR ended, I took a bus to St. Louis, where my parents picked me up and we drove back to Carbondale. I did not stay for the commencement ceremony and had the university mail my diploma to me.

"Well, now that you have a bachelor's degree, what do you plan to do next, Nasib?" Papa asked when we reached Carbondale.

"I'm thinking of finding a job for a year before I decide on graduate school and a career path."

"Sounds good, but what kind of job?" Papa asked. I had majored in religious studies and minored in philosophy, so I didn't have an obvious career path.

"I don't know, but I'd like to go live in New York City and look for a job there."

Mama suggested calling Auntie Rosa Lee. After all, she seemed to know everyone in New York. I agreed, and Mama immediately got on the phone.

Auntie Rosa Lee jumped at the idea of my spending a year in New York, though she didn't seem to give serious thought to the question of a job. "I'm living alone now, and I need a young man to stay with me in this big house," she said. Uncle E.J. had died of a heart attack several months earlier, and Auntie Rosa Lee was likely lonely. "I'd love to have Nasib come and live with me."

I was absolutely elated.

I spent five days in Carbondale with little to do. My parents' large split-level ranch house was in a bedroom community with nothing but similar houses as far as I could see from the front bay window. Behind the house, there was a yard screened with trees. To go anywhere, I needed a car, which I didn't have, so I spent the week watching TV. At the end of the week, my parents drove me to St. Louis, where I took a train to New York City.

As always, Auntie Rosa Lee welcomed me with a giant hug and then led me up several flights of stairs to my room for the next year. We entered a large room with a queen-sized bed, a night table, a desk, a chair and a small bathroom just outside. "This is your own private bathroom, Nasib," Auntie Rose Lee informed me. She must have seen my surprised reaction.

I thought to myself, Wow, this is definitely an upgrade in my standard of living; it's better than anything I've ever had, even when I lived at home.

I collected my thoughts and said, "Auntie Rosa Lee, I'd like to pay rent; how much is it per month?"

"Now, Nasib, you don't have to do that."

"I must; I insist."

"Okay. You can pay me fifteen dollars a month once you find a job."

I doubted that was enough; I was paying double for a small, shared room in Iowa City. But I figured, she's being nice. Maybe when I find a job, I can offer more, depending on how much I'm paid.

She continued, "Speaking of a job, I have a friend, William Robinson, who's an executive in a company in Manhattan and who may be able to help. I talked with him, and he'll be happy to see you on Tuesday at nine in the morning. Here's the address; you can take the subway there."

I was excited; it looked like it was going to be easy to find a job.

Tuesday morning came around, and I took the subway to Times Square and then walked toward the East Side on Fifty-Second. My appointment was at nine, but I reached the building by eight. Having skipped breakfast, I was a little hungry and decided to stop for coffee and a danish.

At a quarter to nine, I entered a very tall building and imagined myself coming to work there every morning. I gave the receptionist my name and told her why I was there.

A few minutes later, a man of medium height, dressed in a suit, with receding brown hair, and eyeglasses, approached me. "Hi, Al. I'm Bill

Robinson; Dr. Nemir told me about you, and I'd be happy to see if I can be of help. Let's go to the coffee shop and chat over a cup of coffee."

I was about to tell him I had already stopped for a cup, but then I thought perhaps this meeting could clinch a job for me; I didn't want to be rude.

After we got our coffee and sat down, Mr. Robinson asked whether I had a résumé.

I knew what a résumé was, but had never thought of preparing one, and no one at the university had ever alerted me to the importance of having one. In fact, I realized now I knew nothing about the process of getting or even interviewing for a job.

"No, I don't," I confessed.

"Well, why don't you tell me a little about yourself, then? I understand from Dr. Nemir that you just graduated from college. What did you major in?"

"Religious studies and philosophy."

At that, he looked chagrined and disappointed. I'm certain he was trying to figure out how to tell me he didn't have any jobs for me in his organization. "Well, it's very difficult for someone who majors in the humanities to land a job in the corporate business world." He paused, thinking, then continued, "What kind of practical skills do you have?"

I couldn't think of any practical skills I had. "I'm not sure," I admitted, wracking my brain. Then it occurred to me I could do some things. "Well, I can write, count, do mathematics, and things like that."

"Everybody can do those things, and we really only hire people to do such jobs if they have special mathematical skills, like accounting; but for that, you need a degree in accounting."

Our meeting ended up being a huge disappointment for me, though it ended on a nice note. Mr. Robinson told me he would keep an eye out, and if something came up, he would let me know. This was the last I heard from him, and after waiting for him to contact me for some time, I learned when a businessman says, "If something comes up, I'll let you know," that means, "Don't expect to hear from me again."

Still, I left the interview feeling despondent and wondering whether I'd be able to find a job, now it became clear my college major was not an asset. Should I have chosen a field with practical skills, as Papa never stopped telling me? I wondered. This is what happens when I major in religious studies and minor in philosophy. I tried to justify my failure, thinking, I want a job where I can help people; this was going to be an office job and not one I would have been interested in anyway.

It was back to the drawing board.

As I walked out of the building, I realized I wasn't far from St. Patrick's Cathedral on Fifth Avenue. I decided to sit in the church and pray for better job prospects. I entered through the grand gothic entrance, walked to one of the front pews, and knelt to pray.

There were lots of people, mostly women, either sitting or kneeling, who seemed to be in prayer or meditation. I wondered if all of them were asking God to help them find a job. The guy in the pew right in front of me, dressed in a suit and tie, definitely looked like he had a job in one of the corporate office buildings that surrounded the cathedral.

After I prayed, I left the cathedral and walked all the way to West 114th Street, to Columbia University, to look into taking a philosophy course in the fall. I spoke with an advisor in the philosophy department who suggested I take a course with Professor Danto on the Theory of Action. I thought it sounded splendid and went ahead and registered for the course.

Perhaps if I do well in the course and maybe take a couple more courses during the year, I could apply for the graduate program in philosophy here, I thought half-heartedly.

After stopping at Columbia, I went on to see Doug and his wife, Charlene, in their new apartment on Riverside Drive near Columbia. They had recently moved to New York from Iowa City because Doug had been accepted into the anthropology PhD program at Columbia.

I told them of my dismal failure in my meeting with Mr. Robinson and then going on to register for a philosophy course at Columbia.

Doug looked surprised. "Why are you still sticking to philosophy? You'll just end up with the same result in trying to find a job later."

"You're probably right. I've also been thinking about a couple different career paths; perhaps something in an applied area where I could help people, like the social sciences or education. Or, since I've always had interest in international affairs, I could work for the U.S. foreign service."

"But wouldn't you need an undergraduate degree in a field like political science, or history or even languages to get into an International Affairs graduate program like the one at Georgetown?"

"I know Arabic; I could start by applying to the Middle Eastern Studies Department at Georgetown. Then, after an interim degree in that, I could transfer to the International Affairs program."

"That sounds exciting; you should do it," Doug said.

"I could also apply to other universities with similar programs. I know the University of Michigan has a Middle Eastern Studies program. In fact, the director knows my father."

"Wait a minute," Charlene said, jumping into the conversation. "You're talking about the future, but what about now? What about finding a job now?"

A very confident woman, Charlene had been an organizer and leader in the anti–Vietnam War rallies at Iowa, where Doug had met her. She talked incessantly, no matter what the subject. Now, she continued her train of thought, "I just got a job with the Social Services Department here in Manhattan. I know they have openings; why don't you apply?"

"That sounds good," I said.

"You can apply to the departments in Manhattan and in Brooklyn, since you're living there. You'll just need to send two separate applications," she said. "Here, I have some extra blank ones."

I filled out the applications and mailed them the next day, but continued worrying about my future. By working as a social worker, I'd certainly be practicing some of the Catholic corporal works of mercy, feeding the hungry, giving drink to the thirsty, clothing the naked, and sheltering the homeless, but I kept thinking what I most wanted was to get into a graduate program that would enable me to explore issues that would help me improve the lives of the poor, the hungry, the homeless, and the poorly educated.

Two weeks after I sent the applications, the Manhattan office contacted me to tell me I had been rejected. I felt really low and was now convinced I wouldn't be able to find a job any time soon. I felt utterly helpless.

I called Mama, and as I told her about my declined application, I started crying. Mama sounded concerned, telling me, "Just pack your bags, get on the train, and come here to Carbondale."

"What would I do in Carbondale?"

"We know lots of people here; we'll get you a job at the university and you can take classes."

"I'll think about it," I said and hung up.

I considered Mama's offer, but then decided that, after having been independent for two years, I was not about to go back to living at home. Besides, I loved being in New York. I thought to myself, there is a big city out there waiting to be discovered.

Before I could blink, I was on my way to Manhattan, without any particular purpose in mind other than adventure.

30. Feeding the Hungry, or Not

FOR THE NEXT COUPLE OF WEEKS, I BROWSED THE JOBS SEC-
tion of the classified ads in the paper every day, but even in such a
big city, I couldn't find anything I was qualified for.

Then, one day in early August, I got a surprise phone call. "Hi, my
name is Joe, and I'm calling from the Social Services Center in Brooklyn. May I please speak with Albert Badre?"

"Yes, that's me."

"I'm the assistant to the director here; we received your application,
and the director, Mrs. Goldstein, is interested in talking with you. Could
you come in for a meeting tomorrow around nine in the morning?"

I was so excited; I rushed down to tell Auntie Rosa Lee, taking five
steps at a time on the stairwell. Then I called my parents and told them.
It never once entered my mind I didn't actually have the job yet and this
was just an interview.

Mrs. Goldstein was a large, heavyset lady with a wide, kind face. She
looked at me with a motherly smile, and with a deep, affectionate voice,
introduced herself simply as Rose. After we made some small talk, she
asked me, "Why do you think you're qualified to work here?"

"Well, I think I'm a people person, and I'd like to work in a job where
I can meet lots of different people."

"You should know these are not the kind of people you meet in college," she said. "They're poor people with very little education. Most are
high-school dropouts and have trouble making ends meet. Many are on
drugs and have been arrested and served in jail at some time or another."

I thought to myself, this will be a splendid opportunity to practice
the corporal works of mercy.

She continued, "Also, you should know most of them are black
women with children, with no man at home. The neighborhood,

Bedford-Stuyvesant in Brooklyn, is a high-crime area. Only last week, one of our case workers was mugged while visiting a client."

I can take care of myself, I thought.

"Are you okay with all of this?" she asked.

"Yes, ma'am," I responded. Thinking back on it now, I had no idea what I was getting myself into.

She smiled. "Okay, you got the job. You start on Monday." It was a short interview, and I was naïve enough to not realize it showed how absolutely desperate they were for employees.

It felt like a long weekend as I waited to start my new job. I couldn't sit still, so I took the train from Brooklyn Heights to West 114th Street. I got off, walked all the way to the Village, and back again, the entire time thinking about my future.

I had no doubt I wanted to pursue graduate studies of some kind, but was still very conflicted about what area I should pursue. I had many possible career paths I could follow, and each had its attractions and drawbacks.

My mind was filled with questions. Was taking philosophy courses at Columbia, with the idea of exploring whether I should pursue a graduate degree in philosophy, a realistic path, or was I just continuing my undergraduate passion for the theoretical?

I was also still very interested in what was going on in the world, particularly in Europe and the Middle East, and I thought about whether I should elevate that interest to a professional level. Should I pursue a specialized graduate degree in Middle Eastern Studies, leading to a career in the foreign service, as I had discussed with Doug?

Perhaps my job as a social worker would help me sort out whether my passion to help alleviate the plight of the poor and forgotten was a real calling, or just another passing interest.

On Monday morning, I took the subway to downtown Brooklyn, where the social services building was located. I entered the building, and the receptionist directed me to the second floor.

"See Peggy," the receptionist said. "She'll be your supervisor."

I went up the stairs to the second floor and entered a very large room filled with many rows of desks. I asked the first person I saw where I would find Peggy, and he directed me to a woman with short black hair and glasses.

I went up to her and introduced myself.

"Hi, Al. I'm Peggy; I was expecting you. Welcome to social services. The fourth desk in this row will be yours." She picked up a sheet of paper from her desk and continued, "Here are the names of the fifty clients you'll be servicing. They used to be the clients of a caseworker who recently had to leave due to a severe illness. Officially, each client is a family with dependent children; the program we work on is called Aid to Families with Dependent Children, or AFDC."

We walked over to my new desk, and Peggy pointed to the large file drawer beside it. "This contains the folders on all the clients you'll be in charge of servicing and monitoring. We call each client 'a case'; you're their 'caseworker.' You'll have about fifty cases at any one time, and the number of cases changes slightly each month. Sometimes clients are no longer eligible to receive welfare, and you'll occasionally get new clients."

I looked at the folders in the drawer; most seemed to be between two and three inches thick. I was a little alarmed; it looked like a lot of work. In a voice that may have sounded a little perturbed, I asked, "How exactly do I work with each client? What do I do for them?"

"Well, to start, for the next two days, I want you to read every one of these folders so you can get an idea of who your clients are."

That sounded easy enough, but I still didn't know what my job was exactly, or what I was supposed to do for my clients. I asked again, "When do I get to meet the clients, and what precisely am I doing for them?"

"You'll meet your clients when they come in here every once in a while to ask for something. You'll also need to visit each family in their home twice a year on a routine basis, as well as any time there is a problem."

"How do I know when to visit them?"

Pointing toward her desk, Peggy said, "There's a client visit schedule on the bulletin board next to my desk. It lists the visits for each month."

Then, looking back at me, she continued, "After each visit, you'll need to write a report and file it. In your reports, you'll need to verify what was described in the client's folder is still accurate. You can also call clients to check on them and make sure all is going well. You go on your visits twice a week; for you, the visits will be Tuesdays and Thursdays. The other three days, you'll be in the office writing reports, making client phone calls, and seeing clients who come in to see you about problems they may have."

As I absorbed all Peggy said, I couldn't help but think it sounded more like lots of paperwork and not actually helping alleviate the poor's daily suffering. She certainly said nothing about feeding the hungry, giving drink to the thirsty, clothing the naked, or sheltering the homeless. Still, perhaps I would be able to get involved more directly with the lives of the poor and needy of Brooklyn as a caseworker.

I hated how they called them clients and AFDC cases, though. These terms seemed to overlook the fact these were people in need.

31. My First Client Visit

THE FIRST CLIENT I WOULD BE VISITING WAS MRS. JOHNSON, A twenty-one-year-old single black woman with two children, ages two and three. She was separated from her husband, who provided no child support. The family had been on welfare for two years and was living in a two-bedroom apartment in Bedford-Stuyvesant. A year ago, she had a part-time job making some supplemental income. Her own mother babysat while she worked. Unfortunately, Mrs. Johnson had lost her job three months ago and was now unemployed.

I wondered, is this woman and her family able to live on their welfare check alone? Is it my job to find out and see what I can do to help? Maybe this is where I get to feed the hungry and clothe the naked.

As I pondered these questions, I noticed movement to my left. I looked up and saw a tall, muscular man with a kind face, eyeglasses and a sharply receding hairline. With a wide smile, he said, "My name is Tom. I sit right here, beside you."

I stood up and shook his hand. "My name is Al. This is my first day."

"Welcome, Al. I'll be at my desk every Monday, Wednesday, and Friday. I think you have the same schedule."

"Yes." I paused and then pointed to the folder in my hand. "On Tuesday, I'll be going to visit this client who lost her supplemental income. When I go visit her, what can I do for the family?" I was sure he would know what I ought to do for a client who had lost her supplemental income and had two children to feed.

"You can't do anything for them directly. You just look around, ask the mother if there are any problems, make sure there's no man living in the apartment providing extra support she did not report, then come back to the office and write and file your report. That's all you have to do."

"That's fine," I replied, "but shouldn't we help these people when we find problems?"

"No, you don't want to get involved. In fact, the department frowns at any attempt by caseworkers to do any charity work outside the written rules and guidelines."

I was surprised, and with a tone that must have sounded naïve, I asked, "Why not? Aren't we supposed to be helping these people?"

"Yes, but only within the guidelines. If the caseworker does anything that causes a problem, the social services administration would be liable and could face legal action," Tom explained. "They don't want us to do anything other than make visits, observe, and write reports."

Looking amazed, I asked, "That's it? That's all we do?"

"Yes. In fact, many caseworkers don't even do the home visits; they just call the client on the phone, ask a few questions, and write it up. The Bedford-Stuyvesant area—where all our clients are—is very dangerous. Several caseworkers were mugged and robbed last year."

I was starting to understand this job was not the place to do works of mercy, as I had hoped it would be. "What do people do on the days they're suppose to do the home visits, if they don't actually go visit?" I asked.

"Many just stay at home, call the client when they come in the next day, and write their report," Tom said.

I decided on the spot I would visit each client in person.

The next day, a Tuesday, I called Mrs. Johnson and told her I was coming to visit in a couple of hours. I took the subway to central Brooklyn, the "Bed-Stuy" neighborhood, and got off at Nostrand Avenue. As I walked through the neighborhood, I was immediately struck by the numerous abandoned buildings and littered vacant lots. I saw rundown brownstones and filth on the sidewalks along the side streets. On the large avenues, storefronts were unkempt, and graffiti and garbage were everywhere. Boys and men just stood around on street corners, looking bored and without purpose. I thought to myself, this is not the America we learned about in Lebanon, not the country that excited me in 1960 when we first moved here.

Mrs. Johnson lived on the second floor of a five-story apartment building. The hallway walls were covered with graffiti, patches of mismatched paint, and dirt. The odor of garbage was strong. I took the stairs to the second floor and knocked on Mrs. Johnson's door. An attractive, nicely dressed young lady, with curly black hair, opened the door.

"Hello, I'm Al Badre, your new caseworker."

"Come in, please. I'm Jumana Johnson."

I went in and immediately noticed the smallness of the rooms and the staleness of the air; I could tell the apartment was poorly ventilated. But, as Tom had told me, it wasn't my job to do anything about it. All I could do was write it in my report.

I walked into a very sparsely furnished living room, which contained only two chairs and a small table between them. One bedroom had a queen-sized bed and the other had a mattress on the floor.

I asked Mrs. Johnson if she had any particular problems social services needed to be aware of, and she instantly responded, "Yep; about ten days before the end of the month, we run out of most foods and have to live on bread and water. Also, the winter is coming, and I don't think I can afford winter jackets for my babies."

"What about the coats they had last winter?" I asked.

"Well, you know, children grow. Last year's clothes don't fit them anymore."

I felt really stupid.

On the subway back to Brooklyn Heights, I started thinking, maybe I could visit the family toward the end of the month with a bag of groceries and two baby jackets from the Salvation Army. But then I remembered what Tom had said, and I tried to put the idea out of my mind.

Part IV
On Reaching for the
Realm of the Mind

32. A Shifting Mind: Religious Studies to Scientific Inquiry

OUTSIDE OF MY REGULAR COURSEWORK, I READ BOOKS BY Catholic theologians such as Karl Rahner, Edward Schillebeeckx, Yves M.J. Congar, Pierre Teilhard de Chardin, Henri du Lubac, Étienne Gilson, Romano Guardini, Gabriel Marcel, Joseph Ratzinger (who would later become Pope Benedict XVI) and the Trappist monk, Thomas Merton.

I was particularly captivated by Rahner's description of the "Christian commitment" and his thoughts on being a Christian by choice and not because one was born into a Christian milieu. To my mind, it was similiar to the Great Awakening and the revivalism of Jonathan Edwards. The revivalists emphasized personal rebirth and commitment to Christ. Similarly, in his book, *The Christian Commitment*, Rahner argued in the "Diaspora Church," a church subsists within a non-Christian, secular culture, Christians must actively choose to be Christians. These concepts of Christian choice and commitment in a non-Christian culture, perhaps even in an anti-Christian milieu, strengthened my resolve to deepen my Catholic commitment.

The other theologian that intrigued me was Pierre Teilhard de Chardin, and I spent a considerable amount of time studying his theory of the evolution of the universe. I had already read Rahner's book on evolution, *Hominization*, which posited the idea that the relationship between "spirit" and "matter" is characterized by the development of the physical world from the beginning of time, toward the spiritual world in an ongoing process of self-realization. I saw a clear connection between Rahner's "matter-to-spirit" idea and Chardin's concept of continuous evolution toward increasing levels of consciousness. As I read and reread Chardin's books, particularly *The Phenomenon of Man* and *The Divine Milieu,* I was intrigued by his thesis the cosmos is continuously evolving toward higher levels of complexity and consciousness—the "noosphere," as he calls it. The endpoint of this evolution is "The Omega Point," or God. I understood not only was the cosmos in continuous progression toward God, but at the same time, God's presence and love everywhere through the Body of Christ—the church—made the universe the "Divine Milieu."

I appreciated Chardin's idea of the "evolving cosmos" as a new spirituality informed by science. As a result, I became interested in science as an intellectual method of inquiry, very different from the applied science I had encountered in Dr. Armaly's lab.

I began contemplating a career in scientific inquiry as it related to improving the human condition, merging science and human spiritual progress. I discussed the idea with Doug. "I'm thinking about a career in a scientific field that would allow me to work toward helping humanity progress toward the Omega Point, one that would enable me to improve the human condition. What do you think?"

Doug thought about it for a bit, then said, "I don't know what you mean; it's too broad a goal."

"I guess I'd like to pursue some kind of scientific inquiry that would lead to improving peoples' lives, like food production, health, comfort, economic welfare, education, and so on."

Doug was now getting excited at the thought. "That sounds great, but what actual academic field would you pursue?"

"I don't know yet, but this could resolve a problem for me: how to combine my interest in religious and philosophical issues with a practical career to allow me to make a living, as my father keeps telling me I need to do."

My minor was in philosophy, and I was very interested in existential philosophy and the writings of Kierkegaard, Albert Camus, and Jean-Paul Sartre. Unfortunately, I couldn't find any courses on the subject, so I decided to read the works of both Christian and non-Christian existentialist philosophers on my own.

Camus' *The Myth of Sisyphus* particularly resonated with me. The gods condemned Sisyphus to push a rock up a mountain, but when he reached the top, the rock would roll back down to the foot of the mountain, and Sisyphus would have to start all over again. This went on for eternity. Sisyphus endured by focusing on improving the art of pushing the rock. He had eternal hope each time he would do better, and as a result, he successfully fought despair.

Even though it was not a Christian-focused piece, I interpreted it as being about the Christian virtues of hope and doing the best you can in the present moment, no matter how difficult a task is. One should always trust in God, no matter how difficult the obstacle and always have hope.

Whenever I visited my parents, I spent a considerable amount of time discussing—and sometimes arguing about—my major with Papa. He didn't think my major in religious studies would give me any kind of future job security. He was probably right, but I didn't see it that way at the time and didn't care.

In these conversations, Papa would inevitably say, "What kind of job will you get? You should have majored in something practical. Now, after you graduate, you'll need to do postgraduate work in a field where you can get a job."

"I'll get a PhD and work in some university."

Frustrated, he would respond, "Academic jobs in the humanities are very rare. Plus, you'll be competing with a thousand applicants for the same job."

This kind of conversation took place every time Papa and I were together, and it was starting to make me worry about my future and how I could reconcile my interest in history, religion, and philosophy with the practical need to make a living.

On the other hand, over the summer, Ammo Sharl had encouraged me to stay in the humanities, though he continued to insist that instead of philosophy, I should develop my interest in history. He believed I needed to be well versed in the evolution of Western civilization before I could fully engage its philosophy and theology.

I was definitely conflicted. I continued taking courses in philosophy and theology, but was increasingly asking myself how I would apply what I had been learning to the socio-moral-political realm. In fact, these thoughts stayed with me even after I graduated and moved to New York City.

33. The Future on My Mind

AFTER ABOUT A MONTH WORKING AS A CASEWORKER IN Brooklyn, I fell into a daily routine. Three days a week, I would go to my eight-to-five job; on Tuesdays and Thursdays, I made client visits. In the evening, I went to Manhattan three times a week for classes at Columbia. After class, I often went to visit Doug and Charlene or my cousin Edward Said, who was an assistant professor of English at Columbia.

My cousin Edward and I regularly met at a coffee shop near Columbia and had long discussions about philosophy, religion, and politics. International affairs were a frequent topic of conversation, particularly the Palestinian–Israeli conflict. We shared an anti-war sentiment, particularly in regards to Vietnam, but I could tell Edward held a special distaste for those who favored Israel in its conflict with the Arabs. In September of 1968, Edward was not really politically active. In fact, he did not strike me as being the political activist type at all, let alone the international advocate for the Palestinian cause he became in later years.

In early September of 1968, about a month after I started my job as a caseworker, I decided to write down my thoughts about my future in a letter to Auntie Eva in response to one I had received from her. I told her I had given up my original plans to pursue a graduate degree in religious studies but was still conflicted and trying to decide between two different career paths.

On one hand, I was still interested in philosophy, with an emphasis in ethics, and my continuing interest in politics and international affairs made me consider an academic career in social and political history.

But, on the other hand, I wanted a career that would not limit me to conceptual work. I wanted to work in applied social justice somehow, similar to what I was doing in my work in social services.

I concluded my letter by saying, "I hope whatever I decide to do is what I am supposed to do."

I occasionally met with Ammo Sharl at the Harvard Club whenever he was in New York. He was on the speech circuit and was in high demand, giving speeches all over the country. We talked about all kinds of things, and I particularly enjoyed listening to his thoughts on religious philosophy.

While I never overtly told him so, I did not agree with his views on Vietnam. I later learned he knew about mine from Mama. The last time we met, he kept bringing up Vietnam and the communist threat; he was obviously angered by what Mama had told him about my anti–Vietnam War sentiments. He told me I was naïve and should not talk about things I knew nothing about, particularly when it came to international affairs.

I strongly suspected he brought the subject up at Mama's request. She strongly supported the war, and she likely insisted Ammo Sharl talk me into changing my position.

The fact was though I was still a strong advocate for the peace movement, I was much less of an activist than I had been. I was becoming increasingly interested in social justice issues and the plight of the poor.

34. An Ode to Barbara

M Y COWORKER, TOM, AND I BECAME GOOD FRIENDS, OFTEN
having lunch together in a bistro not far from the office. He was
very interested in my Lebanese background and asked me a great many
questions about Lebanon's culture, customs, and food.

One day in early January, I suggested I could introduce him to Lebanese food by taking him and his wife to dinner at the Beirut Restaurant
in Manhattan. He immediately jumped at the idea, and on Friday evening, I walked over to Tom's house, which was just a few blocks from
where I lived in Brooklyn Heights. Tom answered the door and invited
me in, and as I walked into the living room, I saw a beautiful, petite,
blond woman with a wide smile on her face. "Hello, I'm Maggie," she
said. "I'm looking forward to trying Lebanese food; I've heard it's delicious, but have never tried it."

"You're going to love it," I assured her.

I sat next to Maggie on the subway, and she was curious about my background, asking how long I had lived in New York, where I had lived before
that, and when I had come to America from Lebanon. I gave her a short
summary of my history and my time in Beirut, Albany, and Iowa City.

I was about to ask her about her own background in turn when the
train stopped at Penn Station in Midtown. We got off and walked a
couple blocks to the Beirut Restaurant.

We entered the restaurant to the sound of Lebanese music and the
voice of Fayrouz, and I immediately felt at home. The host seated us at a
table next to a large bay window in the front of the restaurant and asked
whether we would like anything to drink.

"I suggest you try a glass of *arak*; I think you'll like it," I said to Tom
and Maggie. They agreed, and I ordered a glass of *arak* and water for
each of us.

Arak is very potent, being fifty percent alcohol, and is a clear, colorless, anise-flavored drink. When mixed with water, it becomes a milky-white color.

Before I even had a chance to look at the menu, Tom said, "Al, you know Lebanese food. Why don't you order for all of us?"

I nodded, then opened the folded menu and quickly scanned it. "Why don't we start with a sampling of the *mezza* and then follow up with a main entrée?" I suggested.

"What's a *mezza*?" Maggie asked.

I pointed to the list in the menu. "It's the starters on a menu, like an appetizer. I'll order the most popular ones."

As we were waiting for the drinks, Maggie said, "I like this music; the singer has an amazing voice."

She was referring to Fayrouz, and I informed her, "Fayrouz is the most prominent singer in Lebanon; she's the diva of Middle Eastern music."

Our waiter soon returned with our drinks. Maggie took one sip of *arak* and announced, "Wow, this is potent—but good!"

The waiter asked if we were ready to order, and I explained, "I want to introduce my friends to the different flavors in Lebanese food," I said. "So let's start with the hummus, *baba ghannouj*, grape leaves, *tabbouleh, fattoush, falafel, labne, mekanek, kibbeh* balls, *chankleesh* and lots of bread. For the entrée, let's share an order of *shish taook*."

After the waiter left, I asked Maggie about her own background. She explained she had come to New York several years earlier from Charleston, South Carolina, where she was born and raised.

That surprised me. "You don't have a Southern accent, though."

"Yep, I lost it many years ago."

Tom chimed in, "Charleston is a real Southern city; charming on the surface, but quite unique."

"How so?" I asked.

"Well, if you're an outsider among the natives, you can cut the air with a knife."

"I don't understand. What do you mean?"

"People not from Charleston—not born and raised there—are viewed with suspicion, especially if they're from the North. It's as though they're afraid of Yankee agents in the 'War of Northern Aggression.'

"I'll give you my favorite example. In one of Charleston's historic graveyards, there's a gravestone for a ninety-five-year-old man with the inscription: 'He moved to Charleston at the age of three, but we love him even though he was not one of us.'

"Just think: this guy lived in Charleston for over ninety years and was *still* considered an outsider."

I laughed, then said, "Tom, I never asked you if you're from New York."

He chuckled. "No, I came here from Michigan because I wanted to be an actor on Broadway. I ended up being a waiter instead. After a while, I got tired of trying to get by like that, so I became a caseworker."

At that point, our waiter and an assistant brought out two trays with all the *mezza* dishes. I showed them how to use the pita bread to eat both the hummus and *baba ghannouj* by tearing a piece of bread and scooping up a little portion of the dish. Both Maggie and Tom loved all the dishes, but especially those two.

As we were about to leave, Maggie said, "While we're in Manhattan, why don't we go visit my sisters, Ruby and Barbara? They live a couple of subway stops from here." Tom and I agreed, and we headed over.

As we approached the old brownstone on West Seventy-First, Maggie warned us, "It's a very small apartment."

Sure enough, as we entered, I found myself in an apartment so small I could stand in the living room and the kitchen at the same time. A very thin, petite, pretty young woman with hazel eyes and long blond hair down to her hips greeted us with a generous smile. With Kafka's *The Metamorphosis* in hand, she sat down in a sling chair, where I was sure she had been sitting and reading before we interrupted her. She offered us wine, which Maggie poured into four wine glasses, and explained that their other sister, Ruby, was out walking the dog.

I was immediately attracted to Barbara, but was so shy I spent most of the visit staring into my wine as if it would tell me what to say.

For her part, Barbara continued to hold her book the entire time we were there, looking down at it now and then as though she couldn't wait for us to leave so she could continue reading.

I thought about Barbara all weekend after that, but was at a loss as to whether I ought to contact her. I belatedly realized if I had actually made eye contact and spoken to her while at her apartment, I might know what to do.

Back in the office on Monday, Tom said Maggie wanted to know if I had liked Barbara. I noncommittally said she was "fine" and left it at that.

When we were both back in the office on Wednesday, Tom asked me if I liked Barbara well enough to take her out on a date.

"Yes, I could see going out on a date," I said carefully.

"Maggie and I would like to see you guys go out," Tom said.

A couple of days later, having decided I needed a push, Tom handed me a piece of paper with Barbara's phone number.

By now, I was definitely getting the message. Still, I wasn't sure whether Barbara actually wanted to go on a date with me. I asked Tom, and he replied, "We don't think Barbara would mind getting a call from you."

Seventeen days after our quiet meeting in Barbara's apartment, and after continuous prodding by Tom on Maggie's behalf, I got up nerve to call Barbara and ask her out.

Her immediate answer was, "Where?"

I froze for a few seconds; I hadn't thought that far ahead. I was merely hoping for a "yes" and would think about where to go later. The only thing I could think of on the spur of the moment was the Beirut Restaurant.

She seemed delighted. "Yes, sure. When?"

I was relieved. "How about this Friday? I'll come by your apartment at seven."

The evening was perfect. We were so comfortable with each other. We both enjoyed the Lebanese food, and she couldn't stop asking questions about Lebanon and my family. She wanted to know every detail of our trip from Beirut to New York by sea.

After dinner, we walked along the streets of Manhattan. We talked and laughed a lot and ended up in Central Park. She told me about growing up in Charleston, South Carolina, and about her family. She was one of five siblings, all girls. She was a part-time art student at the Pratt Institute in Brooklyn and also worked in the dean's office at Pratt's School of Information and Library Science.

I was fascinated; I had never met an art student before. "I know very little about art," I confessed. "You'll need to teach me."

With a big, beautiful smile, she said, "Sure. I'd love to teach you. The best way is to go to the New York Museum of Art. I'll tell you all about every art piece and all the genres."

"Great! I'm looking forward to another date," I said with a grin.

Barbara and I started seeing each other every day. After work, I'd meet her at Pratt, and we'd head to Manhattan, walking and talking. Our favorite place was a bar just around the corner from Auntie Rosa Lee's house, where we always had whiskey sours.

We spent an entire weekend at the Museum of Art, where Barbara told me all about so many different artists and styles. I was totally floored by how much she knew, and by the end of the weekend, not only did I know a little bit about the different genres of art, I had also developed a beginner's appreciation for art history. I also learned a little about how to view a work of art, looking for the subject matter, its use of color, and the artist's juxtaposition of objects, shapes, light, and so on.

Around this time, I composed a poem, but never wrote it down, called "An Ode to Barbara and Many Other Things." I can still recall the title and some of the lines. I would recite it to her almost every day as we walked the streets of New York.

By mid-February, I was spending every waking minute of every day, when I wasn't at work, with Barbara. I would leave Monroe Place early in the morning, before breakfast, and not return until after midnight. Being absent so often, Auntie Rosa Lee left me a note in the entrance foyer at one point, saying, "Where are you? I never see you anymore."

The next morning, a Saturday, I came down to Mary's delicious breakfast, and Auntie Rosa Lee was sitting there waiting for me. "Well, good morning, stranger! Where have you been these last few weeks?"

I looked at her with a smile and said, "I've met a girl. Her name is Barbara, and I really like her. I've been spending a lot of time with her."

Without looking at me, Auntie Rosa Lee picked up the breadbasket and passed it to me. "Have some toast," she instructed. "What does this girl do?"

"She's an art student at the Pratt Institute and also works there for the dean of Library Science."

Auntie Rosa Lee finally looked up at me. "Why don't you bring her over for dinner today?"

That took me by surprise; I wasn't ready for that yet. After all, there was nothing officially serious between us. "Not today," I said. "We're spending the day at The Cloisters to see the tapestries and carvings. We'll eat there."

After two hours of viewing the beautiful tapestries, rugs, and Eastern religious icons and being amazed by the sixteenth-century wooden rosary bead carved in minute detail, we found we had seen everything we wanted to see and decided to head back to Brooklyn Heights. We spent the rest of the day strolling along the Brooklyn Heights Promenade, feelings inspired by the gorgeous Manhattan skylines and the magnificent Brooklyn Bridge, and then stopping for our favorite courting drink, a whiskey sour.

35. Getting Married

By the end of March, after spending almost every single day with Barbara for the past three months, walking up and down Manhattan, and talking and laughing all the way from Columbia to the Village, I realized how much I wanted to spend the rest of my life with her.

One day after work, on our way from Pratt to Barbara's apartment, we stopped at an Irish bar and ordered two whiskey sours. With my glass in my hand, I seriously and sincerely asked, "If things continue to go as they are, would you like to marry me?"

After taking a sip, she looked at me. "'If'? Yes." Even though there was a long, deliberately hesitant pause after "If," I took it as a definite "Yes."

I reached across the table and took her hand. In less than ten seconds, the old man behind the bar came out, slapped my hand, and said in a thick Irish accent, "We don't allow this kind of behavior here." He clearly didn't approve of young people showing affection in public. We quickly left and couldn't stop laughing about it as we continued to walk toward Barbara's apartment.

"'If'? Yes," didn't take long to become only a "Yes." Only one week after I popped the question, we started talking about a wedding.

This also meant we had to tell our parents and families, who would likely be horrified we wanted to get married after only knowing each other for a few months. Still, I decided to call my parents to tell them the news. Mama sounded surprised and a little apprehensive to hear the news, but she didn't seem to disapprove. She questioned whether it was prudent for us to get married so soon, but agreed and sounded eager to meet Barbara during her trip to New York for the Church Women United Board.

Barbara was raised Baptist, but since coming to New York, she had become increasingly interested in Catholic beliefs. We both wanted a Catholic wedding, but Barbara was not a Catholic yet, and that meant we would not be able to marry in the church.

Having had many years' experience with the Newman Center at the University of Iowa, I felt a priest at one of the universities in the city would be more likely to be sympathetic and suggest how we could have a Catholic wedding outside of the church. I was already familiar with the Catholic Center at New York University from when I was a student there in the summer of 1967, and Barbara also was familiar with it from her involvement in peace marches and anti-war protests. Plus, because NYU was in the Village—the heart of the countercultural revolution of the sixties—we would likely encounter a less conservative priest there.

As it turned out, the priest at NYU was young and friendly. We introduced ourselves, and I started by explaining, "Father, we want to get married and have a Catholic wedding. I'm Catholic, but Barbara is not." I hesitated a little, then continued, "She has been wanting to become a Catholic for some time now."

He looked at Barbara. "What is your religion now?"

"I was baptized into the Baptist church, but I now share Nasib's Catholic beliefs."

The priest looked at us sympathetically. "I can't marry you in the church, but you could be married as a Catholic if an ordained priest was willing to marry you, and I happen to know such a priest. His name is Paul Mayer; he left the priesthood to marry, but because he was ordained, he can still legitimately administer the Sacraments of Marriage and the Eucharist."

"Does he live in New York City?" I asked.

"No, he lives a short train ride from here, in New Jersey."

He gave us Father Mayer's home and office numbers, and we left feeling hopeful and thankful there was a way for us to get married by an ordained priest.

Next, I went to see Auntie Rosa Lee. "Barbara and I plan to get married in May."

Auntie Rosa Lee looked surprised. "Oh? Don't you want to wait and think about it a little longer?"

"Not really," I said. "I'm sure I want to marry her. There's no reason to wait."

She looked a bit doubtful, despite my assurance. "Why don't you bring her to dinner tomorrow night?"

I agreed, and the next day, I met Barbara after work at Pratt, and we came directly to 7 Monroe Place.

Auntie Rosa Lee welcomed Barbara in her usual gracious manner. She took Barbara's hand and led her to the living room, where Auntie Rosa Lee's son, Alfred, and his wife, Aminy, were waiting, along with Auntie Rosa Lee's daughter, Elaine. They were the first of my relatives to meet Barbara. They were all very gracious and made Barbara feel welcome.

As we were having dinner, Auntie Rosa Lee asked, "So you've decided to get married?"

"Yes; we're hoping for a May 3rd wedding," I responded.

The entire family stared at me. Elaine chimed in, "That soon?"

"Yes. Why wait? We're absolutely sure of each other," I said.

Elaine continued, "But you just met. And there's a lot to be arranged in a wedding."

Auntie Rosa Lee then graciously broke in, "You know, we've had several weddings in this house. How would you like to have yours here?"

Barbara and I looked at each other, and I answered, "Thank you, Auntie. That's a great idea. Let's have the wedding here."

Because both of us wanted a Catholic wedding but could not marry in a church, Auntie Rosa Lee's generous offer was positively heaven-sent.

A few days later, I met Mama at her hotel on Manhattan's westside. She immediately wanted to know all about Barbara and her family. "How did you meet this girl?" she asked.

"I met her through her sister, Maggie, and her brother-in-law, Tom. Tom is my co-worker in social services. They live not far from Auntie Rosa Lee in Brooklyn Heights."

She looked approvingly at me. "And what about her parents? Where do they live?"

"Her mother lives in Charleston, South Carolina. I'm not sure where her father lives now; her parents are divorced."

At that, Mama's expression changed. There had never been a divorce in our large extended family before. It scared her I was about to marry a girl who had already experienced her parents' divorce; it might make her consider divorce normal. "Are you sure you want to go ahead with this?"

"Yes, I'm sure. Don't worry, Mama. Barbara's mom is very devout and doesn't believe in divorce, either. She simply felt she had to separate herself from a bad situation." I hugged her, and she looked less anxious.

"Okay, let's go meet Barbara."

"Great! Her and her sister's apartment is not far from here; we can walk."

Barbara knew I was going to bring Mama by to meet her, and so she was nervously waiting. The moment they saw each other, though, they were in each other's arms.

"I'm so glad Nasib found the right person to marry," Mama said.

"I'm so very happy to meet you," Barbara responded. Then, pointing to the couch, she asked Mama to sit down so we could talk.

"Nasib tells me you're an artist."

"Yes, I'm actually an art student at Pratt Institute. That's one of my paintings," she said, pointing to a piece on the wall across from her. It was an oil painting of an old man looking at a field with a pond. It was in the impressionist style, with lots of greens, blues, and browns; whenever I gazed at it, I felt a sense of calm.

"Very nice," Mama said. After that, the conversation quickly shifted to the wedding. "Nasib tells me you plan to get married on May 3rd. Have you started the invitations?"

Barbara nodded, and I said, "Barbara is using her talents to create a beautiful invitation. Here's a sketch." I placed the draft on the coffee table and continued, "Notice all the Arabic words: *salam* [peace], *muhabba* [love], *musawa* [equality] and *wahida* [unity]. Also, notice all the symbols, like the cross, the dove, and the universe."

Mama looked pleased. "Very nice; this combination of words and symbols definitely offers a powerful message. It's also very kind of Rosa Lee to offer her house for the wedding."

Soon after, we took a day off work and went to Macy's to shop for our rings. We bought two beautiful thick-banded gold rings, but had to pick them up a week later, as they needed to be resized.

Two days later, we took the invitation Barbara had designed to the printer and ordered one hundred copies. We knew most of our relatives and friends would not be able to come from Lebanon, Iowa, Charleston and beyond for the wedding, but we wanted to announce our marriage to the world all the same.

Our next challenge was to find a place to live after the wedding. Barbara's sister, Ruby, was thinking of moving back to Charleston or to Atlanta, where their sister Pat lived. Ruby needed to stay in New York for another two months, so we planned to move into the apartment after Ruby moved out. But in the meantime, we needed to find a temporary place to stay for two months.

I often walked from Times Square to Columbia and would see a residence hotel called The Greystone on Ninety-First Street where weekly and monthly rentals were offered. We decided to check it out. The clerk at the front desk informed us all rooms came with kitchenettes and there were two rooms available for rent. The room he showed us looked old and worn out, and the halls had various unpleasant cooking smells, but we decided to rent it anyway since we would only be staying for two months.

The next day, after we picked up our wedding rings, I called both numbers the priest at NYU had given me and left a message, asking Father Mayer to call me back at the 7 Monroe Place phone number. Early the next day, I got a call from him. He suggested Barbara and I come meet with him at his home in New Jersey.

We made the trek to his home, where he greeted us warmly and introduced his wife. "Hello, I'm Father Mayer, and this is my wife, Naomi." He told us that just as he had been a priest, Naomi had been a nun before they got married. It was all very strange to me; I had never met a married priest before, let alone a married nun.

He invited us to sit down and then got right to business. "So you want to get married and have a Catholic wedding, but you can't get married in the church?"

"Yes, we'd like to get married on May 3rd, in about five weeks," I said.

He looked at his calendar. "That won't be a problem. Do you want to have the Eucharist administered?"

"Yes, we do," I said for both of us, "but not everyone attending will be Catholic."

"That's okay. People will know what to do, and Barbara can receive if she wants to. By the way, Naomi will make the Eucharistic bread."

"Will we also have the Cup?" I asked.

"No, offering the Body of Christ is enough for this ceremony." He made some notes, then continued, "But we should get together again closer to the date to talk about the details of the wedding ceremony, how many people will be attending, Gospel readings, hymns, etcetera." We agreed to meet again at Doug and Charlene's apartment five days before the wedding.

We went back to Manhattan feeling everything was coming together nicely. The only thing we had not yet settled on was a honeymoon destination. We had both grown up near ocean, and we wanted our honeymoon to be at a beach somewhere on the East Coast.

We initially considered the island of Nantucket or some location on Cape Cod, but given it was still early May, we decided to go further south, where the water would be warmer. We looked at going to Florida, but the cost of a flight and a hotel was too high for our budget. After that, we looked around and discovered the beaches in Virginia were not very far away and the airfare was reasonable. We made reservations at a small oceanfront hotel in Virginia Beach.

Time passed quickly, and soon it was time for our final meeting with Father Mayer to go over the final preparations. Naomi came along, and I introduced them both to Doug and Charlene.

As before, Father Mayer quickly got down to business. "We'll start the ceremony with blessings and a hymn, followed by the readings you've selected."

I jumped in. "We've already selected the readings: one from the Gospel of Matthew and the other from the book *Divine Milieu* by Pierre Teilhard de Chardin."

"That's good. What about the hymns?"

"We've talked about that, too," Barbara answered, "and chose three we really like: 'Lord of the Dance,' 'They'll Know We Are Christians,' and 'The King of Glory.'"

"Naomi knows two nuns who play the guitar and sing. I'm sure they know these hymns. They may add a couple more to round things out."

"That'll be great," Barbara said.

"Doug here will be my best man and the ring bearer."

Barbara quickly added, "My father is ill and won't be able to come. I work with Dean Sharify at the Pratt Institute. He's like a father to me and has agreed to give me away."

After writing everything down, Father Mayer asked, "How many people do you expect to be at the ceremony?"

"Around twenty."

With that, he wrapped things up. "We'll see you on Saturday," he said with a grin.

At long last, Saturday, May 3rd finally arrived. Barbara came to 7 Monroe Place early, before any of the guests arrived, and Auntie Rosa Lee immediately took her upstairs to the second floor, saying no one should see her before the wedding began.

Among the attendees were my parents, Leila and Maria; my brothers, who lived in California and Illinois, couldn't make it. There was also Auntie Rosa Lee; Aminy; Elaine; Alfred; Barbara's mother, Ruby; Maggie; Tom; and Barbara's sister, Pat, with her husband and their two children. Mr. and Mrs. Molineaux also came down from Albany with ten of their children—Lorraine had a previously scheduled engagement and couldn't make it. Doug and Charlene were there, as well as Barbara's art school friends, Doreen and Maria. Two of my friends from Iowa, Liz and Bill, had recently moved to New York, and they also came to the wedding.

The wedding was a blur for me, and I went through the motions—standing next to Barbara in front of the priest, repeating the wedding vows—in a sort of a daze. The combination of stress and excitement stifled my appetite, despite all the delicious-looking food at the reception.

Barbara was in far worse shape, though; right after the ceremony, she dashed up to the bathroom on the second floor and threw up. After she had rested on the bed in Auntie Rosa Lee's room for a bit, we took a cab back to Barbara and Ruby's apartment in Manhattan. Ruby was staying with Maggie and Tom for the night, so we had the place to ourselves.

I suggested we cancel our flight to Virginia Beach in the morning, but Barbara, who often got sick due to stress, knew she would be fine by the morning and nixed the suggestion. Sure enough, she was much better by the next morning, and we were soon on our way to the airport for our honeymoon.

The morning of our first full day on our honeymoon, we took a walk along the beach. All our stress fell away, and we both felt refreshed and exhilarated as we listened to the splashing waves, sat in the bright sun, and enjoyed the ocean breeze.

The beauty and serenity of the ocean was a sharp contrast with the noisy, smelly and crowded New York City we had become accustomed to. For the first time since arriving in New York City from Lebanon, I lost the feeling it was the city I wanted to live in forever, and we contemplated how great it would be to live in a place like Virginia Beach.

After our beach walk and breakfast, we took a walk-through a nearby residential neighborhood. While we both appreciated the high-rises of Manhattan, the simple homes that lined the clean, paved streets truly delighted us in a new way.

As we continued our walk, we saw a small church with a life-sized crucifix on the front of the building. Seeing the crucifix, I immediately knew it was a Catholic church. "Let's go inside," I suggested.

As we walked inside, a priest came down from the altar, where he seemed to have been busy moving items around. He walked toward the entrance of the church and greeted us, "Hello, I'm Father Just. Welcome to Star of the Sea. Are you visiting Virginia Beach, or do you live here?"

"I'm Al, and this is my wife, Barbara. We're on our honeymoon here in Virginia Beach for four days, and we wanted to know more about this parish. What time are the masses on Sunday?"

"Sunday mass is at eight, ten, and noon." He reached over to a table and picked up what looked like a pamphlet and said, "Here's a bulletin; it gives you the times and tells you a little about our parish and activities."

On our way back to the hotel, we talked about that nice little church surrounded by palm trees and flowers, and how we wished we could be a part of the community. At that moment, New York City seemed too big.

36. Trouble in the City

O N JUNE 29TH, WE MOVED INTO THE APARTMENT BARBARA and Ruby had shared. Even though I had been there many times before, as we first entered it together with the intention of making it our first home, I noticed for the second time just how tiny it was.

The next day, we went out to buy furniture. We started at Gimbals and purchased a red couch, a mattress, and a bookcase. The king-sized mattress literally fit in the bedroom wall-to-wall.

Since the Audis owned a furniture store, we figured we would go there and get the "good" stuff; they were family, so we thought we could get some good deals. Unfortunately, the only deal they offered us was a rocking chair that had a defect. Since I could not live without a rocker, we went ahead and got it anyway. The good Audi furniture was too expensive for us. This was yet another time when I really missed Uncle E.J.; he would have given us many good deals, as he had done for my parents.

One day, I went into the office and almost immediately got a call from the lobby telling me I should come down. One of my clients, Shirley, was there, and she was agitated and wanted to see me immediately.

I looked at her folder and read over the reports written by her previous caseworker; nothing seemed particularly troublesome. Grabbing my notebook, I went downstairs to a booth where my client was waiting.

I thought I would start by being friendly, so I addressed her by her first name. "Hello, Shirley."

She answered with a weak smile and an anxious face, "Hello. I'm desperate. There's a week left in the month, and I ran out of money to buy food for my babies. I don't get my next check until the first. Can you help me?"

I knew the welfare department wouldn't issue additional checks unless it was an emergency, and they didn't consider not managing your money to last the entire month an emergency. Often, welfare clients would spend their money on drugs and then come back and ask for more, sometimes claiming they had to pay for a doctor's bill or medicine for their sick child.

"I'm sorry, Shirley, but I can't get you more money. The department won't approve it," I said.

Her smile immediately dropped from her face. With a deep frown, she insisted, "You have to get me money. My babies are hungry."

"I'm really sorry, but there's nothing I can do; it's a department policy."

At that, she suddenly leapt from her seat, grabbed my shirt collar, lifted me from my chair and pushed me up against the booth's wall. "You'll get me a check right now if you don't want me to beat the shit out of you on your way home tonight."

This was the first time in my life I had ever been completely terrified. All I wanted at the moment was to get out of that booth, maybe even out of this job and social services in general. I was desperate to get back upstairs, away from this maniac. In a very low tone, I said, "If you let go of me, I'll go upstairs and see what I can do." I knew security wouldn't let her follow me up there.

She took her hands off me and said, "Okay, you go and come right back."

I immediately went to Peggy and told her what had happened. She instructed me to stay up on the second floor and she would call security and have them escort Shirley out of the building.

Later that day, as I was ready to go home, I remembered Shirley's threat she would "beat the shit" out of me on my way home. I approached the building's front door very slowly and cautiously and opened it just enough to let me stick my head out and look in both directions. The sidewalk was bustling with people, and Shirley was nowhere to be seen. I slipped out, walked to the subway station across the street very quickly, hurried onto the train, and went home.

A month later, I went into the office, and, as I sat down at my desk, Peggy came over and informed me Shirley had moved into a new apartment, so I had to go visit her. Whenever a client moved, the caseworker had to inspect the new apartment to verify things like the number of rooms and living conditions, such as running water and electricity.

I immediately started sweating. "Are you serious?" I asked. "I have to go visit her after what she did to me? After threatening me?"

Peggy looked serious. "Yes, you are. This is your job."

"Peggy, I know it's my job, but this is a special situation. Can't you find someone else to do it?"

Peggy sat down on Tom's chair next to me and sighed. "Look Al, every caseworker here has a Shirley they have to deal with. You have to learn to deal with yours."

At that, I tried to convince myself perhaps it wouldn't be so bad. After all, our previous meetings had started out friendly enough. Perhaps she had gotten over her anger by now.

Peggy wanted me to visit Shirley the next day as part of my regular field visits. I tried to call ahead to let her know I would be coming by, but couldn't reach her—her number had been disconnected. The prospect of making a surprise visit to Shirley caused my fear to triple. But I had no choice; I had to go.

The next day, I went over to Shirley's new address and knocked at the door. After about a half minute, she opened, wearing a headscarf, which she hadn't worn when I saw her at the office before. She was also barefoot and wore a long dress that went down to her ankles.

"Hello, Shirley," I greeted her pleasantly. "I'm here to make a quick visit, since you recently moved."

With a stern but surprisingly gentle voice, she answered, "I've changed my name to Halima. I recently became a Muslim. If you want to come in and look around, you'll need to take your shoes off and move around the apartment on your knees."

I had never heard of the "moving around on the knees" custom among the Muslims of Lebanon, but I complied. As I entered the apartment, two guys walked out of the backroom and left through the front door. I knew they shouldn't have been there, and I strongly suspected

Shirley was trying to make extra money on the side, since the welfare department wouldn't give her any. Furthermore, they weren't on their knees and neither was Shirley/Halima. I was the only one on my knees, and I quickly realized the demand was to humiliate me and discourage me from entering.

"I've seen enough," I said and left. The entire episode caused me to become more realistic and less passionate about my idealistic cause. Even though I continued to visit my clients, I was growing more hesitant about meeting them face-to-face and increased my interaction with them by phone.

It was an election year, and the New York district attorney had recently launched an investigation into welfare fraud, making the practices of the Department of Social Services an election issue. The City decided some caseworkers were reporting bogus, fictitious visits to clients in order to increase the recipients' welfare checks in return for kickbacks. I knew of no one that did such a thing; at worst, many caseworkers simply had phone interviews with their clients, rather than visiting them in person. I could hardly blame them. After all, it was well known the Bedford-Stuyvesant neighborhood, which our office served, was a dangerous one where it was common for caseworkers to be mugged while on client visits.

Still, as a result, we were suddenly asked to prepare extensive justifications for any recommended increases in welfare checks. An uncomfortable feeling grew among my coworkers that we were being watched, resulting in low morale pervading the atmosphere in our building. Our supervisors became tense and often took out their frustrations on the workers by being rude and abrasive.

In addition, living in New York City had become extremely unpleasant. While it had been an exciting adventure when I first got there, it was now becoming uncomfortable, even scary at times.

Auntie Rosa Lee was mugged in Brooklyn Heights while walking home. When the mugger snatched her purse, he dislocated her shoulder.

Barbara's handbag was stolen while she was on a crowded subway. She didn't even realize it was missing until she got home, with only the strap on her shoulder. This resulted in a frightening evening, waiting for the crook to use the stolen door keys to come in and rob us. We ended up putting a new lock on the door and changing our bank account numbers.

One night, we heard a commotion on the street below our window. We looked out and saw police officers using flashlights to examine the outside stairs leading down to the building's cellar. The next morning, when we walked out of the building, we saw the chalk outline of a body at the bottom of the stairs, right in front of the cellar entrance.

A couple weeks later, we woke up one morning to find the restaurant one block from our apartment—a place we sometimes stopped for a bite—had been totally destroyed by a bomb.

My stressful work situation and the anxiety of living in New York City was enough motivation for us to get serious about leaving. My focus turned to deciding which graduate programs to apply to, with the idea Barbara could finish her undergraduate art studies wherever we ended up for my graduate education.

Before I could decide on a graduate program though, I needed to consider what I wanted to do for a career. This was difficult because my heart was still with philosophy and theology, but my common sense—influenced by years of my father's insistence I should settle on a practical career, one where I could make a good income and be financially secure—pushed me toward my other passion, foreign affairs.

I decided to keep my options open. I applied to the PhD program in religious studies at the University of Toronto to study theology under Leslie Dewart. I also decided to move forward with my idea of working for the U.S. foreign service. I knew I would likely first need to get a master's degree specializing in a particular region, and since I knew Arabic, a master's degree in Middle Eastern Studies made sense. As such, I applied to the University of Michigan's top-notch Middle Eastern Studies program.

Barbara was pushing for me to go to Georgetown for such a degree; she loved Washington, D.C., and wanted to live there, but I felt Michigan had more to offer.

"I'll most likely end up at Georgetown, in the Foreign Service program," I assured her. "But I'll have a better chance of getting in if I already had a specialization in Middle Eastern Studies. Plus, I visited Ann Arbor last year, and I really liked the campus town. The university is very highly ranked in many fields, including Middle Eastern Studies."

In late August, we decided to visit both universities and submit my applications in person, then go see my parents in Carbondale. We caught a late train to Toronto and slept in our seats, arriving early in the morning the next day. After depositing our bags at the hotel, we headed for the university.

I was a little dejected because Dr. Dewart was traveling, and I wasn't able to see him. It never occurred to me I should have contacted him in advance of our trip to Toronto to find out if he was going to be there. I also felt rather apprehensive and a little melancholic about not being in the United States, the nation my family had immigrated to nine years earlier. The United States was my home now. I told Barbara, "I don't feel at home here."

I submitted my application anyway, and the next day, we took a bus from Toronto to Detroit, and then on to Ann Arbor.

The moment we got to Ann Arbor and saw the tree-lined streets and green lawns, we both loved the city. We walked around, found the Union, and stopped for a Coke. From there, we went to the administration building, where I submitted my application and paid the application fee. The receptionist told me since I was applying to start in January, I should receive an answer by mid-October. That evening, we walked around, seeing as much of the town and campus as we could.

The next day, we took the bus to St. Louis, where my parents met us and drove us to Carbondale.

37. Leaving the City

*T*HE GOOD NEWS CAME IN LATE OCTOBER: I HAD BEEN accepted into the Middle Eastern Studies program at the University of Michigan. We went out to dinner to celebrate and talk about our plans. We wanted to be in Ann Arbor to look for an apartment and get settled at least a month before the start of the semester, which meant we would leave New York around early December.

Barbara immediately started planning the details of moving our furniture and belongings. "Should we contact a moving company?"

"Probably, but if it's too expensive, we should look into renting a U-Haul instead."

"We'll also need to buy a car," she pointed out. In New York City, we used the bus or subway to go everywhere. We had no need for a car. In fact, having one would have been a burden; we'd have to worry about where to park it and pay for insurance and maintenance. But in a college town, where public transportation was not necessarily so rampant and reliable, having a car would be essential.

The next day, Barbara called a moving company to check their prices. They had a minimum price, which was very expensive, given that we had very little furniture, so we decided to go with the U-Haul option. The only problem was Barbara didn't have a driver's license yet, and I obviously couldn't drive both a truck and a car at the same time.

Fortunately, Doug and Charlene came to the rescue. They agreed to drive the U-Haul while I would drive the car, which we had not yet purchased. Doug even offered to help load and unload our furniture. In return, we offered to buy an airline ticket for them for their return trip to New York.

We had been looking at cars even before we heard the news from Michigan, and in November, after we got the acceptance letter, we hurriedly bought a Simca, an inexpensive French car. Then, a few days later, a friend told us it was difficult to find garages that could repair Simcas. We were worried we had been too hasty in buying a car before we did our research. Since we had not yet picked up the car and driven it off the lot, we hoped we could cancel our purchase.

We went to the salesman and asked to be released from our contract, but he refused. He told us this was a binding contract and the dealership owner had never canceled a contract before. At that, we became very anxious and asked to speak with the owner. At first, the owner told us the same thing: he was not in the habit of canceling a sale once a contract has been signed; but, when we pleaded with him, and he saw we were really scared, he agreed to cancel the sale. This was our first experience of buying a car, and we had no idea a contract was binding. We thought buying a car was like purchasing any store item. You can return it within a certain period of time. This was what I had learned nine years earlier when I first bought stuff in American stores. We were naïve but lucky we had a car dealer kind enough to cancel the sale.

We had wanted a small car from the start, one with a reputation for fuel economy and reliability. After our Simca fiasco, we went to look at a Volkswagen Bug. We liked what we saw, but the salesman told us in order to get financing, we needed to have a credit history, which neither of us had. He suggested we get someone, like a parent, to co-sign the loan. We called Papa, who was more than happy to help. He came out from Carbondale in late November and went with us to the Volkswagen dealer. We purchased a green Volkswagen on November 25, just two days before leaving New York City for Ann Arbor.

We picked up the U-Haul on the evening of November 26, and the next morning, we loaded the truck with Doug's help. We were on our way to Ann Arbor by noon. The feeling of freedom Barbara and I experienced as we left the city was indescribable. I drove our Volkswagen, and Doug drove the truck in front of us, with Charlene and her maps sitting beside him.

As we got on Interstate 80 in Pennsylvania, our car suddenly stopped. Our first thought was they had sold us a defective car. With no other options, we decided to wait for Doug to notice we were no longer behind him and double back for us.

However, Doug, who wore thick glasses and had to focus on the road ahead of him, soon disappeared around a curve. We sat there wondering when he would realize we were no longer behind them.

About twenty minutes later, Doug reappeared and parked the truck behind us. I got out of the car and jokingly said, "I thought you'd get to Ann Arbor before realizing we weren't behind you anymore."

"What happened?" he asked.

"The car just stopped. The engine won't start."

"When you picked up the car, did you fill it up?"

"No, should I have?"

"When you get a new car, the dealer doesn't fill the tank," he explained. "They give you just enough gas to drive home or to a gas station." We were surprised and felt a bit foolish.

"We didn't know that, and we're nowhere near a gas station. I haven't seen one for a while. What should we do?"

"I saw a gas station a little up the road. I'll go fill a tank and bring it back. It should be enough for you to drive there and fill it all the way up."

After filling up at the gas station, we agreed for the rest of the trip, we would drive in front, and Doug would follow our little green Volkswagen.

The idea when you buy a car, you need to go fill gas was news to me. In Beirut and Albany, I was always a passenger in a car and gas-filling was not part of my car experience. Even in Iowa City when I drove my parents' car occasionally, I never had to fill gas. Filling a car with gas, or looking under the hood, or inspecting the tires, or even getting a car washed was never part of my car experience. Barbara, who did not drive, knew even less about cars than I did.

38. Exploring the Realm of the Mind

AS WE GOT CLOSER TO THE BUSY UNIVERSITY TOWN OF ANN Arbor, we saw many Volkswagens, and, like ours, a great many were green. There were a lot of traffic lights, pedestrians, and lane changes, so Barbara and I became concerned we would lose the U-Haul in traffic. We needed to stop and talk to Doug.

We turned the corner from Huron onto Main Street and saw there were several available parking spots, so we pulled into one and parked. We were sure Doug would see us do this and do the same. But as Doug got closer, another green Volkswagen pulled out of the space in front of us. Before we could get out and flag down Doug, he drove the U-Haul right past us, following the other Volkswagen!

We decided to wait for Doug to notice his error. We had a good spot near campus, which he was apt to return to. As we expected, the U-Haul soon returned. Doug hopped out and said, "When the guy pulled into an alley to park his car, I knew it wasn't you, so I backtracked."

At long last, we reached the Bell Tower Hotel where we would stay. Tired and relieved to finally get out of the vehicles, we checked in and immediately started looking for an apartment, since we needed to drop off our furniture and get rid of the U-Haul.

The bulletin board at the student union had an advertisement for the Medford Apartments about eight minutes away from campus. We headed over and a tall, soft-spoken man dressed in overalls and who looked like a farmer showed us a one-bedroom apartment. We loved it: it was clean, spacious, and bright. It felt like a mansion compared to our cell-sized New York apartment.

We rented it on the spot, but the manager told us he still needed to finish some work on the kitchen appliances and paint the living room.

He said it would be ready in a week, and in the meantime, we could stay in a furnished apartment on the first floor and store our furniture in the basement. It didn't take long to unload the furniture and return the U-Haul.

Doug and Charlene returned to New York the next day, and Barbara headed to the University of Michigan personnel office to look for a job. There were many posted positions for which she qualified, and she decided to apply for a secretarial job in the math department. It paid $450 a month, about what both of us had been making put together in New York. Barbara got the job and started right away, working for George Piranian and Lamberto Cesari, a renowned Italian mathematician.

Before the semester started, I went to meet with Professor McCarus, chair of the department of Middle Eastern Studies, for an advising session and to find out what courses I should take. I was hoping to find classes on Middle Eastern history or thought, but the only classes offered in the department for the winter trimester were a course on the Quran with James Bellamy and another on Arabic with Ernest McCarus.

Bellamy's class involved students reading an Arabic text and translating as they read. He never lectured in class. I could definitely read Arabic, but had some difficulty translating without an Arabic-English dictionary.

After several sessions, I told Barbara, "I'm not sure what the goal of Bellamy's class is. I know I can read Arabic, and with good dictionary, I can translate most of what I'm reading, but what does it have to do with learning about the Middle East as a region?"

"Maybe you should give it some time."

"Okay, but I don't think anything will change."

"Well what about your other class, with McCarus?"

"Well, it's a course on Arabic. Most of the students don't know Arabic very well, and some don't know it at all. Most of what he's teaching, I learned in elementary school in Beirut."

I stuck with it for another trimester, taking courses in Islamic history and Arabic literature, but by the end of the spring session, I had decided I didn't enjoy the subjects I was studying and I wanted to leave the program.

I was reading Teilhard de Chardin's *The Future of Man*, which posed the idea human evolution was not only biological, but also cultural. The entire human family was culturally converging toward the Omega Point, the Kingdom of God on Earth. This cultural convergence was teleological, goal-directed, and enhanced by education. The notion of understanding human progress in terms of goal-directed improvements in education and advancements in knowledge acquisition intrigued me.

My focus began to shift to education as a field where I could contribute to the cause of advancing human progress. But then I wondered how this could work practically, given the miserable conditions I had seen through my work as a social worker in New York: young men loitering, standing idly on street corners, wasting their existence; mothers struggling to feed their families; and children who couldn't read or write.

I told Barbara of my thoughts: "How can humanity progress when a huge segment of society has been left behind in the gutters?"

"By lifting those people up from their poor conditions," she said.

"Absolutely, you're right. If we help the poorest and more disadvantaged move forward and improve their quality of life, then our entire society will be elevated as well."

When I had been working as a caseworker, Barbara and I had frequently talked about how education was the key to lifting children on welfare from the poverty they were raised in. But obviously, whatever we were doing in the schools was not working. I was convinced improving the way teachers teach was vital to progress and to elevating the human condition.

I decided gaining a better understanding of how people acquire knowledge and skills in an increasingly technological environment was essential for developing more effective strategies for teaching and learning. I had no background in educational theory or the psychology of learning and teaching, so I decided to take a course in educational psychology with Robert Dixon.

The course was a general introduction to theories of human development as applied to learning styles and the instructional process. I was very excited about everything I learned in that course and was now absolutely certain I wanted to focus on the psychology of learning, knowledge acquisition and instructional practice. I decided to change my program of study and officially enrolled in the School of Education.

While Barbara enjoyed working in the Math Department, she was unhappy with the environment and particularly with her supervisor, a micromanager who got on everyone's nerves. She interviewed for and got a job at the Mental Health Research Institute (MHRI) working for Manfred Kochen. The new job came with a promotion in her job title and a substantial salary increase as Kochen's research assistant.

Shortly after Barbara started working for Kochen, he wanted to know more about her and what had brought her to Michigan. She told him about our meeting and courtship in New York and how we had come to Michigan when I was accepted as a graduate student. She also told him about my interest in educational psychology. At that, Kochen said he would be interested in meeting me and had her set up an appointment for us.

When I entered Kochen's office, I saw a small-framed man with bushy grayish-white hair sitting at his desk and writing. Barbara introduced me as "Nasib," but told him I went by "Albert" professionally. He greeted me with a smile and a handshake and addressed me as "Nasib." After I sat down and he sat back comfortably in his chair, he asked about my research interests.

"I'm interested in modeling and improving the learning and knowledge acquisition process."

He seemed excited by my response. "I'm very interested in learning theory and how the brain stores and retrieves information; perhaps we have a common interest here."

A couple of weeks later, Kochen offered me a research assistantship in his lab and offered to be my graduate advisor, which I was delighted to accept.

Fred Kochen was an applied mathematician who primarily worked on mathematical models in the behavioral sciences. He was a prolific author with some two hundred and fifty publications to his name, including multiple books. He had an active, curious mind, and seemed to always be at his desk writing.

As I got to know him well, I found he had a broad range of interests and unlimited energy. His interdisciplinary approach to scientific problems, unbound by the focus of a single discipline, was contagious, and it affected the way I approached problems in my future research.

The more I got to know Fred Kochen, the more I was fascinated by his active mind, his curiosity, and his incessant ability to ask profound questions about difficult research problems. Under his mentorship, my interest in modeling the learning processes of individuals and communities deepened.

At MHRI, I became increasingly aware of the importance of getting research grants—which would enable me to do research in my specific area of choice—and also of the fact being able to list a research grant award on my curriculum vitae (CV) would improve my chances of getting an academic research position in an extremely competitive job market. As part of this newfound awareness, I wrote a grant proposal for the U.S. Department of Education to support my dissertation research work, in which I would investigate the effects of shifts in a person's mental model when they are faced with a problem to solve or a lesson to learn.

Surprisingly, I had a great deal of trouble getting Kochen to help me write the proposal, or to even review what I had written. The only thing he agreed to do was to attach his CV to the submitted proposal.

When the proposal was funded, he told me he would have to be the principal investigator (PI) on the research grant, saying MHRI did not allow graduate students to be a PI. I felt frustrated by the MHRI policy; being credited with getting a proposal funded, particularly when I had written the proposal with no help at all, would have looked good on my CV.

I was very hurt, and Barbara and I discussed my leaving. She advised me to talk to Kochen and explain I needed to be listed as a PI on the proposal as it would help me later, when I was looking for jobs. I went to see him the next day, and he agreed we could be co-principal investigators.

My doctoral research was focused on how people learn to cope in ill-defined situations by shifting problem representation. These are situations in our lives where there is a perceived problem, but it cannot be stated precisely. These ill-defined problems tend to be most of the situations we encounter in our daily lives, and so we need to learn how to cope with them in order to survive and succeed. By studying and improving how humans learn, acquire knowledge, shift representations, and solve daily problems, I sought to improve the human condition in general.

While working on my dissertation research, I took psychology courses in cognition and memory, which helped me expand my research focus to explore how learners process information. I was beginning to perceive a relationship between human information processing and a learner's interaction with an emerging information technology—the computer.

The research I did for my dissertation and with Kochen led to many publications and technical reports. He and I coauthored and published three journal articles on the subject of learning and knowledge acquisition. The paper that got the most attention was on measuring a learner's performance by the quality of the questions asked.

With a PhD in hand and a goal in mind, it was now time for me to find a faculty position where I could pursue my mission of computer modeling to understand and improve the way humans learn and acquire knowledge. The job market in academia—and particularly in the behavioral sciences and educational psychology—was dismal. On the other hand, academic jobs in information science were somewhat more plentiful. My information science credentials were mostly from the research I had done with Kochen; I had no coursework in the area. Thus, the only way I could land a job in the field of information was through Kochen's network of colleagues, so I went to him for help.

He told me he had a colleague at Georgia Tech, Vladimir Slamecka, who was the director of the School of Information and Computer Science (ICS) there, and he had asked Kochen if he had any graduating students looking for an assistant professor position. Kochen offered to recommend me to Slamecka, which he did.

He also mentioned a friend at the University of Pittsburgh had told him of an open assistant professor position. He suggested I send my CV to his contact at Pittsburgh, which I did.

Two weeks later, I got a call from Slamecka inviting me down to Atlanta for an interview. As the plane flew over the city, I saw it was shrouded in a thick green canopy. Atlanta, Georgia was a city dressed in old, established trees, shrubs, flowers, and expansive green spaces. I was totally awed and thought to myself, "This beautiful city would be a great bonus if I get this job." I couldn't wait to call Barbara and tell her about all the trees.

In the course of my presentation on my research and the subsequent question-answer and discussion sessions, I noticed some people were friendly and supportive of my work, while others were critical and dismissive. I immediately realized there was some kind of rift in the department—those who supported Slamecka's goal of building the department aligned with his vision of an emerging information society, and those who vehemently opposed it—and my work fell into one of the two camps.

Later that evening, I had dinner with Slamecka. He told me he thought my research was very relevant to what they wanted to do in ICS and if they decided to make me an offer, he would want me to work on a project he was directing on computer-assisted learning and information processing, including acquisition, storage, and retrieval. It sounded like it was right up my alley, and I told him as much.

Exactly three weeks after my visit to Atlanta, I got a letter offering me a position as an assistant professor. Right after I accepted the offer from Georgia Tech, Kochen's contact at Pittsburgh called with an offer. I told him it was too late. I felt like I was on top of the world.

39. Building a Life in the Realm of the Mind

WE PACKED UP OUR APARTMENT AND DROVE TO ATLANTA IN early August. We found a large two-bedroom apartment at the Lenox Forest apartments, within one block of the Lenox Mall. Georgia Tech paid to move our furniture, and the truck arrived three days after we signed the lease on the apartment.

In late August, I went to meet with Slamecka and get the keys to my office. He introduced me to some of the people I would be working with on the learning technology project, the Audio-Graphic Learning Facility, or ALF. ALF was a computer-assisted instructional system that stored an instructor's lectures, including both text and graphics, which a student could retrieve, review, and study at his or her own pace.

Among the people working on the project was Pete Jensen, a research engineer, who was responsible for the ICS computer laboratory. Jensen came across as a nice guy, with a gentle demeanor and a kind voice. He spent some time explaining what the project was all about. John Gehl was another researcher on the project who helped write the reports for many of Slamecka's projects.

One day during my first year there, Slamecka came into my office and said we would be getting funding for a project on an information system for internal medicine and we'd be working with a doctor from Emory University on it.

"I want you to read the proposal for the project and get ready to work on it starting next month," he said. "Also, I want you to go see Pranas Zunde; he has a funded project he could use your help on."

At first, I was surprised, because he didn't seem interested in the research I wanted to pursue. I told him I had projects I was continuing with Kochen, as well as ideas for new projects that would continue what

I had started on my dissertation. In response, he asked if I had funding for them and explained, if not, I should work on funded projects.

At that point, I began putting two and two together. I had been hired to work on Slamecka's and Zunde's funded projects because that was where my salary was coming from. In fact, they were the only ICS faculty members with funded projects. I was very grateful to Slamecka for having given me a position, but now I felt like a hired hand and like I didn't have time to continue the research I had started with Kochen.

I told Barbara, "Compared to the academic, scholarly environment in Michigan, this place is a shop, 'Slamecka's Shop,' where I'm expected to produce work for pay and not pursue my own interests. I have to figure out a way to liberate myself by getting my own funding. The problem is I don't have any time during the day to work on my own projects and proposals; I even have to help write proposals that will extend the work I'm doing for Slamecka and Zunde!" I liked both of them personally, but their demands weren't going to further my own career.

It didn't take me long to notice friction between some of the senior faculty and Slamecka. It was possible this seeming conflict stemmed from the fact Slamecka was always on their cases about not getting funding for their research. Because I was working with Slamecka on his projects, and because Slamecka had great respect for Kochen, he saw me as one of "the good guys." I made sure to maintain that friendly relationship and also nurture similar positive relations with the other faculty members. But, as an untenured assistant professor, I was caught in a trap between the Slamecka–Zunde axis and the senior faculty.

When I joined ICS in September 1973, the faculty was eclectic, with varied backgrounds. Slamecka had a vision—somewhat mercurial and, to my mind, vague—that had to do with the "future of information," and he hired people in tenure-track positions that would fit with his vision. Except for one computer scientist from Stanford who worked on artificial intelligence, the 1973–74 faculty came from backgrounds that included philosophy, linguistics, physics, library/information science, psychology, applied mathematics, industrial engineering, electrical engineering, and behavioral science.

This mixture came with both positives and negatives. It made for very interesting research collaborations, be it in human information processing or computer issues dealing with retrieval, processing, and storage. On the other hand, it also created problems in how the individual faculty member's background and training dictated their approach, often leading to disagreements on the proper methodology to tackle a problem.

It also led to especially strong disagreements on what the goal of this new "information discipline" should be in general and of the school in particular. This was a fundamental disagreement that caused the senior faculty to divide into two camps: those who wanted to move the school toward strictly computer science, and those who sang the praises of the broader information science. For an untenured assistant professor, faculty meetings were often tense and even downright unbearable, particularly when there was a crucial vote. Abstaining was not an acceptable option and a minute felt like an hour.

At that time, there was no way of telling for certain which direction the field would move in. If you looked around the academic world, you could see the footprints of computer science growing larger.

At Georgia Tech, the demand for computer science and programming courses was on the rise. I later learned many within the department feared if ICS ignored this demand, the School of Electrical Engineering would capitalize on it.

It didn't take long for ICS's trajectory to begin to take on a very clear path toward computer science over the next few years. I may very well have been the last non-computer science hire. Information science and the Slamecka vision were losing.

To Slamecka, anything that had to do with "information" or "knowledge" belonged in ICS, so he asked me to develop and teach a course on how humans process and manage information.

I excitedly prepared my lectures and selected the readings for this graduate class, using it to rekindle and further develop my passion for improving the human condition through effective learning strategies. To make the course relevant and interesting to students whose main interest was computer technology and computer science, I focused on human information processing in technologically changing environments.

In preparing my lectures, I found I had to draw on many different fields of study, including computer science, cognitive psychology, learning theory, philosophy, linguistics, cybernetics, ergonomics/human factors, mathematics, and decision theory. This was not difficult, given the interdisciplinary environment Slamecka had created in ICS.

Developing the course's multidisciplinary content gave me the freedom to pursue my lofty goals of understanding how people adapt to their technologically changing environment. This was when I started exploring research questions about the interactions between humans and computers. When I had time, I worked on a proposal on this subject, which eventually got funded. I also developed the first course in the nation on human-computer interaction.

Being in this interdisciplinary milieu was very important, as it allowed thinking outside of the disciplinary box, which lead to innovation. At both MHRI and ICS, I had been in research milieus that encouraged interdisciplinary "borrowing." In the early to mid-seventies, Thomas S. Kuhn's *The Structure of Scientific Revolutions* and his ideas about "paradigm shifts" were very popular among scientists. Kuhn argued paradigm shifts happened at the edge of a discipline—where you were free to borrow methods, theories, and concepts from other fields—not in the course of "normal science." This was "revolutionary science," and many of us imagined it was what we were doing.

The interdisciplinary atmosphere at Georgia Tech was primarily limited to our school until a very forward-looking Regents Professor from civil engineering named Paul Mayer established a faculty lounge in the middle of campus. Around the end of 1974, he used the lower level of the library to provide bagels and coffee for faculty every morning. Within two months, it became so popular he decided to provide catered sandwiches and drinks for lunch as well. Mayer convinced the administration to fund the effort, and soon, the lower level of the library became "the faculty lounge." It quickly became a very important space for sharing ideas across departments and schools. The lounge was where many faculty collaborations, research ideas and joint papers were initiated. An ICS professor, Lucio Chiaraviglio, and I coauthored a paper for *The Journal of Exact Philosophy*, which we conceived, drafted, and completed in the lounge. It may very well be the Georga Tech interdisciplinary tendency had its beginnings in this lounge.

During my first year at Georgia Tech, Barbara and I became close friends with Phil and Margit Siegman. Phil, a professor at ICS, was very bright, but had a cynical view of the research being done in the school.

While I was engaged in pursuing my professional activities at Georgia Tech, Barbara and I were quietly building our life in Atlanta. She enrolled at Georgia State University and completed her BA in art. We made many new friends, including Jimmy Gough and his gentle, Southern-mannered wife, who made Barbara and me feel very welcome in Atlanta. We also often hung out with the Siegmans, enjoying foreign films and political conversations.

Barbara and I joined the parish of the Cathedral of Christ the King, where we met Father Lopez, a young, enthusiastic priest. We nurtured a close relationship with him, one that intersected friendship and spiritual advisement.

Since our marriage in New York had not been in a church, we decided to be remarried in the church in Atlanta. We asked Father Lopez to officially baptize Barbara into the Catholic Church. He agreed to guide Barbara through the catechism, and soon after, she was baptized and later confirmed into the church. After that, we also asked him to remarry us as two baptized Catholics into the Catholic Church, which we did at the Cathedral of Christ the King. This beautiful neo-Gothic church would also be the location for the marriage of our son, David, to Sejal Shah in 2003.

Other than the two witnesses Father Lopez brought, no one else was invited to our second wedding. We decided to make it a private ceremony, renewing our vows to each other and to God alone. In the years ahead, this story of our two marriage ceremonies would surprise people and provide fascinating conversations.

We never discussed our faith with most of our colleagues and friends. I often felt academic culture was foreign to my belief and faith. I could not have religious or theological discussions—or even philosophical ones—with my colleagues, as most of them were either not religious or outright anti-religion. I felt awkward about bringing up topics I felt passionately about, so I largely did not even touch on the subject. My professional and spiritual life coexisted but never mingled. I enjoyed being an academic making impactful scholarly contributions, and the university provided me with the milieu to pursue this goal. I also wanted to continue nurturing my interest for asking deep theological and spiritual questions; my family life gave me the venue, and my church the community to pursue this personal passion. I was totally comfortable with my life of science being separate from my life of philosophical and theological inquiry. Both life passions allowed me to reach and work in the realm of the mind that began for me with my love of reading going back to my Beirut Baguettes nights.

The promise I had made to myself when I left Lebanon in 1960 seemed to have been fulfilled. I had a career in the realm of the mind I enjoyed. My path was always morphing and evolving. Eventually, my research would shift from education, cognition, and the behavioral sciences to human-computer interaction. When I left Georgia Tech years later, I knew the words I had spoken around the dining room table in Beruit years before had come true.

I am happy with my life. As a Lebanese American, a life time academic and a Catholic, I am of two cultures, both of which make my life complete.

Epilogue:
Return to Beirut

*I*N 1971, PAPA, MAMA, LEILA, AND MARIA WENT BACK TO LEBA-
non when Papa went on sabbatical as a visiting professor at AUB.
After one academic year back in Carbondale, Papa accepted an offer
in the fall of 1973 to become the president of Beirut University College
(BUC). He remained in that position for eight years before coming back
to the United States.

We kept in touch regularly by phone and correspondence. Then, in
the winter of 1974, Mama wrote a long letter to Barbara and me insisting
we visit them in Lebanon. Papa repeated the invitation when he came to
visit us in the spring, and another letter from Mama informed us everyone in Lebanon was looking forward to seeing us that coming summer.

The more I thought about going back to Lebanon after fourteen
years, the more my enthusiasm for the idea grew. The thought of recon-
necting with childhood friends and relatives filled me with anticipation.
Barbara, who had never been outside the United States, was thrilled
about the idea of making her first foreign trip. It was an opportunity we
couldn't refuse.

All we had to do was get there. My parents were living in the spacious BUC penthouse, and we could stay with them. They had shipped
their own car from the United States to Lebanon, so transportation
would be taken care of as well. In late spring, we decided to make a trip
to Lebanon in August, with a side excursion to Egypt.

We flew from Atlanta to London. In London, Barbara and I got on a
flight to Beirut, with only a short stop in Athens.

As our flight approached Beirut in the early evening, I looked down
from the plane's window, dazed by jetlag and the cloud of cigarette

smoke that surrounded me, and saw the glittering skyline of a sprawl-ing metropolis, the Beirut I had left as a boy of fourteen. As my eyes started tearing uncontrollably, I wondered, Would this be the same Bei-rut I left all those years ago? After all, I had changed, why not the city?

In the fourteen years since I had left, I had become an American, undergoing a total cultural transformation. In Beirut, we had been socially privileged, not because we were wealthy, but because my fam-ily belonged to the intellectual and social elite. In Albany, we had been nobodies, and we had to build a new life. In Iowa City, I became a Cath-olic. In New York, I met the love of my life and got married. In Ann Arbor and Atlanta, I forged a career that would enable me to make a positive impact, focusing on the way people learn and interact with technology.

But then, my thoughts turned back to the city below me, the city of my youth. As the plane got closer to the ground, I could see the area of Beirut where I had grown up. On the left was the seashore campus of AUB. Adjacent to it was my primary school and the Ras Beirut neigh-borhood where we had lived.

I pointed these out to Barbara, and I could tell she was getting excited. "I can't wait 'til we get down there, and I can see the neighbor-hood where you grew up—your childhood playground—up close," she said. "I have a feeling seeing where you grew up is going to tell me a lot about you."

The plane landed and taxied to the middle of the tarmac, where it came to a stop. As we exited the plane, climbing down the stairs, my parents were there at the bottom with a car and a driver. Because Papa was the president of a college, he had special privileges, so Mr. Had-dad, an important executive at the airport and the husband of Mama's cousin, took our passports to process them. We didn't even have to go through customs.

As we entered the airport visitors' lounge, an entourage of smiling relatives and family friends greeted us. The only two I immediately rec-ognized were my sister Leila and my cousin Habib, who had visited Barbara and me in Atlanta eight months earlier. In Lebanese fashion, Barbara and I were greeted with hugs and air kisses on both cheeks.

I had not seen so many relatives in one place in all my fourteen years in America. I was elated to see them, but it also emphasized just how different my life in Beirut had been compared to what I had become accustomed to in Albany and Iowa City and New York and Ann Arbor and Atlanta. It reminded me in Ras Beirut, you couldn't walk along the streets for a minute without meeting at least a dozen people you knew. Our extended family lived within walking distance of one another, and I remembered how we would visit friends and relatives every day, a practice that was absent from our life in America.

As we drove to Beirut University College and my parents' penthouse on top of the largest building on campus, my first impression was one of amazement at how narrow and winding the streets were. I told Barbara, "During all my years in America, whenever I thought of the streets of Beirut, I thought of very wide streets and large sidewalks. But they're nothing like how I remember!"

"These streets are small," she agreed, "and with the way people park on the street, two cars couldn't pass each other."

Just as she was commenting on the narrowness of the streets, we came to an intersection with no traffic light or stop or yield signs. Cars were coming from both sides of the cross street, but our driver didn't seem to be slowing or planning to stop or yield. I thought we'd hit each other for sure. But then, in the blink of an eye, we were safely on the other side of the intersection. Barbara took a deep breath and said, "I guess when you drive here, you have to know how to play the game of chicken."

"Yes, driving in Beirut is very different from what we're used to back home."

We entered BUC from an entrance that connected directly with a seven-story building. We took an elevator to the top floor, and as we entered the penthouse, the first thing we noticed was the amazing view of the brightly lit Beirut skyline. Mama introduced us to Maryam, the kitchen maid, and Antoinette, the housemaid. Maryam was tiny, and her smile made us feel so welcome. She seemed genuinely delighted to see me. I felt like the prodigal son returning. Antoinette was memorable for her obsessive, almost compulsive, need to clean everything in sight.

The next morning, I took Barbara on a walk around Ras Beirut to show her all the primary sites of my childhood. We set off through the BUC campus, immediately noticing how the campus was surrounded and enclosed by a solid wall—very unlike most universities in the States. It was beautiful, with walkways, green lawns, flowerbeds, and classroom and dormitory buildings constructed from colorful stones from the Lebanese mountains. As we strolled toward the front gate, we saw students sitting on benches reading and conversing.

We exited the front gate and walked toward the part of Ras Beirut where we had once lived and where I spent my childhood. I almost immediately knew where I was in the city and how best to navigate the streets. It was like I had stored the information in the environment itself, and all I had to do to know where to go next was retrieve it from the environment. It was an amazing experience that made me feel very comfortable with my surroundings. I felt totally at home.

We strolled down busy Hamra Street with all its shops, restaurants and cafes. We zigzagged along the narrow Beirut streets, sometimes having to walk in the street to get around the many shoppers and the cars parked half on the curb and half on the street.

Barbara marveled no one got parking tickets or even seemed to notice the confusion this created. She commented that, to her, downtown Beirut was like what would happen if you took a busy New York City street and compacted it down into a much smaller area. It was fascinating to see Beirut through Barbara's eyes. Everything seemed simulatensously new and fascinating and also old and familiar.

Unlike New York's tall skyscrapers, Hamra Street had much smaller buildings housing both shops and apartments. Residents sat above everyone on balconies, watching the clatter of people below. People talked and laughed while going in and out of shops selling everything you could imagine, making a constant buzz of sounds.

As I began to hear Lebanese Arabic being spoken all around me, a feeling of easy comfort settled around me. The pace of activity on this busy street seemed slower than what I was now used to. My personality seemed to become gentler, and I felt much more comfortably tolerant of people around me.

I also realized speaking and thinking in English was now much easier for me than doing the same in Arabic. This was somewhat surprising, and reminded me of my early days in Albany, struggling to speak and think in English. After a while though, as I heard more and more Lebanese Arabic being spoken, conversations in Arabic became much easier for me.

We walked from Hamra to Artois Street, and suddenly there was the Halim Hanna building. I pointed to the second floor and said, "That's where we lived. See that balcony? That's where Leila and I played and she chased me with the rug beater. That window leads to the dining room, where Mama and Papa announced we would be moving to America." My voice cracked at the emotional memory. I could almost see the scene that had played out fourteen years ago.

Barbara hugged me and said, "These are precious memories; you should treasure them."

Then I looked across the street, hoping to see the tiny old grocery store where I had gotten candy. It was gone. A newer small building stood in its place. I pointed to the building and told Barbara, "That's where Im Jozef's store used to be and where I got my favorite chocolate wafer."

My grandparents had lived in a three-story building that used to be across the street from our building. It was also gone, and in its place was a multi-story condominium building. I pointed it out to Barbara, adding, "I feel a little sad, but I guess progress has to go on."

We walked a block down the street so I could show Barbara the Nassif house, where we used to play marbles in the front yard. It, too, was gone, and in its place stood another large multi-story building.

I turned to Barbara with what must have been a dismayed expression, because she immediately said, "It's okay; after fourteen years, you would expect lots of changes." She then asked me to describe what the Nassif house had looked like, and I described the large, one-story house with French windows and the large front yard with the beautiful flower garden, both of which were now gone.

Despite all the new buildings, stores, and cafés, I could still see the outline of the Beirut I had known. It seemed like a good metaphor for all of the changes I had experienced as well.

We continued walking west toward AUB, and there was the Uncle Sam's Restaurant in front of the AUB main gate, just the way I remembered it. I told Barbara about how often we frequented the restaurant, the only place in Beirut that served hot dogs.

As we walked along Bliss Street toward my old school, I could still see parts of the buried tracks from where the tramway used to go, traveling from downtown to the Beirut lighthouse.

The International College, where I spent the first eight years of my education, looked very much the same as I remembered it, though the buildings seemed much smaller than I remembered them being. I told Barbara funny stories of my antics there.

We soon made our way back at BUC, where we met my parents, who were taking us to Brummana, where I had spent many of my childhood summers, for the weekend. Along the way, we stopped to see many of the sights, including the Shrine of Our Lady of Lebanon at Harrisa, where we had an extraordinary Lebanese lunch made entirely with local ingredients.

We arrived in Brummana in the afternoon, and Barbara and I immediately set off to take a walk into town so I could point out some of the familiar sites from my childhood. We first went to the Brummana High School and the school's tennis courts, where I learned to play tennis. I showed her the house on the school's campus we shared with Uncle Fuad, Auntie Ellen, and their family for several summers.

Walking with Barbara through the streets of Brummana—with its quaint, colorful shops and cafés—and breathing in the fresh mountain air filled my mind with warm, pleasant memories of summers in Lebanon, when we left school for three months of uninterrupted fun in the mountain villages.

Taking in all the fresh air, the beautiful scenery and the serenity of the village, Barbara said, "I could truly see us spending every summer here for the rest of our lives."

I concurred with a heartfelt, "I would love that."

On our return to the house, we all sat on the balcony for tea and the mandatory pastries. That night, we slept soundly with the windows open to let in the cool mountain air.

Early the next morning, my parents took us to Dhour El Schweir, our family's ancestral home and the Lebanese mountain village where we spent most of our summers in Lebanon. It was only a fifteen-minute drive from Brummana and sat on a higher mountain ridge.

The summer home of Papa's cousin, Ammo Jamil, was in Dhour, and we stopped at his house. We spent a pleasant hour reminiscing and telling old stories.

At one point, Jamil suddenly looked at me with a smile and said, "Look over there." He pointed to a hat rack near the door with an old, worn-out, and yellowing cap hanging on it. "Do you recognize it?"

"No," I responded honestly.

"That is the cap you left here the last time you came to visit fifteen years ago. It's been there ever since; I've never removed it. I always hoped you would come back one day, be sitting right where you are now."

I thought to myself, "I have nothing left from my childhood here; it would be great if I could take the cap back with me."

Aloud, I said, "Wow, can I have it back?"

"Absolutely not," he said with strong emphasis. "It has become part of the décor."

I was disappointed, but decided not to push the issue, as I was now a mere visitor.

After driving around town and showing Barbara the main square and the cafés where we spent many of our summer days, we drove down to see the Badres' ancestral home. The house was situated at the edge of the village, not far from the family gravesite. It was vacant and in utter disrepair.

We returned to Brummana that afternoon and were greeted by many of my aunts, uncles, and cousins, as well as several of Mama and Papa's friends. The party was held outside on the terrace, surrounded by huge Lebanese pines, whose fragrance reminded me of my childhood summers in the mountains. Chairs and tables were scattered across the terrace, and a large table in the center was filled with numerous Lebanese dishes. A nearby side table held drinks.

Because I had not seen many of these relatives and family friends in over fourteen years, we spent quite a bit of time chatting, both retelling stories of yesteryear and catching up on all that had happened since. Unfortunately, we didn't sing as we so often did at such gatherings, because my parents' summer house did not yet have a piano.

This was Barbara's first time experiencing one of our large family gatherings, and she seemed to really enjoy it. She was amazed everyone spoke English with her, and their kindness made her feel very welcome and completely at home.

It was a wonderful reunion party.

We spent the next few days going on various tours of Lebanon. I wanted Barbara to see the full extent of the country's history, culture, and natural beauty, and she fully embraced the opportunity.

At one point during a tour, when we were enjoying a quiet moment in a garden, I said to Barbara, "Remember when we were in Brummana, and you said you could see us spending every summer in Lebanon? I want to do that. I want us to come back here every year."

"Well then, why couldn't we?" she asked. "Let's do it."

That same day, we had lunch at a restaurant right on the water of the Sufa River—a place I remembered from my childhood. The restaurant's long tables sat on an outside terrace under a canopy of grapevines. It was lovely to simply sit and breathe in the fresh mountain air. Streams of rushing water ran alongside the restaurant, and patrons could place bottles of soda and beer in baskets in the water near the tables. It was wonderful to pluck a can of Coke from the stream next to my chair, and sure enough, it was ice cold.

Some of our relatives joined us for lunch, and in response, Barbara remarked, "Now I know why all the restaurants in Lebanon have long tables . . . because you never eat alone!"

We laughed, but also realized how different and uniquely family-oriented Lebanon was compared to the United States, where, due to peoples' mobility and the size of the country, it's common to live far from family.

Soon after that, Barbara and I went on a short jaunt to Cairo, Egypt. We had an amazing experience, going on a private tour of the Cairo Museum and the Giza Pyramids. We went to the Old Cairo *souk* district, where the father of one of my Georgia Tech students, Mr. Muhsin, used his haggling skills to bargain for alabaster jars and silver and copper inlaid trays for us.

In the evening, we went to Sahara City, an entertainment venue in a large tent in the desert thirty minutes' drive from Cairo. We saw a popular Lebanese singer perform and watched the *tanoura*, an Egyptian whirling-skirt dance. When we left Sahara City at two in the morning, we looked up to see a beautiful crescent moon hanging over the night's sky.

On our final day in Cairo, I made a mistake. We had been told not to drink water because it could make us sick. In the late afternoon, we went back to our hotel for a cool drink after a day of wandering around. The waiter convinced me to try their signature drink, a fruit soda. It was delicious, but I didn't realize it had ice in it. The ill effects of the ice didn't show up until the evening of the next day, when we arrived back in Beirut. I ended up being rather sick for a few days.

Two days before we returned to Atlanta, I told my parents there was one more trip I needed to make: to Dakkoun, the Maronite village where two of our maids, Wasima and Shafia, lived.

Wasima and Shafia were so happy to see me they both started crying; when I saw their tears, my eyes also began to well up.

They both looked much older than I remembered or even would have expected. I knew they were poor and they and their families had suffered a great deal in life as a result. After we left that day, my mother told Barbara and me she and Papa had been sending them money.

Wasima and Shafia invited us into their living room and offered us Turkish coffee and cake. They didn't speak English, but they both told funny stories about my childhood in Arabic, which Mama translated for Barbara. Shafia recounted the tale of Im Josef and her "free candy," which, to my surprise, my parents didn't remember.

Because of the language barrier, they did not interact with Barbara very much. However, I did notice them frequently staring at her, and I could tell they were thinking, What a beautiful bride Nasib has brought back with him to Lebanon.

It was an emotional reunion and truly a gift for me to have all of the women I have loved the most gathered together in one room.

Back in Atlanta, Barbara and I vowed to henceforth spend our summers in Lebanon. We felt changing our cultural environment for a few months every year would be intellectually and spiritually enriching for both of us. Unfortunately, the Lebanese civil war broke out in the spring of 1975 and lasted for the next fifteen years, until 1990. Thus, our plans were shelved. We did go back to Lebanon a few times during that period, but not as often as either of us had hoped. Instead, I turned my attention back to my career, to our starting a family, and to living my Catholic spirituality.

Postscript:
The Present Day

40. Career

I KNEW IF I WANTED TO KEEP MY POSITION AS A PROFESSOR AT Georgia Tech, I needed to qualify for promotion and tenure. The "publish or perish" reality of the academic world hit me squarely in the face. Publishing in highly ranked journals was the most vital requirement for getting promotion and tenure, followed by getting letters of support from top people in my field. But to get such letters, you'd need to have made an impact and developed a reputation in your field. In addition, I needed to demonstrate success in getting grants and research funding.

I set out to publish and compete for research grants, and I succeeded in both. Among the people the promotion and tenure committee sought letters from was a reputed experimental psychologist and National Academy of Science member, George Miller. His letter, along with my list of publications and funding resulted in my promotion and tenure in 1980.

Not long before my promotion, I created a course at the request of IBM that explored the relationship between computers and their users. The course proved to be popular, and I offered it in many IBM locations worldwide. Seeing the success of this industry course, I created both graduate and undergraduate versions at Georgia Tech, calling both "Human Factors in Computer Systems." These were two of the first courses on the interaction between humans and computers ever offered in a college curriculum.

At that time, there was considerable scientific interest in the fields of ergonomics and human factors in engineering, but not so on the interactions between computer software and the end-user, primarily because the personal computer and graphic user interfaces had not yet been developed. Still, they were just around the corner.

Even though the idea of improving the interactions between users and computers was novel, I thought it would be helpful to organize a workshop to explore directions such a novel field would take. In 1980, I proposed organizing a workshop in the interdisciplinary area of the relationship between computer technology and people; the Army Research Institute awarded me a grant for it. The participants were all top experts from academia and industry research, and it was probably the first professional meeting of this type.

As a byproduct of this workshop, I coedited a book entitled *Directions in Human-Computer Interaction*. It was one of the very first books published in the field. Little did I realize or anticipate human-computer interaction would become a major field of research in computer science.

My career continued to evolve as I increasingly focused on humanizing computer technology. In 1997, I established and directed the master's degree program in human-computer interaction at Georgia Tech. It was the first interdisciplinary program of its kind in the country. Before I stepped down as its director in 2003, the program was featured in the *U.S. News and World Report* issue on Best Colleges and Programs and was attracting over three hundred applicants a year.

In 2002, I authored the book, *Shaping Web Usability: Interaction Design in Context*. It was a top seller in the usability area during the first five years of its publication.

41. Family

SEVEN YEARS AFTER WE GOT MARRIED, BARBARA AND I HAD our only child, David. David is a Biblical name meaning "beloved." My maternal grandfather's name was "Habib," which means "beloved" in Arabic. Thus, "David" is the English version of "Habib." In addition, Barbara's paternal grandfather's name was David, so it seemed perfect.

In 1980, my father retired from his position as president of Beirut University College, and he and my mother, as well as Leila and Maria, moved to live near us in Atlanta. My father passed away in 2010, and my mother still lives in Atlanta with my sister, Maria. Leila is now married and lives with her husband and two children near Des Moines, Iowa. My brother, Sami, became a banker and then later a real estate agent in Los Angeles. He and Janet have two children. Ramsey started his own business as a financial consultant in the health industry. While he had a nationwide clientele, he was based in Chicago for many years. He and his wife now live on St. Simon Island, Georgia, near his daughter and son-in-law, both of whom are doctors.

David, his wife Sejal, and their two sons, our grandchildren, Shawn and James, now live in Providence, Rhode Island, where he is a tenured professor of cognitive neuroscience at Brown University.

I left Georgia Tech in 2003, but continued to do usability consulting and visiting professorships around the world for many years. A few years ago, Barbara and I moved to Providence to be near our son and his family.

Forty-four years after I last saw her, I reconnected with Lorraine. I met her, her husband Conrad, and her mother in Atlanta while she was there for one of her children's wedding. Shortly after that, Barbara and I visited them at their home near Albany. During our visit, I learned

Lorraine was still a very devout Catholic and had gotten a graduate degree in Catholic theology.

I brought up my Catholic conversion and told her I was trying to deepen my prayer life. Two weeks later, I received a gift from her, a daily prayer book called *Give Us This Day*. I now subscribe to it and use the book in daily mass.

While visiting Lorraine, we went to Mrs. Molineaux's house for a visit. Mr. Molineaux had passed away some years back. There, she presented Barbara and me with a book of poems she had written.

While in Albany, I reached out to Bill. He was quite surprised to hear from me since it had been forty-seven years since we last saw each other. We all met for breakfast and then made a personal history tour, including my house, the old Molineaux house, the house where Bill had lived when we met, the neighborhood where we used to hang out, the St. Vincent De Paul Church, and the VI school building, which had closed in 1977 and was now converted into condominiums.

I remained in touch with Doug, either by post or Christmas card. After getting a doctorate in anthropology from Columbia, he got an academic position at a small college in Iowa. After getting tenure and publishing a couple of books, he and his second wife, Pia, decided to go into the business world and make some money. They moved to Philadelphia and started their own market research company and became extremely successful doing so.

Soon after I retired from Georgia Tech, Doug called me and told me he had gotten a Catholic annulment for his first marriage and was now focusing on building his spiritual life. He asked if I would be interested in going on a retreat with him. I agreed, and ever since, Doug and I have gone on retreats together twice a year.

42. Spirituality

*I*N THE WAKE OF VATICAN COUNCIL II, I BECAME INCREASINGLY aware the Catholic Church was beginning to view the world with greater openness. While Pope John Paul II put the brakes on for a slower evolution, I could see the Church windows starting to crack open slightly and let the authoritarian air of Medieval Catholicism out. A focus on God's love and mercy was beginning to replace the neoscholastic approach that had driven my intellectual conversion to the Catholic Church. I had been steeped in apologetics arguing why I should be a Catholic and not a Protestant and why the Catholic Church was the one Christ had established, rather than in a theology of love and mercy.

Both the Second Vatican Council and the Catechism of the Catholic Church advocated tolerance for and openness to other Christians and religions. The Catechism states:

> Those who, through no fault of their own, do not know the Gospel of Christ or his Church, but who nevertheless seek God with a sincere heart, and, moved by grace, try in their actions to do his will as they know it through the dictates of their conscience— those too may achieve eternal salvation.

I interpreted these statements to mean all people, from the beginning of time to the end, who live just and righteous lives will achieve salvation and see God. This has led me to view all people as children of God, but at the same time, I continue to believe the real presence of Jesus Christ in the Eucharist is what distinguishes Catholic spirituality from all others.

Over the years, Barbara and I practiced our Catholicism by going to church and receiving the Eucharist. Our spirituality evolved and became more inclusive, focusing on love, service, and constantly reaching for God's presence in our everyday lives. My personal spirituality had grown to focus on receiving the Eucharist daily and the conviction being a Christian in the modern world means making continuous choices on a daily basis. For me, that means practicing the corporal and spiritual works of mercy in the community where I live, including organizing food for the hungry, serving in meal kitchens, leading Bible studies, and organizing parish community spiritual activities.

Today, I continue to live life as a proud immigrant, a devout Catholic, and one who has contributed to the realm of the mind. All three aspects make up who I am today.

Acknowledgments

THE STORY IN THIS BOOK HAS BEEN ENRICHED BY INPUT AND feedback from family members, relatives and friends. I thank only a few here by name but I am grateful to all of them.

When my family first immigrated, my father stayed behind, first year in Beirut followed by two years in the Congo. During those three years, my mother corresponded with him regularly telling him about our daily life in Albany. My brothers and I wrote occasionally as well. When my father passed away in 2010 at the age of 98, we found all of the letters. I am grateful that my father saved all our letters, and especially thankful to my mother for her detailed letters, and to my brothers, Sami and Ramsey, for providing valuable anecdotes in the letters they wrote. Reading those letters triggered a load of memories and motivated me to write these memoirs, first for my family, and also for those interested in the life of an immigrant to the United States.

My deepest thanks go to my wife, Barbara, who reviewed an early draft making detailed and constructive comments. Her insights and attention to detail were extremely valuable. I am also greatly appreciative for her steady support throughout the writing journey. My gratitude goes to my sister, Leila, for sharing with me her reminiscences from our last years in Beirut, of our trip to America and the first three years in Albany. My son, David, his wife Sejal, my sister Maria and my mother, (who is now one-hundred and three years old), graciously listened to me read to them early versions of the first several chapters, giving valuable comments and feedback.

I am indebted to freelance editor Elisabeth Chretien, who edited and made extensive comments on an early version of the manuscript. Elisabeth has a remarkable ability of turning my often lengthy, wordy sentences into succinct prose.

I am immensely grateful to MaryAnne Hafen for being an outstanding editor and advisor. MaryAnne's suggested changes and edits made the manuscript narrative flow naturally with a purposeful thread.

Finally, I want to thank the WiDo Publishing team for their dedicated focus on getting the book published in a timely manner. I am especially grateful to Karen Gowen of WiDo Publishing for her enthusiastic support and encouragement.

About the Author

D<small>R. ALBERT NASIB BADRE (PHD, MICHIGAN, 1973) IS PROFES-</small>sor Emeritus of computing at the Georgia Institute of Technology and an international consultant specializing in designing technology to enhance the human experience. Dr. Badre was an early pioneer in the field of human-centric design, with over 35 years of experience in human-computer interaction, learning technologies, and human-centric e-learning. His background combines expertise in the empirical methodologies of the behavioral sciences and the design approaches of the computing sciences. He is a frequent consultant and lecturer to the data processing and computer industry in the U.S., Europe, Middle East, and South America in the area of Human-Computer Interaction.

Dr. Badre authored numerous technical papers, is co-editor of the book *Directions in Human Computer Interaction*, and the author of

the book *Shaping Web Usability: Interaction Design in Context*, which was adopted in several dozen courses worldwide.

Dr. Badre was the founding Director of the MS Degree Program in Human Computer Interaction at Georgia Tech. This was the first interdisciplinary HCI Program worldwide, combining the school of Psychology, the school of Communication and Culture, and the College of Computing. The Program was featured in the *U.S. News and World Report* issue on Best Colleges.

Today, Dr. Badre and his wife live in Providence, R.I., near his son and family, where he leads a very active volunteer life in service to the community.